Soul Awakening

Soul Awakening

The Journey from Ego to Essence

Birthing the Luminous Self Trilogy
Book One

Karen Anderson
and
Barry Martin Snyder

Luminous Self Media

Front cover artwork by Jean-Luc Bozzoli, www.jeanlucbozzoli.com

Back cover butterfly crop circle photo provided by Remko Delgaauw,
www.xld-sign.com

Back cover photo of the authors by Martha Ekstrom Wilhelm

Luminous Self Media
http://www.luminousself.com

ISBN 978-0-9835990-0-5
Printed in the United States of America

The Birthing the Luminous Self Trilogy

Humanity is in the midst of the most enormous evolutionary shift in its history. For millennia, the veils of soul-amnesia have occluded our consciousness, making it a challenge to remember who we truly are. The litany of wars, unequal distribution of resources, and environmental destruction attests to this fundamental forgetting that as souls, we are all one. Our collective soul-forgetting has brought our species and the planet to the brink of destruction.

Yet in the midst of this crisis, a luminous, soul-awakened human species is being born. Individuals everywhere are beginning to stir from their sleep as the divine light within the core of their being ignites. Birthing the Luminous Self is the process of awakening to, merging with, and expressing our divine magnificence through every facet of our mind, body and world. As this occurs, we shed the thick, opaque skins of the false self to reveal the brilliant radiance of the true, multidimensional Self. This is the process that is underway in those who are at the forefront of human evolution. One day, all of us will shine forth in our true splendor as awakened souls, blessing one another and our planet with our Presence.

Each of the three volumes in the trilogy presents an essential facet of the process of Birthing the Luminous Self. Volume One, *Soul Awakening*, offers an in-depth treatment of the all-important step of reconnecting with our inner divinity -- directly, consciously coming home to our core Self. Once we have reestablished that conscious connection, we are capable of serving as conduits of grace through which the Divine can pour Its blessings. This is the subject of the second volume, *Agents of Grace*. Finally, we reach the ultimate stage in the human experience: transcending all human limitations and stepping forth as a full and complete embodiment of the Divine. Now, we follow in the footsteps of the being who demonstrated absolute freedom from the laws of the physical plane through the resurrection and ascension of his body into an eternal, infinite body of light. Each in our own way, we realize *We are the Awakening Christ*, the title of the third book in the trilogy. Together, the three volumes of the trilogy describe and catalyze the progressive journey into the full realization of the Luminous Self.

Contents

PART THREE
The Living Laboratory of Soul Awakening

Foreword

By Kiara Windrider

As we come closer to an evolutionary doorway in consciousness, there are many questions we need to ask ourselves. Who are we really? Why have we chosen this time to be on Planet Earth? What hope can we look for in the midst of the apparent chaos we experience today on all levels of human existence?

Many have spoken of a collective awakening that could transform human aggression into harmony, violence into peace, separation into oneness. Is this mere wishful thinking? And if not, how or when might this happen? Is there a map or a vision that can inspire us to continue moving forward?

Most of us tend to identify with ourselves as a human personality, separate in time and space, restricted by limitations we have collectively imposed on ourselves. What if we instead began to identify with ourselves as an infinite soul, multidimensionally immense, self-existing beyond all limitations of time, space, and matter? Waking up as a soul rather than as a personality is the evolutionary shift required on the planet at this time.

Everything we are seeking is already available and awaiting this discovery. All the suffering, conflict, disease and fear we experience in our lives is the result of living in the consciousness of separation from this soul identity. This is true individually as well as collectively. Our collective awakening is the key to transcending all the crises that face us today, whether environmental, social, political or personal. Nothing less will suffice.

The stories, perspectives and insights shared in this book will challenge you and inspire you to make your own journey of awakening, for remembering who you are as a multidimensional soul is a prelude to the collective awakening. The book offers an induction, a holographic transmission of the soul realm frequencies in a way that is meaningful and relevant to us in these times, no matter what our individual life circumstances may be.

In these, the last hours before the dawn, a silent revolution is happening on levels we know little about. Our journey as a human caterpillar is about to end. And in the quiet darkness of the chrysalis, something very new is preparing to emerge!

Introduction

Eco-death or Ego-death?

There has never been a time like this on planet Earth. Whether we're scanning the internet, listening to the latest news, or quietly communing with our inner world, we can't help sensing something immensely powerful going on. Crisis, change and revolution are in the air. As we write, millions in the Mideast are rising up to claim the sovereignty that is their birthright. Billions more the world over still suffer from repressive regimes and unequal distribution of resources. Climate change, weather anomalies and earth changes are on the increase, and, combined with the nuclear catastrophe in Japan, present a dire specter that appears to be approaching apocalyptic proportions.

The winds of change are blowing through our individual worlds as well, accelerating the rate of evolutionary transformation with each passing day. The same desire for freedom, peace and fulfillment that is spawning mass uprisings reverberates within each of our hearts. As we feel the increasing dis-ease of a way of life that is no longer workable, our inner worlds erupt with unresolved emotions seeking healing and acceptance. Daily life is pervaded with a rising sense that major changes are needed, and a knowing that so much more is possible.

The myriad problems we face are complex, multifaceted, and interwoven. Consider the ways that energy, pollution, economics, the food supply, and global power politics are intertwined. Where do we begin, when everything is so interconnected? Through earthly eyes, the situation can certainly look hopeless. We are challenged as never before to discover a vaster, more inclusive, and more hopeful perspective.

The two of us are convinced that everything going on "out there" echoes one fundamental issue "in here" -- we human beings have lost touch with who and what we truly are. Asleep in the human condition, we have forgotten that we are vast, limitless souls, facets of the Divine that know how to live in harmony with all other forms of life. Our overwhelming crises stem from egos running wild, obsessed with gaining ever more for themselves with no thought of anyone else, much less of preserving the very planet we all live upon. To some degree, each of us participates in this wholesale destruction of life. For all of us, the way beyond it will be revealed as we return to the soul. For this is our true identity as facets of the One Great Being.

What mystics, saints and sages have always known is now being confirmed by quantum physics, transpersonal psychology, and holographic brain theory: Outer reality is a direct reflection of what is present within our individual and collective consciousness. Our ubiquitous crises can't be fixed or changed "out there." They will resolve only as a function of a radical, collective change "in here." The solutions to humanity's dilemmas will not be found within the level of understanding that created the problems. They can only emerge from a state of consciousness that can hold them all within a vaster, unified field of awareness. That unified perspective is the natural state of the soul, the presence of the Divine within each one of us.

Futurist Barbara Marx Hubbard has dedicated her life to reframing the crises that beset us into an unparalleled evolutionary opportunity. One of this visionary's favorite statements is "Our crisis is a birth." From this perspective, the challenges we face personally and planetarily are evolutionary drivers shepherding us toward the quantum leap our species must take if it is to survive. In this light, the ultimate solutions cannot be found in new technologies, greater energy efficiency, or revamped organizational structures. Similarly, to truly flourish, our personal worlds need far more than a new diet or drug, a change of career or relationship, or more money.

Soul Awakening: The Answer to all Crises

When we are in touch with the soul, we directly experience that we are all one interconnected being. It is impossible to exploit, dominate, injure or destroy another human being when we are awake to this reality. As souls, we view all of life, including the very planet we live upon, as sacred. Destroying life for monetary gain becomes unthinkable when our identity rests in the soul, rather than the ego. In a soul-awakened species, wars, domestic violence, poverty, political and religious divisiveness, racism, and all other forms of separation simply do not exist.

The soul is inextricably rooted within the deeper intelligence that sustains and furthers all life. This unfathomable intelligence orchestrates the billions of processes that keep our bodies healthy and alive. It is omnipresent as the essence of every lifeform, informing and choreographing the unified, harmonious interplay of all species. When we are in communion with the soul, we attune to this larger, collective soul, which then guides our every action in perfect harmony with it. Since their awareness is embedded within this intelligence, indigenous peoples know exactly how they must live in order to remain in harmony with the larger forces. They don't need computer models or studies to know what furthers life; their inner sensings tell them everything they need to know.

In contrast, when consciousness is oblivious to the soul, we feel an inner emptiness, an insatiable hole that we try to fill in countless ways. We endlessly endeavor to acquire and consume whatever we believe will assuage the emptiness, but all our efforts come up short. The existential pain and suffering we are left with spawn all forms of addiction. Our insatiable cravings have gotten so out of control that we have become addicted to consuming our very planet, as Al Gore famously expressed.

In all of our outer seeking, we never find what we are truly looking for: the love, light, and life of the soul. Everything we have ever sought without is always, already hidden within us. It is important to remember that the soul is not something we **have**; we **are** the luminous, divine presence that is our soul's core nature. The peace, satisfaction, abundance, joy, and all other divine qualities we hope to acquire "out there" can only be found as we reconnect with the soul, our true Self.

Ego-death or Eco-death? The doorways stand before us. Which will we choose? Only a soul-awakened species will survive the perfect storm that lies directly ahead.

Birthing the Luminous Self

Fortunately for us all, awakening to the soul as our true nature is exactly the evolutionary vector that lies before us. This immense change is not adequately described by the word transformation. What we are experiencing could more accurately be called a transmutation -- transformation on steroids -- for we are literally becoming a new species. The ego-based structures that surround us are crumbling as new, soul-awakened ways of being come forth. As the old decays and disintegrates, it forms the compost for the new life that is already beginning to emerge. This is as true within us as in the outer world.

Decades ago, Sri Aurobindo and his consort, The Mother, foretold the birth of a new species with superhuman capacities, and explored the consciousness such beings would embody. Incan Q'ero shamans tell us we will go through a radical death and re-birth after which we will emerge as "homo luminous," a spiritually advanced species. Hopis, Aztecs, and Mayans anticipate the end of the current age, believing that a great purification will be followed by the birth of an enlightened humanity. Pierre Teilhard de Chardin, a philosopher and Jesuit priest, believed humanity and the Earth would arrive at an omega point, which would spell the end of the human species as we have known it and be followed by a "Christification of the Earth." He asserted that in the newly emerging unified consciousness, all will know their oneness with God.

The prophetic cosmologies of many of the world's great spiritual traditions predict chaos and apocalypse at the end of the age. They also foretell the coming of a messiah, whether as the Second Coming of the Christ, the Kalki Avatar in Hinduism, the Imam Mehdi in Islam, or the Maitreya Buddha. While most conceptualize this incarnation of divinity in the form of a single, godlike human, the understanding is emerging that, while divine beings may descend to Earth, a *collective divine incarnation* will manifest as humanity awakens.

The end of the age is here. The long-awaited spiritual "savior" is beginning to incarnate in and as each one of us. While the evolutionary process may take many hundreds of years to complete, the transmutation is underway in our minds, bodies, hearts, and souls. The Luminous Self has lived within us forever, waiting for the moment when it could finally fully radiate out into the world. As we birth the Luminous Self, we bring forth the contribution only we can make to the collective awakening. We understand why we have returned to Earth at this pivotal time, and at last fulfill our destiny as a soul in the human experience. Joining in oneness with other awakening souls, we co-create the world we envision in our heart of hearts.

From Human Caterpillars to Multidimensional Souls

Long ago, when we incarnated into these human forms, we compressed our multidimensional vastness into third-dimensional bodies so that we could explore life within the material plane. In the process, we forgot our boundless, divine origins, believing that only what we could see, hear, taste, smell, and feel was real. Like caterpillars, we have "crawled" on the earth for millennia, exploring physical reality while we slowly evolved during each lifetime.

Now, at this extraordinary time on the planet, we are re-awakening to our true, unlimited nature. A stirring inside tells us we are about to experience life in a whole new way. As soul-awakened, multidimensional butterflies, we will soar free of all earthly limitation and suffering. Yet we cannot get from here to there without a complete metamorphosis of our being. We must die to who and what we thought we were, so we can be reborn as the brilliant butterflies we have always been, deep inside.

Like earthbound caterpillars, many human beings are as yet unaware that they are about to undergo a radical transformation. But the first reawakening souls have already entered the chrysalis, the evolutionary crucible in which our old identity literally dissolves away. At times, this process feels like a death, for in order for the butterfly to emerge, virtually nothing of the caterpillar can remain. Just as a caterpillar's solid form literally liquifies within the chrysalis, our previous identities and ways of being are disintegrating so that entirely new expressions can be born.

Humanity is now beginning its collective metamorphosis. All around us are signs of the total, systemic breakdown that must occur so that we can be reborn as multidimensional butterflies. Individually and collectively, we must surrender who and what we thought we were in order to be born into who we truly are. In the process, we will let go of all we thought life was about, all we believed possible. As the old, third-dimensional structures dissolve, within and without, we will emerge as illumined, multidimensional beings.

How will we get from where we are now to this amazing eventuality? In nature, the mysterious metamorphosis from caterpillar to butterfly offers some helpful clues. Within the chrysalis, as the caterpillar dissolves into an amorphous mass, something magical happens. New structures called "imaginal cells" begin to appear, and they contain the living template that will unfold as the butterfly. Similarly, the divine presence within each of our souls begins to come forth as we become aware we are not the limited, human "caterpillar" self we had thought, but something far more glorious. As we deepen in the soul, we activate the "imaginal cells" of our divine essence, which have been waiting for us to consciously participate in the transmutational process. Now, we are finally ready to actualize all of who we can be.

Millions of us are now realizing that we are imaginal cells within the collective body human, here to help catalyze the shift from limited, earthbound caterpillar into the full, radiant awakening of the butterfly. Since you have been drawn to this book, you are most likely one of these souls. Like the two of us and countless others, you are in the process of bringing forth the multidimensional, luminous presence that is who you really are, beneath the disguise of your earthly form. Your soul, the core essence that radiates from your heart of hearts, is the seed crystal around which the old that is dying will re-form itself into the New that is now being born.

For those who have already entered the chrysalis, transformation has become the central focus of life. Just as a caterpillar doesn't know how to become a butterfly, or what life will be like when the transmutation is complete, we, too, are asked to surrender and submit to the unfolding mystery of the process. While a part of us may want to hold on to what has been, another, bigger part is ready to soar free into a whole new way of being.

The true chrysalis lies within. In the inner realms of our soul, the alchemical transformation that is taking place will naturally, gracefully outpicture in new expressions of life that are magnificent beyond imagining. Everything that is occurring, within and without, is a part of this birth. Even the innumerable crises that surround us are nothing other than the pathways through the birth canal of our individual and collective soul into the light of the New Heaven and New Earth. In perfect timing we shall emerge as the Luminous Ones, shining forth in radiant splendor, living free and unencumbered of all that weighed us down during our caterpillar past.

Soul Awakening: Humanity's Evolutionary Imperative

Although the divine light has been shining in our heart of hearts all along, we may not have been in touch with that inner radiance. We might have spent decades searching the world for what can only be found within -- the love, wisdom, compassion, and limitless healing power we discover when we return home to the true Self. When we directly experience our luminous radiance, we realize the soul is who we really are, not the small, limited human being we thought we were.

Establishing a conscious connection with the soul is far more than a spiritual exercise or meditation technique. Reconnecting with our inner divinity forever alters our experience of who and what we are. The answers we seek, the guidance we need, the resolution of painful patterns and issues -- all of this and more becomes available as we awaken to the soul. The two of us often joke that connecting with the soul is "one-stop shopping," for all issues and dilemmas find resolution when we turn them over to the true Self.

In the days ahead, as the old, dying patterns of human culture dissolve and Earth changes and other evolutionary catalysts increase in scope and strength, our conditioned, habitual ways of being will become increasingly untenable. The only compass each of us can rely on to take us through the times to come is the inner voice of the Divine, informing us of our unique path through this all-encompassing death and rebirth. Living in communion with the soul may well become our most precious survival skill as we journey through the crises and into the new golden age.

As we awaken to the soul, our divine essence pours forth from the core of our being. Our human expression becomes filled with who and what we truly are, and outer life gradually transforms into a reflection of our inner wholeness and divinity. Relationships alter as we become capable of connecting with other human beings soul to soul, without ego-games and personas. Aware of our oneness with all of life, we naturally embody the Golden Rule. As the gnawing sense of lack dissolves, addictive attempts to fill the inner emptiness with the things of the outer world fall away. The life-enhancing intelligence of the soul supports healing from within and informs us of what we need to do in the outer world to resolve dis-ease on all levels of our being. As the divine template within the soul unfolds, we activate the "imaginal cells" of our sacred essence. Letting go of the concepts and perspectives that have bound us to our caterpillar identity, we blossom into the unique expression of the Divine we were always meant to be.

Now is the time. The radical shift from ego to soul is humanity's next evolutionary step. It and it alone is the key to moving beyond all the crises we face. Consciously connecting with the soul and awakening our divine nature is the most rEvolutionary act available to us now.

Our Own Journey of Soul Awakening

The two of us were brought together through a magical, mysterious set of circumstances, far different from anything we had ever experienced in previous relationships. Almost immediately, we were taken on a journey of discovery, a "university of the soul" orchestrated by a grouping of higher-dimensional beings, that taught us how to facilitate conscious communion with the Divine within. Since 1989, we have been sharing what we've learned with people the world over through groups and sessions, via teleconferences and in person. While we were expanding our capacity to catalyze the transformation of egoic shadow material into realization and freedom during sessions, our own lives became a living laboratory of awakening. In the potent evolutionary crucible of daily life, everything that occurred became part of the divinely orchestrated curriculum.

This book distills all that we learned about reconnecting with the multidimensional Self through facilitating sessions and in our own process of soul-awakening. The stories of our own voyages from ego to essence reveal the challenges we faced all along the way. While our egos often stubbornly clung to life, the deeper impulses of the soul did their best to come forth. At times we wondered if we would make it, as all that was not of the soul disintegrated around us. But calmly and quietly, our inner divinity showed us the way through everything we faced, within and without.

We have come to know the love, wisdom, and power of the essential Self through living into those qualities, one step at a time. Because what we share is not theoretical or abstract, but based in real-life experience, our stories provide a *living transmission* of the journey of soul awakening. They illustrate many of the archetypal passages we all encounter as we come home to the true Self. In our groups and teleconferences, people often tell us that hearing our stories reminds them of what is real and true in their own lives. Our experiences also convey what is possible as we let go of the ego-mind's illusions of limitation and open to our magnificence. Neither of us can take credit for the "miracles" of grace that have blessed our lives and sessions. Most of the time, these breakthroughs occurred *despite* the two of us, not because we are special or unique in any way. We are as amazed as anyone at what is possible when the ego~personality gives way and the Divine steps in.

Each of the transformational passages related in this book shifted our awareness into a more awakened, soul-embodied state. Since we have literally lived into everything we know about the soul and the Luminous Self, each of our books is imbued with the frequencies of the soul realms. The holographic imprints of the shifts in energy~consciousness that occurred are embedded in our stories. Thus, they can function like tuning forks, resonating your own inner divinity to come forth more fully.

Instead of simply reading these stories, we suggest that you live, feel, and enter into them, just as you would while watching an engrossing movie. Invite the transformational energies each passage contains to resonate throughout your own being. In this way, it becomes possible to experience the inner shifts described here without having to actually live through the events that precipitated them. *Soul Awakening* contains many seeds that will germinate within you until it is time for them to sprout into outer expression. The more you let your awareness enter into our stories and experience them as if you were there with us, the stronger the transmission and the deeper within your heart of hearts the evolutionary seeds will be planted.

Soul Awakening is designed to catalyze your unique process of awakening to the soul. As you read the words and absorb all that is between the lines, the energy and consciousness of your core being will be stimulated and activated, especially if this is your conscious intention. In truth, there is only one of us, and the paths the two of us have traveled contain many archetypal phases common to us all. Invite the evolutionary transmission contained within *Soul Awakening* to resonate your divine core and catalyze the birth of your Luminous Self.

Preface

While the names and identifying details of our clients have been changed to protect their privacy, everything you are about to read is presented just as we experienced it. Nothing is made up or embellished to make a better story.

In Part One of *Soul Awakening*, we describe all that led us up to the pivotal moment when we learned that it was possible to directly experience the soul. This revelation gave us our primary purpose for being on Earth during this pivotal time: to facilitate as many experiences of the beauty and wonder of the true, divine Self as we are meant to share.

Part Two presents what we discovered about how to expedite this life-altering experience, along with many clients' descriptions of their immersions in the soul realms. This section contains the guided soul-induction process we have used in sessions and groups for more than two decades. Utilizing this over time will enable you to cultivate and deepen a conscious connection with the energy~consciousness of your own soul.

Part Three relates further adventures in our ongoing, ever-unfolding journey of soul awakening and embodiment. As we continued to shed caterpillar identities, we were brought ever more fully into the soaring peace and deep serenity of the butterfly Self.

Throughout the book, we take turns telling our stories. Sections are clearly delineated with our names so that Barry's and Karen's voices are easily differentiated. Often, after a story, we join voices to describe the impact of the experience on us both. These sections are separated from the body of the story by a small symbol. Wherever you see no introductory name, the story is told in our joined voice.

A note about the language in this book: All language is representational, composed of symbols that attempt to point the way to truth but can never fully convey it. We use terms including soul, God, and Christ to evoke the experience of particular levels and facets of being. Some of these words may speak deeply to you while others may not feel resonant at all. If the words get in the way, ignore them or substitute your own. We recommend that you focus on connecting with the underlying energy and consciousness words can never fully communicate. Read between the lines; allow the words to spread out and take time to be absorbed; experiment with letting what is written evoke the living experience of whatever is being described. You may find yourself transported into a realm that transcends language altogether.

After this Preface you will find a Glossary that provides our definitions of words central to the book's themes. We suggest exploring the Glossary before starting to read the book, to gain an overview of the language and concepts developed within it. Familiarity with the Glossary may help you to more easily resonate with and integrate all that is presented in *Soul Awakening*.

Glossary

Throughout this book, we use terms such as ego, soul, oversoul, and God. These are somewhat arbitrary differentiations within a totality that is seamlessly woven together. In truth, it is impossible to point to where the soul ends and the oversoul begins. These levels of energy and consciousness continuously blend, intermingle, and overlap. Gradually, ego, soul, and oversoul are realized as being but different octaves of the one, true Self. As it evolves back toward the Source that originally sent it forth, the soul is reabsorbed into the oversoul, whose vast beingness is in turn incorporated within the Absolute that is often referred to as God or the One.

Working with distinctions and levels of definition can be helpful to the mind, but we must remember that reality is far less describable than the mind likes to think. All such descriptions are only relatively real and accurate, and can ultimately become a limit to authentic perception. The only absolute reality is the Oneness within which all of life arises. Everything else exists at a relative degree of differentiation, resting within that unimaginably vast interconnectedness.

The following definitions reflect the ways we use these words; they may differ considerably from dictionary definitions.

Chakra Energy~consciousness vortex within the human subtle anatomy; from the Sanskrit word for "wheel." Seven major chakras are located just in front of the spine and in the head. Each regulates and affects a particular sphere of human experience; for instance, the throat chakra influences communication, among other functions. When chakras are clear of distortion, they allow divine energy~consciousness to freely flow into outer expression. When chakras contain blockages or are shut down, the corresponding area of life does not operate at its full potential.

Christ Source, the "Father," or the Creator, fully made manifest; God experiencing Its creation from within it. The full awakening of the soul results in Self-realization, which in its ultimate demonstration manifests as the Christ. A being who is enlightened, God-realized and fully embodied; a divine human who has transcended all earthly limitation. A universal reality that is not exclusively identified with the man called Jesus.

Dis-ease Literally, a lack of ease on any level of the subtle anatomy -- physical, etheric, emotional, mental, or spiritual. The hyphen is used to emphasize that the manifestation of bodily illness or injury reflects a lack of ease on the subtle levels that has now precipitated a physical condition.

Ego, ego-mind The outer-acting facet of the soul's beingness; the sense of self or identity that arises from the projection of the soul into time, space, and dimensionality. In most human beings the ego often operates in separation from the soul, and is thus referred to as the separate ego. Our definition of ego is not synonymous with the classic psychoanalytical model. (See: self, separate self)

Energy~consciousness We use the little squiggle, or tilde, between the two words to connote their inextricability from one another. In truth, energy cannot be separated from consciousness; they form the indivisible unity that indicates life is present. At times we use each term separately when its qualities are more pronounced in the context.

Etheric The level of the subtle anatomy that encompasses and contains the blueprint for the physical body. The etheric body surrounds and interpenetrates the physical body, existing at a less dense level of energy~consciousness than the material form. Disease patterning first occurs in the etheric body before it manifests in the physical body.

Holographic, hologram Science defines a hologram as a three-dimensional image created by the interference pattern of light waves reflected from an object illuminated with a laser. The image looks as lifelike as the object, but is evanescent and intangible.

    Holograms arise within fields of consciousness as subtle energetic patterns that generate recurring circumstances in our lives. Ongoing material-level poverty, for example, may holographically reflect subtler levels of belief, judgment, and so on. Religious, ethnic, cultural, and national holograms color the beliefs and emotions of large groups of people.

    We also use the term to refer to a projection of energy~consciousness into matter in a manner that encapsulates the Whole within a part of itself. For instance, the soul is a holographic projection of the oversoul, which in turn is a holographic extension of the All in All. Each level contains everything inherent within its "parent" level.

I AM   The individualized aspect of the Divine that resides within the soul lotus.

I AM Presence   The individuated aspect of God that resides 15 - 50 feet above the physical body and anchors in the heart of hearts. A core principle in the I AM or Ascended Master Teachings brought through by Godfre Ray King.

Languages of Light   Higher-dimensional, holographic symbol~patterns (again, the tilde is used to indicate the two are inextricably woven together) that may pour in during a soul activation to expand consciousness and accelerate soul evolution. They can consist of geometries, patterns, color infusions, sacred languages such as Hebrew and Sanskrit, sounds, and other manifestations of vaster realms and presences.

Lifestream   All the lifetimes of a given soul. Lifestream issues and themes may influence many lifetimes until they are resolved and transcended.

Multidimensional   The sphere of existence that transcends third-dimensional physicality; the vaster field of being of the true Self. This term and **higher-dimensional** refer to the levels of Creation beyond the three dimensions of length, width, and height.

Overlight   Higher-dimensional presences often oversee earthly endeavors and shepherd human beings through their evolutionary processes, guiding them toward the experiences and contacts that will support their flowering as souls. The vaster illumination of such presences enhances and expedites soul development.

Oversoul   The extension of the I AM Presence that overlights and organizes all of its individual soul extensions in matter. The aspect of our being that always resides above and beyond physical, embodied existence; the higher Self, the source of the embodied soul.

Pacemaker   The sinoatrial node in the physical heart muscle that stimulates the heart and regulates its contractions to circulate blood throughout the body. The soul attaches to the body at this point for as long as it wishes to embody in physicality. When the soul withdraws at the end of a lifetime, the pacemaker stops functioning and physical death ensues.

Shadow   Subconscious or unconscious material that, when it impels behavior, can lead to projection, blame, and other distortions in outer experience and relationships. When it is brought to light, shadow material can transform into healing blessings.

Soul The individualized aspect of God that contains every quality and attribute of its Source and exists as an extension and subset of the Whole within manifest creation. Its divine nature preexists as a potential that is progressively realized in the process of soul awakening.

Soul center, soul space The location in the body where the soul focalizes its energy~consciousness and is most clearly apprehended and experienced. The primary soul center is located above the physical heart in the center of the chest. The soul center is distinctly different from the heart chakra and operates at a subtler, vaster level.

Soul lotus The soul lotus resides in the core of the heart soul center and enfolds the I AM, the individualized spark of God/One/All That Is. As soul awakening progresses, the soul lotus unfolds, blossoming forth in outer, manifest expressions of the soul's essential nature.

self, small self The third-dimensional, ego~personality level of being. (See also: ego, ego-mind, separate ego)

Self The multidimensional, unmanifest, oversoul level of being.

Sense of self, self sense The perception of who we are that is based on sensory input and experience. That which we identify with and attach to colors our self sense and contributes to the rise of duality in our experience, as in "I am this and not that."

Separate ego The ego operating without reference to the soul, unable to tap into the soul's love, wisdom, and power. Its basis is founded in fear and doubt.

Soul The unique spark or facet of the One that takes embodiment to evolve and express its divine essence within matter. The immortal, immaterial spirit that animates the form.

Soul Star The eighth chakra, located a few inches above the head; the doorway to the higher-dimensional, nonphysical realms.

Source Prime Creator; the origin of all manifest creation in all dimensions and universes.

PART ONE

✦ ✦ ✦

Awakening Begins

✦ ✦ ✦

1

Here We Go Again

Barry: A Difficult Reentry

It's 1950 in planet Earth time, a perfect moment to begin another lifetime. There's a mixture of feelings as, from between the worlds, I look down at the matrix I will be entering. It's the right one for this lifetime, but it won't be easy. Yet I also know that despite the pain that awaits me, this is the life that will finally bring the spiritual birth that all my lifetimes have prepared me for, the culmination of my larger purpose for coming to this planet. In order for this flowering to take place, though, all that remains unresolved from my many incarnations will need to be faced and transformed. It is comforting to know that I will not have to do this alone, and that I will not fail.

The script for the opening scenes of this life called for a rough entry. The parents that seemed appropriate lived in a small, rather poor town in central Pennsylvania. Mom took amphetamines, and when Dad found out he was to become a father, he started drinking more and running around with another woman. The imprints of these emotional upheavals were subconsciously recorded in the mind of that little fetus.

After gestating for nine months in this emotional stew, I didn't exactly feel excited about emerging into the world. Due to a blood Rh issue, the doctors feared I could be a "blue baby," born without sufficient oxygen, so they used forceps to speed up my birth. The world I first experienced was shocking to the senses. Beneath the blinding white light of the operating room, the first humans to greet me were hidden behind masks, emanating waves of fear.

I had no sooner emerged than I was separated from my mother and put in isolation. I was black and blue from head to foot and my skull had been misshapen by the forceps, with one ear sticking straight out and lower than the other. When the nurse took me to my mother for the first time, her first embrace included laughing at my appearance and joking that I looked like a prize-fighter.

My mother's pain overflowed into our home in the form of angry, psychotic episodes. Terrified and overwhelmed by the psychic bombardment that was often directed toward me, I tried to run away from home, but that was destined for failure. At four years of age, two blocks from home seemed like the edge of the universe. With no hope of breaking free of it all, I found another way. When mother raged and catharted, I escaped by withdrawing into my inner world. I could also live according to my true nature by escaping into nature. I spent a lot of my free time playing and creating imaginary worlds. This kept the joy and magic alive.

I first became aware of the idea of "God" when my parents forced me to go to church and Sunday school. Everyone seemed to feel that praying to Jesus and his Father, the powerful, grandfather-like man up in heaven, was more important than anything, including enjoying life. Sitting on those hard pews, all I could think about was how great it would be to get home and go out to play. But I either had to go through this painful tedium every Sunday morning or stay inside the house the rest of the day. I realized my parents thought they were doing something that was good for me, but how could something that felt so bad possibly be good for me?

Like most young humans, I saw my parents as godlike figures and tended to sign on for anything they thought was true. But a whole lot of it didn't make any sense. Except for Christmas Eve and Easter, when I could feel the presence of something special, church felt totally dead. The God they talked about always seemed to be judging us humans. The smiting, pestilence and plagues he meted out to the poor unfortunates in the Old Testament really scared me.

Worst of all, although everyone espoused the teachings of Jesus, I didn't see anyone doing a very good job of living them. The people I knew perpetually judged one another and talked about their neighbors and friends behind their backs. The teaching about loving one another, the one thing that made the most sense, wasn't something I saw much of in my day-to-day life.

Yet even through all of that, the light of the Divine did oc-casionally shine. One of the first truly "spiritual" experiences hap-pened while playing in my back yard one evening. As I looked up at the dark sky, I felt awe and wonder at how the universe went on and on forever, dotted with millions and trillions of planets and stars. Looking down at my hand, it seemed to melt away and I saw another whole universe full of planets and stars within me. For the first time, that child-mind pierced the veils and perceived the true nature of things -- oneness.

A recurring lucid nightmare also seemed to link me to something beyond what I experienced in daily life. In the dream, which seemed as real as waking life, I found myself falling down and down, spiraling into deeper and deeper layers of a suffocating darkness and density. I felt as if I were being compressed and overwhelmed by a force that was deadening my soul. Inevitably, having fallen off the bed, I would awaken on the floor in a fearful sweat. The night terror felt so deeply troubling that I often cried.

While I wasn't conscious of the message of the nightmare at the time, a subtle knowing indicated it was something significant from beyond. The largely unconscious terror of the "fall" would go on to inform this entire life, just as it had pervaded all previous em-bodiments. The apparent archetypal fall from grace, the core cause of my suffering, was driving me onward in search of the larger truth or reality beyond the trauma and pain of earthly existence.

Karen: Childhood's Eternal Now

While Barry seems to have come into this life with the fur-rowed brow he wears in his baby pictures, I had a much softer landing. Both of my parents wanted and cherished their first child. I felt secure and safe in my little world of swing sets and neighbor-hood friends and books.

When my awareness travels back to those early days, eve-rything exists as it was then, in the ever-present now. At age four, I'm out in the yard collecting sparkly rocks. They are more beautiful and precious to me than anything else in the world. I fill jar after jar with them, loving how each one twinkles in its own special, unique way.

At night, I'm outside again, watching the fireflies and at-tempting to collect them, too. The next morning, I'm heartbroken to see them lying lifeless at the bottom of the jar. Nonetheless, each evening I hope that this time it will be different. Armed with a new, clean jar, its top punctured with holes, I go out into the mysterious darkness to catch more. I want the fireflies as friends, and I have to

3

find out if they glow in the daytime. But neither desire is ever fulfilled.

When we move to another town, Mom discards every last jar full of sparkly rocks, having no idea what a lifeline to my true Self they are for me. "You'll find more at our new house," she says. Yet in my heart and soul I know this is not true. These rocks were somehow part of me, and there will never be more like them. I am devastated.

At our new home, just as I'd somehow known, there are no magical, twinkling stones to collect. Instead, I seek solace within the sheltering enfoldment of the neighbors' enormous weeping willow tree. The kind, elderly couple sometimes invites me inside for lunch. I bask in their loving care within the homey warmth of their house, where the light filtering through the lacy curtains makes intricate patterns on the ornate rugs and plump, welcoming furniture.

It's summer now, in yet another town. The windows are open and I'm in the kitchen singing along with Elvis, whose tinny voice coming through the radio pulls me to my feet. Dancing barefoot on the cool, linoleum floor, I feel free and happy, letting the music move my little body.

Now I'm in first grade, in the third school I've attended by age six. After my best friend is moved to another class because she and I talk too much, I leave school at lunch time and walk the long, scary ten blocks home. My mother's first words are, "What are you doing here, young lady?"

"I hate school. I'm never going back!"

"You most certainly are, and you'll apologize to your teacher, too."

Like home, school offers little room to live in and few opportunities to exert my own will. And when I do, punishment often follows. Does anybody see me? Does anyone know what it is like to be a bright, inquisitive little soul who just wants to be free to follow her own energy and have fun? I feel like a prisoner in a world of adults caught up in their own agendas.

At age twelve, I tell my parents that I am done going to Sunday school; the teachers don't seem to practice anything they preach, and the whole thing seems like a colossal waste of time.

Mom's response is, for once, agreeable: "OK, we'll stay home. We were really only going to church for you kids, anyway."

Having left Protestantism, I begin to wonder about the big questions -- for instance, is there a God? In the philosophy tomes I cart home from the library, I am thrilled to discover a name for my state of not-knowing: I am an agnostic!

I read on, more befuddled than enlightened by the abstruse concepts and philosophical systems I encounter. Something in me wants to know what is really going on behind this strange, often puzzling earthly life. There is no one to talk with about these things, no one to guide my search for understanding. But the quest has begun.

A few years later, my gentle, elderly music teacher becomes my first spiritual guide. Ruth attends psychic development classes taught by Jane Roberts, a reporter in our upstate New York town who set out to debunk all things metaphysical and instead became convinced of the reality of the nonphysical realms. To her great surprise, her own experiences catapulted her into a whole new chapter of her life. It would not be long before a medieval philosopher named Seth would begin to speak through her -- first, to the small groups that met in her home, and later to the millions of people who read the Seth books.

Every so often, Ruth and her husband invite me to their home for dinner and a slideshow journey through one of the European countries they have visited. One evening, as we gaze at a photo of a narrow, winding street in the old quarter of a city, Ruth remarks, "I knew exactly what it would look like around that corner -- I must have been there in a previous life." Never have I heard anyone speak of such things. I am enthralled.

Reflection

Barry:

From a human perspective, my childhood hardly qualified as a great start. But it was a perfect beginning for a soul who wanted to make sure he woke up this time. The primal pain and suffering of those early, formative experiences would eventually provide the fuel to propel me on a search for a way beyond the early traumas and those that would follow.

During childhood, I lived with constant fear of abuse. My early wiring set up a foundation of fear and vulnerability, which would later catalyze the development of certain essential divine qualities and attributes necessary to complete the faceting of my soul. The story line had to be particularly intense, both to drive me toward my destiny in the appointed flow of time and space and to make sure that I would continue to seek until I awakened. With nowhere else to escape, I turned to nature to keep my inner world alive, and inward to the only place ultimate solace can ever truly be found.

I chose to enter a particularly dense set of circumstances, for it was important that I fall nearly totally asleep. There wasn't much spiritual upliftment in my family matrix or home town. Even the joyful memories of my early childhood are pervaded by a dark, heavy, psychic miasma in the field of consciousness. Rarely did the light of the soul shine through in those around me, and when it did it was dim, due to the many overlays they carried.

But the soul can never go totally asleep. Mine occasionally broke through, as when I glimpsed the infinity and oneness in everything, and in the recurring dreams when the trauma of the compression of the soul into the tight confines of the human form left me terrified and crying on the floor.

Karen:

My birth was not nearly as traumatic as Barry's was. In fact, my mother had attended natural childbirth classes, a rarity in the early 1950s. But when the time for my earthly entrance arrived, my mother's doctor was out of town, so my birth proceeded in the usual way. Still, I feel fortunate to have had a mother who sought out an alternative to the usual birthing practices of the day.

During childhood, my sparkly rock collection and the twinkling fireflies reminded me of the incandescent splendor of my celestial home. They were a lifeline, a link to who I really was. So much of Earth life seemed inscrutable; I often felt confused and perplexed by what was going on around me. The beauty of nature -- the world of trees, glittering rocks and flowers -- provided soothing infusions of comfort that resonated with my soul. Collecting sparkly rocks kept me in touch with the realms of magic and mystery beyond the veils of this world. Not knowing how important keeping this awareness alive was for a budding soul in the human experience, my mother threw all my pretty rocks away. Since her own higher-dimensional awareness had been lost early on, she was unable to help it flourish in her child. Some variant of this story happens in the life of virtually every newly incarnated soul, especially in the Western world.

Entering school, I discovered I was different from the other children. Having learned to read before kindergarten, I often felt bored and restless, and attempted to liven things up by talking to whoever was nearby. When my best friend was transferred to another class, school became a cruel and punishing place. My wounding lay in the perception that my teacher was unable to see me as the curious, lively little person that I was. She had no idea how to provide the stimulation I craved. And when I reached home, my mother was not sympathetic, either. According to the rules of the culture into which I had been born, children belonged in school, and that was that.

If my soul could have expressed itself, it might have said, "No one can see my celestial nature because they have lost touch with theirs." The pervasive sense of not being seen as a child caused me to go underground, to hide many of the vibrant, sacred aspects of my nature. In a world that often seemed dense and obtuse, they seemed to have no place to go, nowhere to be expressed. Few humans seemed capable of registering anything subtle, and rather than see them be disparaged, I hid these aspects of my nature, as everyone else seemed to be doing.

From time to time, I wondered, *Where are my people?* I sensed there must be others like me, but had no idea where to find them. I thought I might meet some of my people when I entered high school, but they did not appear to be there. *Maybe I'll meet my people when I go away to college,* I hoped, but they were not there, either.

On rare occasions, I met someone that inhabited a wider world than the one most people seemed satisfied with. Ruth, my music teacher, was one of the first with whom I could share the more sensitive sides of my nature with no fear of ridicule or rejection.

The journey of soul awakening in a given lifetime starts the moment we are born. Actually, it begins even earlier, as, between the worlds, we plan our next lifetime and then enter into the womb of the mother we have chosen. Soul awakening continues from one lifetime to the next, from the moment we emerge out of the heart of God to the instant we dissolve back into it.

Before each earthly re-entry, we choreograph a life script that addresses the unfinished business from previous lifetimes and prepares us to fulfill our soul purpose for this incarnation. Everything we set up for ourselves, no matter how painful and wounding, propels us toward our destiny. However difficult and even horrific our circumstances may seem, at no point are we a victim. As souls, we agree to enter into the conditions of our life script because they offer the exact catalysts we need to evolve.

Buddhist teachings stress that the way we begin a life largely determines the soul's progress in that lifetime. Our time in

7

the womb and the quality of our birth process enormously affect the rest of our lives. The mind is like an empty canvas awaiting its first brushstrokes, the formative events that will become key elements in the life pattern that will emerge. Our initial experiences set up the foundational neural networks that form the basis for our perception, and they go on to powerfully influence how we experience and create our lives.

We have all seen the light of the Divine shining through the eyes of a newborn baby. Why does that light seem to dim for so many of us as we grow up? When childhood wounding occurs, as it does to some degree for nearly every soul in the human experience, we tend to recoil and shut down to protect ourselves. Unfortunately, this energetic shutdown also veils our awareness of the light emanating from the core of our being.

As we "go to sleep" to our vast, luminous, celestial nature, we no longer experience its peace, happiness, and joy as a steady state. This becomes the greatest wound of all, which is then compounded by all the subsequent upsets that occur in the presence of other sleeping, wounded souls. With each trauma, our awareness of the light that we are gradually dims until we lose touch with our immense, multidimensional consciousness.

But our wounding is not all bad news, for the gift hidden in each trauma is that its resultant suffering causes us to seek relief and healing. We all carry the intuitive remembrance of the joy, happiness, peace and luminosity of our true nature. Barry felt himself leaving it behind in his recurring free-fall nightmare, while Karen found reminders of it in her sparkly rocks and fireflies. Recovering our divine essence becomes the motivating force that causes all human beings to search for something to relieve the pain and fill the gnawing inner void where we once experienced our sacred nature. Without our wounding and its attendant impetus to search for a way through and beyond it, we might simply acclimate to the circumstances of the world and coast through life, instead of actively engaging it out of necessity.

A second hidden gift in our wounding lies in the fact that as we transform wounds, they become blessings. Our very presence then offers the possibility of a more rapid, graceful resolution to those facing comparable challenges. Having evolved through our own crises, we are able to understand, empathize and bring compassion to the suffering of others. We can embrace their pain while simultaneously holding the deeper truth of the divine gift within the experience. Many of us purposely set up the circumstances of our childhood wounding so we could contribute in this way. In truth, there is only one being residing in and behind the nearly seven billion souls in body on planet Earth. Whatever we go through as individuals immediately and directly affects every other soul.

But not everyone goes to sleep when they come here. As vast frequencies of light and consciousness increasingly bathe our region of the galaxy, more and more souls are remaining awake to their true nature as they enter Earth-life. These new, transitional generations of beings have been called Indigo, Violet, and Crystal children, among other names. Because they remain aware of their true identity and know their beingness transcends their human forms, these souls catalyze awakening in their parents, teachers, and other adults, as well as their contemporaries who have gone "lights out."

Micah, a six-year-old boy we once met, actively helped his parents to awaken. Micah not only knew why he was here on Earth, he also could tell which of his friends remembered where they came from and what it was like there, and who had forgotten. Upon hearing about our work, Micah directed his father to do a session with us. During that pivotal experience, his father reconnected with his galactic home, and received much-needed and deeply appreciated spiritual sustenance. Now he knew that he was not alone here on a strange and painful planet.

As we reawaken from the trance of our amnesia, we are able to support others in staying awake, as Micah did with his father. Even if we have not encountered them ourselves, we can celebrate and nurture the realities our children experience, so they do not have to send parts of themselves underground. And in simple, unobtrusive ways, we can affirm others in who they really are.

Years ago, a father came into the bookshop where Karen worked, his infant son suspended in a baby-carrier on his back. While Dad browsed, Karen made eye contact with the baby, and soon recognized him to be a very regal, dignified soul. Without changing her facial expression, she continued to gaze into his eyes while silently sending him the message, *I'm so happy to see you are back! It's wonderful to have you here for another lifetime.*

The baby's solemn countenance immediately broke into a radiant smile, and he laughed with glee. Later, his father revealed that the boy's name was Rex -- the Latin word for king!

As the level of consciousness on our planet lifts, ever more parents are inspired to create beautiful, gentle ways of welcoming their babies into this world. Home births, water births, and a variety of other rituals and approaches focus on easing re-entry for souls embarking on yet another Earth-life. When one or both parents lovingly participate in a child's birth, that degree of conscious presence becomes a gift to all beings everywhere.

2

When on Earth,
Do as the Earthlings Do

Karen: Trying to Pass

From the earliest age, I knew I was not like most other human beings. Most of the things that interested them seemed strange or pointless to me. And conversely, much of what fascinated me seemed uninteresting to those around me. Worse, they often ridiculed the pastimes I enjoyed, like lying beneath a big tree and looking up at the sky, or wandering in the woods without a plan or destination.

I often wondered how I'd ended up in my family of origin. I seemed to have so little in common with these people! In contrast, my brother appeared to be having a much easier time fitting in; he seemed to be a lot more "normal" than I'd ever been.

Nonetheless, all through school I tried my best to fit in and be "normal." I hid the parts of me I imagined would be mocked, and did my best to excel in the areas that came easily to me. Because I loved reading, I became a good student, but when this drew attention I felt embarrassed. Being noticed by others had often been a painful experience; all I wanted was to be anonymous.

Yet even in this seeming wasteland of soul, transcendent moments occasionally occurred. Participating in the band and choir, I experienced the sublime magic of group synergy when we played or sang particularly beautiful pieces. In music class, I listened with awe to compositions from centuries past that exquisitely expressed the ineffable stirrings within my own soul. I was too awkward and shy to act in plays, but painting scenery became a satisfying creative outlet. And those of us with similar interests and energies found one another. Friendship segued into romance with my first real boyfriend, who shared his poetry with me along with long conversations about the inscrutability of life.

In college during the Vietnam era, I became a political radical, while a close friend from high school who shared my disillusionment with the government's policies began to attend meditation groups for world peace. One evening, I accompanied him to a gathering to find out what it was all about. Afterward, I vehemently stated, "That's not going to do it, Jim. We have to *do something* about the problems in the world, not just meditate on them!" Jim pointed out that everything in the visible world begins as energy, and that as the energy shifted, the outer manifestation would inevitably transform to reflect the inner change. Many years would pass before I began to grasp the wisdom of Jim's perspective.

I became a special education teacher, and focused on creating a safe, welcoming classroom for the kids no one else seemed to know what to do with. Because I had so rarely felt deeply seen as a child, I wanted to see these little beings with appreciation and welcome out what lay within them. My young charges included June, who dressed impeccably and washed her hands a dozen times before lunch. In contrast, Mike was oblivious to the fact that his shoes were on the wrong feet and his shirt was inside out and backwards. During that more innocent time, he delighted in delivering a weather report each morning to the class through the microphone he had fashioned from tin foil and string. Brenda had such irrepressible good spirits she loved to dance on the tabletops. When Tony was suspended for punching me in the ribs, a social worker discovered he had an alcoholic mother and an absent father. This was a rare situation in that suburban neighborhood during the 1970s.

As much as I tried to create a little oasis of freedom in my class, I found it difficult to assimilate into the institutional setting of a public school. Teacherly duties like having to make sure the class was quiet and well-behaved as we passed through the hallways -- not to mention simply showing up every single weekday for work -- felt utterly foreign to my nature. Sitting at the long table in the teachers' lunchroom, I found it nearly impossible to think of anything to say to my colleagues, whose lives seemed to exist in a parallel universe. Unlike them, I had no desire to invest in a house and its furnishings. The goals others found fulfilling and fascinating left me disinterested and unengaged. Professional advancement had no allure, either. I would never be comfortable in that world.

With no interest in worldly success, it never occurred to me that teaching was a poorly-paid profession; I was glad to be earning any money at all, and felt wealthy compared to my student friends. Not wanting to add to the pollution choking the planet, I had no desire to own a car. Eventually, the difficulty of my long commute, which involved waiting for two buses and walking a mile in each direction during the bitterly cold Buffalo winters, caused me to succumb to the cultural pressure to buy a vehicle.

I loved these kids, yet a persistent inner feeling hinted there was something more I was supposed to be doing with my life. But what was it?

Barry: Finding A Place In The World

Grade school was difficult. I found sitting in classes all day only slightly less boring than going to church. What came naturally to me seemed foreign in the outer world, and vice versa. When I couldn't take it anymore I'd fake being sick so I could stay home. Real, painful cramps often knotted up my lower abdomen; fear and self-doubt colored my attempts to cope with the dual stresses of school and home life.

Yet somehow I accessed enough intelligence to get good grades, and most of the teachers felt I was an excellent student. By high school, I no longer experienced the roiling anxiety in my belly. In fact, I didn't feel anything there, or anywhere else in my body. When anxiety arose, I found that I could simply ignore it, and smoking a cigarette made everything seem OK again. I was starting to feel like I fit in, even though a nagging emptiness and subtle depression pervaded my experience.

College provided a brief moment of freedom. I was on my own now, and could explore life without the pressures of parents and teachers. Career ideas dropped away as marijuana and LSD opened up dimensions of reality that felt more real than much of what I had been experiencing in the outer world. There was nothing I really wanted to do with my life when I "grew up," whatever that meant. I only wanted to explore and be free.

The hard realities of what it might mean to be an "adult" hit home during the Vietnam war. I drew an extremely low draft lottery number, which meant I was assured of an all-expenses-paid vacation in the jungle, with people trying to kill me -- people I had absolutely nothing against. I studied political science and read alternative newspapers, which made it clear that this was an unjust, immoral war fueled by American imperialism. Faced with the specter of having to carry a gun with the intention of killing others, I knew if it came down to them or me, it would probably wind up being me. I just didn't think I had what it took to pull the trigger. A deer-hunting experience when I was twelve reverberated in my mind. As I'd looked down at the beautiful animal I had just killed, I burst into tears.

I set about securing a medical deferment, vowing if that did not work I was off to Canada. Luckily, I came into this life with a congenital back deformity. With a note from my doctor and a corset-like back brace, I was able to convince the Selective Service that I wasn't what they were looking for. The relatively innocent, happy college years ended with the comfort of knowing that at least I would not be dead or maimed through war during the next few years.

The issue of getting a job and becoming a productive adult remained. There was nothing I really wanted to do, but the hard reality loomed: Within a short time I would be out on the street, having to make money to live. Part of me felt overwhelmed and didn't have a clue about how to make it in that world. Still, I would have to figure out how to survive and fit in.

As I looked out at the world of adulthood, careers, and financial responsibility, the nagging, perpetual feeling of being a stranger in a strange land, the feeling that had begun at birth, surfaced yet again. Would I ever really fit in here? Probably not, but once again I had to find a way to bend, push, prod and otherwise make myself into something that would pass.

My grandfather was a strong, self-made man who loved me very much and wanted to see me do well in life, as he had. He decided I should go into banking. He and my uncle had risen to become presidents of small banks, so this seemed as good an idea as any, especially since I didn't have any others. I hoped that some of what they had lay dormant in me.

A gray, depressing pall settled over me at the thought of losing my freedom and entering such a strange and non-resonant world. As I'd imagined, it felt painfully stressful at first. But gradually, with the help of alcohol, nicotine, and caffeine, I learned to function and fit in.

I turned out to be good at business, and within a few years my career was blossoming. The college student without a clue now carried a briefcase, wore three-piece suits, and flew all over the country wining and dining CEOs, attempting to get their business. In this surrealistic world, the ego found a lot of nourishment. It liked the idea of success; power, money and approval felt good. I could buy new cars, enjoy expensive vacations and acquire the accoutrements that allowed me to fit into the world. Everyone else seemed to think these were the goals of life, so why shouldn't I? *Might as well get in there and win the game,* the mind insisted.

Everyone around me was getting married, so I did, too. It seemed to be part of the formula to succeed and become happy. I also felt pretty lonely in this new life, and hoped a partner would relieve some of the emptiness. But a few hours after my wedding I found myself calling my best friend, telling him I thought I had made a mistake. The loneliness and emptiness only increased.

Reflection

ᘒᘒ

Karen:

While Barry felt called to investigate and accumulate the things of the world, they never held much fascination for me. When my parents visited during this time, Dad looked around for a chair to sit on, and realized the big floor pillows were the extent of the furniture. "You never were very materialistic," he commented.

My goal as a special education teacher was supposed to be to help children reintegrate into regular classes, but what I saw going on in them made it nearly impossible to feel excited about that. They seemed designed to make the children into good little robots, meek and compliant and unable to think for themselves. As a political radical and sensitive soul, I couldn't support that. To me, it looked like death. For years after I left teaching, whenever I'd see a school bus, tears welled up. Each time, I felt all over again the unbearable tragedy of enforcing compulsory education on tender little souls just coming into this life.

Although I had entered "the world," to a degree, and pursued a profession that provided meaning and some satisfaction, I never felt that teaching fulfilled the ultimate purpose for my life. The promise of financial security was eclipsed by the need to be true to the inner feeling of rightness within me. In those days, I would not have called that the soul; it was simply a feeling that had always led me through life, and I had learned that when I followed it, life felt good and right.

Now, something beyond the safe, secure world of my teaching career was calling, though I had no idea what it was. All I could do was follow the inner sense of rightness as it led me out into an unknown future.

Barry:

As I gradually learned how to cope with the wounds of childhood and the demands of parents and school, I found a way to be in the world and pass as a relatively normal adolescent. The magical world of childhood with its endless summers of playing in imagined worlds I created in the nearby woods or my backyard slowly disappeared. Less and less of me flowed outward and more of the world flowed in. Gradually I lost touch with the inner fountain of joy and happiness and my inherently playful nature.

The inrushing world brought with it expectations, demands and a grey heaviness that all but paved over the wellspring of my deeper nature. Like all children, I wanted to be loved and approved of, and I felt very afraid of criticism and rejection. More and more energy was spent in learning to respond to the dictates of my parents and teachers. As time passed, a Barry emerged that was a reflection of the world's values and ways of being. In the process, the light and life of the soul waned.

Nagging, subsurface feelings of depression, despair and fear attempted to surface from time to time, but I had become adept at stuffing them back down and ignoring them. Even though I wasn't conscious of the pain, much of my life was about avoiding it and looking for anything that made me feel better. That took me into the world of drugs and alcohol.

College provided a safe and sheltering womb, compared to what might lie ahead. The process of leaving college and going out into the "real world" became a painful replay of my birth experience. This time, I faced the possibility of serious injury or death in the jungles of Southeast Asia. Yet once again grace was operating, allowing me to avoid what I felt was a certain disastrous fate.

Despite the sigh of relief, I still had no desire to go out into the world of careers, money, and responsibility. It all seemed very strange and divorced from my remaining sense of self. But it looked like the compulsory next step in the human experience, so I did my best to fit in. Even though I began to play the game successfully, I grew more and more miserable. The real, deeper me that was still alive sensed there must be something more, even though my ego continually denied it.

I tried to make my world more fascinating and searched for something in it that would get me what I was looking for, but I was not really sure what that was. I yearned for a sense of fulfillment, something that would make me feel good about myself and life. I was hoping to find a direction in the outer world that would feel right and good and fill the nagging sense of emptiness within me.

Unconsciously, I always felt something was missing; there was a hole inside of me that was the source of my primal pain. I kept hoping I would finally find something that would fill that hole. But the more I looked in the outer world, the more that inner sense of lack grew, and with it the suffering.

During this time, both of us were in the throes of the socialization process, developing a sense of self as defined by the prevailing cultural milieu. At this point in the journey, having lost the fundamental connection with our eternal, true inner nature, and faced with a world that is antithetical or even hostile to who we are, we do our best to sculpt a self that will be functional in that inscrutable, inherently conflicted outer world. The more we believe this false self is who we are, the more painful the gnawing sense of disconnection from our true nature becomes.

An inner tension develops as we continue to sculpt this separate ego~personality sense, attempting to get the reinforcement of the world even as the inner emptiness grows. During her early life, Karen focused on being a "good student" and then a "good teacher." She tried to fit into the "teacher" archetype, all the while knowing there was far more to who she was than her job description. Meanwhile, Barry put on the three-piece suit of a banker and played that role as well as he could. *If you do all of this right,* he believed, *you'll finally be happy.*

All the while, as the ego-self does its best to fit in and become what the culture asks, the soul quietly waits within. It surfaces when its presence is essential, as when Barry faced the possibility of going to Vietnam. His inner knowing, the voice of his soul, indicated that it wasn't for him to go there, and provided the guidance that led him through the challenge.

Although we may lose touch with it, the soul never goes away. It never abandons us; it is we who turn our backs on the divinity that lives within us as our true Self. That Self is always operating below the surface, doing whatever it can to prevent us from falling totally asleep or going too far in the wrong direction.

Even when we go off track, even when we do the unthinkable, the infinity of the One forever holds all that occurs within its endlessly allowing embrace. It knows that everything that happens during our earthly embodiments serves awakening, and that one day, we, like all sleeping souls, will remember our true nature. All that we've experienced -- wounding and being wounded, falling asleep and reawakening -- has its place within the divine plan.

3

Soul-Seeds are Planted

Barry: Awakening To An Inner World

One day I noticed an ad for something called Transcendental Meditation. The text said it would bring peace and a quiet mind, two things I didn't experience very often. The next weekend found me sitting in a room with two men in suits, the bag of flowers and fruit I'd been told to bring in front of me. The men gave me a little background on TM and then initiated me with a mantra.

Closing my eyes, I began to quietly repeat the pleasant-sounding but absolutely meaningless two-syllable word. The next thing I knew, a man's voice was calling me back into the room from a place that seemed far away. Opening my eyes, I felt somewhat disoriented, but the peace, joy, happiness and bliss were way beyond anything I had ever felt, even during my best drug experiences. The clock revealed that nearly 45 minutes had passed. I had absolutely no recollection of any of them.

For two days the state remained, but then it quickly faded. Try as I would, meditating didn't bring it back, although I did feel a bit more peaceful. Outer reality quickly began to pave over the memory, and during the next few years I rarely meditated. Yet an opening had occurred and a seed had been planted. It would soon begin to sprout -- but not in ways I would interpret as being "fun" or in my best interest.

Karen: Glimmerings of More

Something prompted me to join a yoga class offered through the adult education program in my school district. The teacher shared quotes from Meher Baba, a guru who, she said, never spoke, but wrote on a blackboard. The saying that stayed with me was "Don't worry, be happy." That sounded like a much better way to live than the anxiety-fraught existence I'd known. But I had no idea how to get from where I was to the blissful, carefree life the phrase promised.

Still, something kept leading me on, and the next step seemed to be a weekend yoga and meditation retreat led by Swami Rama. I didn't understand his discourses, and felt inept at meditating. When we were asked to volunteer for some type of service, I signed up for kitchen duty. There, I watched Addie, the kitchen manager, gliding about the kitchen as she quietly, effortlessly concocted meals for the dozens of participants. As we worked side by side in total silence, I felt a deep, wordless harmony and joy.

After the retreat, I sometimes visited Addie at her home. "Why would you want to spend time with me?" she'd ask. She saw herself as utterly uninteresting, and imagined I'd be bored in her presence. True, she seemed to have no interest in the busyness of the world. Instead, she pursued simpler, quieter pastimes. For instance, she'd cultivated the ability to roll out perfectly round chapatis for her Indian husband's meals. She gathered paperback books and delivered them to shut-ins in her aging red Volkswagen Beetle. In warm weather, Addie sat with me on the front stoop and petted her cats, laughing at their feline ways. We visited her mother's tangled, magical garden and marveled at the new growth on the bushes, the way the sunlight filtered through the trees, and the little ornaments placed in surprising locations. We said little, and enjoyed much.

Reflection

Barry:

Even as I pursued the worldly life I had decided was the goal of human existence, the true Self was standing behind the scenes. As it watched me go even further asleep, far larger powers than my small, human ego were at work, and they managed to get me to the TM meditation. For the first time since very early child-hood, I experienced the peace of the inner realms that always lies within, beneath the busyness of the mind and sensory awareness. That peace rapidly receded, and although I continued to meditate, I would not return to the depths of the inner worlds for some time. Yet a seed had been planted, and a conduit opened between the outer, waking consciousness, asleep in the personality self, and the inner realms of the soul.

Karen:

Addie was a new kind of friend, one who had clearly placed spirituality at the center of her life. She exuded a quiet grace unlike anything I'd ever witnessed in another human being. The ways of living that seemed natural to Addie, which she was sure anyone else would find dull and unexciting, magnetically drew me toward her. All my striving to fit in and be normal had left me parched, thirsty for even a little of the peace that pervaded her simple life.

At a magic moment in each person's existence, the soul begins to come forth. It often starts with an awareness of being unhappy or unfulfilled, and an intuition that an entirely different experience of life is possible. We may find ourselves mysteriously drawn to a book, technique, or workshop that catalyzes an opening to the long-forgotten spiritual realms. The opening may not last, but now we are on the path home, whether we are completely conscious of it or not.

Barry's TM experience was the first time he became aware that something other than his normal, waking state of consciousness existed. In that meditation, discovering a fountain of peace within himself, a seed was planted that would soon sprout and change his life forever.

During evening yoga classes and the weekend retreat, Karen glimpsed a wider world that transcended earthly concerns. It would be some time before that world more fully revealed itself, but the journey had opened up new potentials. Her newfound friend Addie exemplified a radical possibility -- to live not according to the dictates of the world, but from the inner peace and generosity of the soul.

4

Life Starts to Unravel

Barry: The Meltdown Begins

When, in 1974, I was offered a promotion that included a transfer to southern California, I snapped at the opportunity. Los Angeles offered more money, more success, and the good life of oceans, palm trees, and glamorous places and things to experience. Despite the glimpses of the soul that were beginning to occur, I still wanted to climb the corporate ladder and have titles, power, and lots of money. Sure, I was far from happy. The drinking and smoking only increased as I took another step into my cultural role. Everyone I worked with drank a lot, too, and it seemed like the "in" thing to do.

Even with all the stress and addictions, I seemed to be on my way to finding the happiness everyone promised would come once I "grew up" and learned how to succeed in this world. Little did I know that Life had something else planned.

One evening I returned home early from a business trip. Thinking I would surprise my wife, I didn't call her first. When I got to the house, she was not there -- and she did not come home at all that night.

As I lay awake in bed, I felt my life beginning to fall apart. Within a few weeks, the divorce papers were filed. The "perfect marriage" part of the American dream had gone up in smoke. I plunged into an abyss of fear and pain beyond anything I had ever experienced.

Determined to hang on to something solid, I managed to keep the house, even though that meant selling nearly all the furniture to pay the first and second mortgages every month. Lonely and afraid, I got back together with my high school sweetheart. This relationship, too, quickly began to disintegrate, catapulting me deeper into a seemingly bottomless chasm of emotional pain and chaos. My drinking spiraled out of control, while my cigarette consumption doubled.

Yet it seemed as if the possibility for happiness was still just around the corner when an opportunity to fulfill the American dream fell into my lap. Still buying into the dream, still thinking my happiness would come from something out there, I left my corporate career to embark upon a business venture that looked like my ticket to becoming an entrepreneur, my ultimate goal in life. The venture with a fledgling computer company seemed to promise quick and substantial wealth. Within a few months, though, the company filed for bankruptcy and what was left of my financial foundation disappeared. I sold the house just in time to avoid bankruptcy, as my new girlfriend left me for another man.

Everything I attempted to do to get my life together again, to find some semblance of happiness, failed. I would muster all my strength, will, and intelligence to push forward, only to encounter some invisible force that pushed back even harder. I felt as though I were in free fall, tumbling into a black hole with no bottom. Everything I thought I was, everything I believed my life was about, was being crushed. What more could possibly happen? Would I be destroyed?

One day, just home from work and still in my suit, I sat on my empty living room floor drinking a beer and smoking a cigarette. As I reflected on my life, what hurt the most was the way things had so abruptly turned around. Just a short time ago, many of my dreams had actually been coming true: My wife and I were steadily climbing the career ladder, the house we had purchased was appreciating, and we often drove to the nearby beach in one of our new cars.

But underneath it all, even then, something was still missing. While everything indicated that I should be totally happy, somehow I wasn't. I often found myself thinking that maybe something was wrong with me. I told myself that if I tried harder, kept advancing in my career, and made more money, everything would eventually work out OK.

On this desolate evening, I looked out the window and my eyes came to rest on the orange tree my wife and I had planted when we bought the house. Full of optimism, we had toasted our future with visions of the rental homes and skyrocketing careers we would have when this little tree finally flowered and bore fruit. Now, as I peered out the window, there on one of the branches was the first flower the spindly little tree had ever produced.

The reality of my life came crashing down. As I collapsed to the floor, the ocean of pain broke through the floodgates, and I cried and cried. Shattered and empty, I finally had to admit that I was unable to cope with what life had thrown at me. I felt powerless, completely incapable of righting the ship of my life and finding any semblance of peace, joy and happiness. I needed help.

I found myself praying to a God I wasn't sure even existed. It had become clear that I really didn't know much about anything. I was failing at life. In that moment, without knowing how I knew, I saw that I had to completely let go of all my ideas about who I was, why I was here, and what life was all about. I had to release the egoic belief that I could do it on my own. There was nothing else to do but wipe the slate clean and begin to learn how to live again, even though I had no idea how that would ever happen.

Karen: Death Without and Within

At 28, I found myself living with a handsome man who was bright and funny and strong-willed. Our Scorpio-Taurus polarity provided plenty of passion, and although he saw me as "too spiritual" and I judged him as "too materialistic," we found a lot to enjoy together. Had I met my life partner? I wasn't sure. Other romances had come and gone, and that had not always been easy. Only time would tell.

On New Year's Day, 1980, I awoke with the inner knowing that, despite the love that we shared, my boyfriend and I were not meant to go on together. As much as I had hoped that maybe he was "the one," it suddenly became obvious that our lives were headed in different directions. I wasn't totally sure what they were, but I knew they would not overlap.

Part of me wished I could make the inner knowing go away. A deep sadness at losing the closeness we did share coexisted with a sense of inevitability. My inner knowings had never been wrong; I knew we were finished. Still, it was painful to walk away from my first "adult" relationship, and a man I loved and enjoyed being with.

Within weeks, on a day that began like any other, I picked up the phone to learn that when my mother didn't show up for work, a neighbor had been called. This kind woman had the unfortunate task of discovering my mother's body in the garage, slumped in her car with the motor running.

We had talked just days before; I'd picked up no inkling of anything amiss. My mind numbly went over how desperately alone and hopeless she must have felt to end her life. *Why didn't I know?*

Why was there nothing I could have done? And why is this happening to me?

My father was on the West Coast for business; I arranged to join his eastbound flight in Denver. We flew across the country in stupefied silence. What was there to say? During the next month at our family home, I awoke each morning to the same horrendous reality; nothing else seemed to exist.

A family friend came over to help me fill boxes with Mom's clothing to donate to charity. "This isn't normal," Mary flatly stated as we slid Mom's closet doors open. "It's too perfect."

My gaze traveled over the neatly arranged outfits, each with its matching scarf draped over the shoulders. *What do you mean?* I wondered.

This was how Mom had always been. When I was 16, she'd hired me to clean the house. A week later I'd been fired; my efforts were not up to her standards. What Mary saw as "not normal" was the only model of how to be a woman I had known. For decades I've struggled to shed that obsessive perfectionism, determined not to let it take me out, too. I've had to let myself off that hook, even when it meant things were not as tidy and impeccable as a part of me thought they should be.

We'd had our rough years, Mom and I, but during my year of therapy a lot of healing had taken place. By the time of her death we had become close, and I had found a place of forgiveness and peace about all that I thought had taken place between us. Although I still felt dismayed that I hadn't picked up anything amiss in her voice on that last call, there was some small consolation in the fact that our last words to each other were "I love you."

Each day I'd console myself with the inner feeling that was becoming clearer by the day: *This must be happening for a reason. It must be that someday, somehow, I'm to use this experience to help others. There just isn't any other way it could make sense for me to be going through this much pain.*

I continued to wonder how this intensely harrowing personal tragedy could possibly be preparing me to help others. Although I understood "things happen for a reason," I couldn't imagine what the reason might be. Yet somehow, I trusted it would be revealed over time.

Meanwhile, it was enough to make it through each day. How do you manage to go out into the world to buy food and do errands when your mother has just killed herself? The people I ran into seemed so put-upon by the smallest things; they were clueless about how bad it really could be, and I wasn't about to tell them. Dad, my brother and I would do what had to be done, and then retreat home. But home wasn't exactly comforting, either: Mom h. ended her life on the other side of the family room wall.

Within a few weeks of Mom's death, my brother had returned home, and Dad seemed stable enough to be left on his own. I had come into a certain level of stability, too. It was time to resume my own life. When I arrived home, I learned that the bookstore owner needed to economize, and I was laid off indefinitely. Would the shocks never end?

Reflection

Barry:

The further I dove into the world, the more miserable I became, even though I was achieving all the things that were supposed to make me happy. Onward I pushed, in denial of the escalating pain and emptiness as I numbed myself with substances. All the while, as I became ever more lost, an infinitely intelligent, loving and powerful presence was silently observing and allowing until its time to come forth arrived. When it asserted itself, I certainly didn't experience it as a gift of loving grace. Far from it! Everything I had been working for and trying to become looked like it was being destroyed.

A powerful force had entered my life, an unstoppable will that systematically crushed my ego's attempts to stay in control. Each time I pushed forward with my personal agenda, it countered with a greater force that thrust me even further backward. I found myself losing more and more ground. I was worn down until that fateful moment when my ego went belly up and I had to confess that I didn't have a clue how to live my life.

Karen:

Like most people, Barry and I entered adulthood trying to find our place in the world, seeking happiness and fulfillment. Now, each of us had reached a crisis point. While Barry found himself on the floor of his home in Orange County, broken down and defeated, my relationship ended, my mother killed herself, and my job vanished.

of us could ever be the same person after this. We
k; what was had ended. The context we lived within
ded. What lay ahead?

For most of us, individualizing and developing a self sense
capable of functioning in the world is a necessary evolutionary
step. The personality may become quite well-integrated and highly
functional in the world's terms. A steady stream of the goodies of
life may flow our way, including abundance, acclaim, and perhaps
even a measure of fame.

Yet as wonderful as it may seem on the surface, often this
"successful" life is still not a genuine expression of the true, eternal
Self. The personality has formed a highly intricate story: "This is
who I am, what life is all about, and what I am here to do." But this
carefully constructed persona may have little to do with the truth of
the soul.

At a certain point in the journey, the sense of self we constructed to function in the world has to be broken down so the soul
can take dominion. When the moment of crisis arrives, it can be
shattering for the human self. The degree to which we are attached
to and identified with our life pattern and the accompanying reinforcement we receive from the world largely determines how intense the shock and subsequent breakdown process will be. As
the true, eternal Self begins to take dominion, there is really nothing the ego~personality self can do to stop it.

Whether gradually or suddenly, all that the ego has prized,
everything it has worked so hard to acquire and maintain, is revealed as incapable of giving us the fulfillment we have sought.
When the worldly self we have so carefully fashioned starts to disintegrate, we feel as if we are being annihilated. What is really
happening, though, is that the human self has begun to be reabsorbed into the soul.

Eventually, the ego's tight grip on the controls is broken.
For some, this occurs gradually, while for others denial ends suddenly with a big "Aha." Many hit a point at which the suffering that
has always been there, buried beneath layers of compensatory
behaviors, becomes unbearable. Nearly everyone finally has to
admit that all efforts to find lasting peace and happiness in the
pleasures of the world have failed. What remains is a willingness to
surrender and turn within to seek assistance from a higher power.

Whatever it takes for this surrender to occur is, despite
appearances, a beneficent and loving act of grace from beyond.
For at last, the feet are firmly planted on the path Home.

5

New Dimensions Unfold

Barry: A Subtle yet Unforgettable Shift

For weeks, a spiraling vortex of discouraging events and circumstances had seemed to be dragging me down into oblivion. I felt completely worn out, exhausted from the stress, and very, very depressed. The breakdown and surrender on the floor of my living room had caused me to begin to question everything. Although this felt like a new start, I was painfully aware that my life still seemed to be in shambles.

On a chilly October evening in 1978, I sat in a car outside a drugstore in West Los Angeles, waiting for friends to pick up a prescription. There didn't seem to be enough strength left within me to face one more day. And I really didn't even care anymore. I wondered where my plunge into the black hole would end. Would I wind up in a mental institution? I had begun to understand why people commit suicide.

Something inside me felt there was only one choice left: to let go of all efforts to make things different. That evening, as I felt my will to continue the struggle collapsing, I let go and felt myself tumbling down into a deep void, while everything around me dissolved.

Then I felt an almost imperceptible shift, the significance of which I would not fully comprehend for many years. Something rippled through my awareness, as though an energy was descending into and through me from above. It felt very subtle, yet profound. *Something* had shifted. While I wasn't sure exactly what had changed, I did not feel the same as I had moments before.

friends got back into the car, I opened my eyes. I felt
_. couldn't have explained how. Somehow, at the most
_mental level, my experience of who I was had been altered,
though this was only a dim awareness at the time. While at one
level everything seemed the same, I now saw the world through a
subtly transformed lens of perception. Something new was present; something nearly imperceptible yet powerfully significant had
occurred. I did not know it, but I had reached a new beginning.

As the days and weeks passed, the pain lessened at
times, while at others it felt even worse. But something else had
begun to happen. At first it seemed to be a problem with my heart.
At times, for no apparent reason, I had a feeling of increased energy, a sort of excitement, in the area just above my physical heart.
It was puzzling, because it wasn't a "bad" feeling, but it was unex-
plainable. Having been under so much stress, I was worried the
unusual sensations might be the precursor to a heart attack.

I noticed that this excitation occurred at certain times, usually in relation to something I was experiencing in outer life. It began to become apparent that there was indeed an intelligence behind these upwellings of energy. As I relaxed into the feeling, the
anxiety and fear eased, and it actually felt very pleasant. At times it
even felt joyful and expansive.

One day a friend was telling me how helpful acupuncture
could be for stress and emotional imbalance. I had never considered acupuncture; it was outside my sphere of experience and
seemed a bit strange and scary. As my friend went on, the feeling
in the upper heart area came on very strongly. The pleasant sensation gave me the sense that I should investigate acupuncture. It
turned out to be one of the most healing modalities I had ever experienced. My stress level immediately began to drop and I felt
much better.

Over the next few months, I noticed that this energy/
excitation occurred any time there was something that "it," whatever "it" was, wanted me to pay attention to and consider more
deeply. Each time I followed the lead of this mysteriously intelligent
"heart prompting," the results turned out to be very positive.

I began to consciously utilize this inner guiding force. At
the Bodhi Tree bookstore, I'd browse until I got that same excitation and feeling of "yes." I'd buy the book and dive into it, curious
what had prompted its purchase. Inevitably I'd discover something
stimulating and relevant to my journey within it.

Soon, the heart prompting became the primary compass in
my life. Its ability to guide me went way beyond the futile attempts
of my mind. As I responded to the sensations in my chest, doors
opened to new and more life-evoking possibilities. Over time, it

became obvious that my prayer for divine assistance had been answered. A highly intelligent presence that clearly had my best interests in mind now guided me, and somehow it was right within my own being.

During the period that followed, I began to consciously ask the Big Questions: *Who am I, really? Why am I here? What is existence all about?* I checked out all sorts of metaphysical information, and found out things that were strangely compelling. In *Strangers Among Us,* Ruth Montgomery declared that many souls were "walking into" the bodies of earthly souls who wanted to go on to other realms. These beings, she went on, were coming in to assist humanity through a period of great upheaval and cataclysm, after which a new Golden Age would be born.

As I read, I couldn't help feeling that this was my story. Ruth Montgomery's book seemed to be the outer messenger arriving to explain the event in the parking lot in West L.A. During the subtle, pervasive shift that had occurred, a vaster, higher-dimensional presence had descended into "Barry." At a fundamental level, Barry was no longer the same person.

Barry: Who or What Am I?

By now, my whole sense of being had begun to shift. I spent less and less time "in my head" as consciousness increasingly focused in the upper part of my heart. My awareness often felt drawn to rest there, even while reading, driving and engaging in all the other activities of life. I felt deeply attracted to the warm, comforting, peaceful feeling that resided there. As the inner feeling of rightness came to guide my outer life, the sense of peace and well-being deepened into a current that flowed through my existence nearly continuously.

One of those inner feelings sent me in quest of transcripts from a metaphysical radio show. I soon found myself knocking on a door in a rough neighborhood in central Los Angeles. Looking over the shoulder of my pinstriped suit, I realized I was the only white person I had seen for many blocks.

A small, thin black man came to the door and asked who I was. When I told him my name, he said, "I've been expecting you." With a sly smile, he asked, "What took you so long?"

Inviting me inside, Don told me that some time ago he had been given the guidance that I would be coming. He also said there was someone with me -- a guide, who was really a larger part of me. In future conversations he often referred to this being as Martin.

Until this time, I was fairly convinced that the person I saw in the mirror was pretty much the limits of who I was. Don woke me up to the fact that my existence was not limited to the physical, human being called Barry. During many an evening in his tiny apartment, all that unfolded progressively awakened me to the multidimensional nature of myself and the universe.

One of the earliest of these experiences occurred one night when I went to use the bathroom. The small room was illuminated by a rather strange blue light. As I looked in the mirror, my face began to change, becoming more and more wrinkled until it looked at least a hundred years old. The face in the mirror reminded me of photographs of very old native Americans, their faces as etched with crevices as a dry riverbed. The longer I looked at this face, the older it got, until it began to resemble what I imagined a mummy's face might look like.

As I stared at this face in the mirror, I realized that my true age was far different from the nearly thirty years that I had been in this body. In that moment, I suddenly understood that my existence spanned an immense expanse of time. "Barry" was part of a continuous beingness that existed beyond the limitations of this lifetime and this body.

When I came out of the bathroom, Don took one look at my dazed and amazed face, laughed, and said, "Found something out about yourself in there, didn't you?" Time and again, Don demonstrated that his awareness went far beyond anything I had ever known possible. I knew that somehow, he was involved in orchestrating these strange, revelatory experiences that were common during my visits.

While it all seemed unfathomable to me at the time, Don always spoke with a clarity and certainty that rang of the truth. My mind spun, at times, trying to grasp what he told me, and to come to grips with the overwhelming eccentricity and genius of Don's very nature. Early on in our connection, Don explained that the Earth is in the process of a major transition. He spoke of this as the "End Times," or "the end of the world," at least as we know it, and he often referred to the biblical Book of Revelations. Don said he had been "taken up" many times to meet a being he called the "Lord God of Abraham," who had shown him many things about the "End Times."

Although he had shared it with very few human beings, Don allowed me to read the book he had compiled about these experiences. This opened my mind to concepts and possibilities far beyond anything I had previously considered. The metaphors and symbology in his accounts excited and sometimes frightened me.

In the higher worlds, Don had been shown many strange events that were to unfold on the Earth. With the passage of time, much of what Don revealed more than three decades ago has proven to be true. In the mid-70s, no one questioned the integrity of the Catholic Church, yet Don told me that not only was the Vatican one of the wealthiest entities on the planet, it also contained rampant corruption. He said Israel would be the focus of the events that would unfold at the end of time, adding that as we approach that moment, the tension surrounding Israel would mount.

Don made it clear that the events that will unfold are not yet determined. He did say, though, that where it will all end is assured. A new, universal religion would arise, centered on the realization that everyone is a part of the One God. The remnants of the old age would be destroyed and a new, divine Earth and human species would emerge.

During one of Don's journeys, he was taken to a place where a great angel stood before him. The angel had one foot on the land and one foot on the sea, and held a light aloft. The angel's voice boomed with the proclamation, "Time shall be no more." Later, Don came to understand that this was the seventh angel to appear in the biblical Book of Revelations.

On Don's wall hung a painting he had created after this experience. One day, Don pointed to the portrait of this great angel, and told me that the seventh angel somehow influenced my life. He implied that the angel was related to Martin, the larger presence he had often said accompanied me always.

The idea of beings living at higher levels was a relatively new concept, and definitely outside my personal experience. That such a being was with me constantly stretched the limits of what I believed possible. Yet looking at that picture, I felt that yes, somehow, the being Don had painted did seem to be related to me, even though this seemed insanely delusional to my rational mind.

Over time, all that Don shared cracked open my self-definition and identity as "Barry." If I were to believe what Don insisted was true, I was not only a being whose existence spanned many lifetimes stretching into the ancient past. I was also somehow linked with a presence who resided in other dimensions of reality, as well as the seventh angel in Revelations. All of this seemed wildly crazy and unfathomable to the "me" that thought of himself as a banker. But the now-familiar feeling inside told me that it was all true.

Barry: An Awakening into Nonduality

One night in the steam room of the health club, I met a very interesting man who invited me to a meeting with his Sufi teacher, Linda. This opened yet another door to entirely new realms of awareness. Linda shared fascinating, powerful teachings that were based on the work of Gurdjieff and Ouspensky. I began to practice seeing everything and everyone in my life as absolutely perfect, and gave my life up to God -- or, as Linda simply referred to it, "X."

As the weeks passed, I entered into a very quiet and expanded state. The mind slowed down and essentially stopped, and all my fears and worries about life dissipated. As consciousness expanded, the sense of "me" began to dissolve. I seemed to be walking through a waking dream that felt more real than the dream I had been in.

I would lie down at night and watch the body go to sleep, while consciousness was still present. In this deeply restful space, dreams arose and consciousness witnessed the dreaming process as well as the dream. Without "sleeping" I would arise after four hours or so, feeling more rested than I had after eight hours of normal sleep.

The body began to regenerate, giving off a slight radiant glow, especially around the face. Everyone noticed it, and I became Linda's prize student. I soared free of the mind, entering a space of boundlessness -- empty, yet supremely full. Free of my pain and suffering, I felt as though I would expand forever.

The sense of being anchored in the human experience steadily diminished as I drifted into another whole dimension of reality. Its blissful luminosity exerted a powerful pull on my awareness. This definitely was not the world in which I had been living, where everyone else still existed. At times an existential loneliness arose. I felt disconnected from the memory of my previous life experience, which seemed so much more visceral and tactile than this new state. I seemed to be drifting ever further away from certain things I still loved about the human experience, and I wasn't completely sure that where I was heading was what I wanted.

A part of me felt the need to continue to dig up my shadow material. Committed to facing everything within me, I became aware of some unfinished business around my sexuality and decided to see a therapist. Since running, denying and hiding from things were becoming less and less an option, it seemed clear that the path to freedom went directly through these painful inner spaces.

Linda warned me against going into all of this and said it would ruin my state. She taught that these issues didn't matter, and that it was possible to rise above it all. Yet somehow, I felt I had to face these shadows and resolve them. The only choice I had was to stay true to myself.

Gradually, Linda withdrew her energy and attention. She ignored me in class and talked about how foolish it was that some students were seeing sex therapists. As the star pupil became persona non grata, I felt crushed and left the group.

Now, the exalted state began to fade. As the mind started up again, so did the suffering. The more I attempted to quiet the thoughts and hold on to the state, the more the mind reasserted its dominion. I felt myself falling back to sleep, buying into the mind and conditioning. This was a truly hellish experience. As I lost the state, I spiraled back down into fear, pain and density, living out the nightmare of my childhood. I felt so hopeless that thoughts of ending it all again crossed my mind. After having sworn off alcohol, I found myself drinking and smoking heavily again.

The beautiful, clear state I had been experiencing was all I wanted, but now it was evaporating. I had identified my state with the group and Linda, and undoubtedly, the strong transmission from her presence had supported the opening in consciousness. Now that she was no longer in my life, the state likewise faded.

To have been so free of self and mind and then fall back into the clutches of ego left me devastated. I seemed to be replaying the original fall from grace. Yet now the goal had been revealed; I had been there. The longing never went away, even though years would pass before I tasted the clarity of that inner expansion again.

Karen: Life in the Aftermath

My life seemed to be in free-fall. My relationship was over, my job had vanished, and hardest of all, Mom was gone. I decided to give myself a year to mourn her passing as thoroughly as I needed to. A fierce need to protect the grieving process seized me; it suddenly became all-important to let it happen exactly the way it wanted to unfold from within. It must have mystified well-meaning friends when I politely but firmly refused the advice, books, and flower essences they so kindly offered. The inner compulsion to let the process have its way coexisted with the sense that if I fully grieved now, I would not be haunted by Mom's suicide for the rest of my life.

Feeling a need for solid, professional help, I sought out bereavement counseling. Those weekly sessions provided a safe haven, a lifeline during that painful passage. To this day it is hard to imagine a kinder, more compassionate being than Marcia Lattanzi, whose unconditional support enabled me to be with all the feelings that surfaced as I made peace with Mom's passing and found a way through the other challenges I faced.

I wasn't done grieving after a year had passed, but the pain wasn't nearly as raw. I could talk about Mom's suicide without being flooded by emotion. On the first evening of a weekend retreat, each of the fifty or so women gathered around the campfire shared what was foremost in their lives. The themes of death and mothers repeatedly arose, until the talking stick came to me and they coalesced in the story of Mom's suicide.

"If only she'd had a place like this to share her feelings, she might still be here," I concluded. Few eyes were dry as we realized the precious gift of our coming together.

That group of women continued to meet monthly, sharing song, story, and ceremony. We washed the feet of a woman nearing her birthing time, passed a sacred pipe around the circle, and absorbed the wisdom of our white-haired spiritual godmother, who read us passages from Sri Aurobindo's stirring epic, *Savitri.* We danced, chanted, and shared food, caring, and sacred space.

Intermittently at first, my ability to feel joy and happiness began to return. I resumed working at the bookstore, and my finances stabilized. I learned to make beadwork jewelry, continued to create custom calligraphy pieces, and taught hundreds of people the art of beautiful lettering. Mom's death was gradually weaving into the fabric of my being. I might not ever "get over" it, but I was learning to live with it.

Karen: New Vistas

Three years before, I had made the first of the many big moves that would take place in my life. Although teaching had been satisfying in many ways, an inner feeling had persistently hinted there was something more I was supposed to be doing with my life. I had no idea what that might be. Seeing an ad for a feminist therapist, I thought, *Maybe she can help me find out.* Pallas turned out to be as insightful as the goddess of wisdom for whom she was named. My year of therapy gave me the confidence to leave teaching in 1977 and move west to Boulder, Colorado.

I'd been accepted into a Ph.D. program in Developmental Psychology, and I hoped to become a liaison between kids and their parents and teachers, promoting mutual understanding through improved communication. But a few months into the program, I found myself crying in the lavatory between classes. I'd begun to read Carlos Castaneda's books, in which he advocated pursuing "a path with heart." It was becoming all too clear that, for me, getting a Ph.D. was not it. Yet I'd received a full scholarship, along with a teaching and research assistantship. That was no small thing. How could I leave the program? And what would happen to my life if I did?

One day after class, I found myself walking downtown to my favorite used book shop. The next thing I knew, I had a part-time job. For someone as incessantly curious as I was, this was a dream come true. Ten thousand books filled every nook and cranny of the charming old house, and much of my small salary purchased additions to my own burgeoning library.

Boulder offered a perpetual spiritual smorgasbord. The higher education that had drawn me to this magical place continued in a new form, with the world's spiritual teachings as the curriculum. It seemed the Ph.D. program was merely the ruse Life had used to get me to leave my comfortable existence and move to this alluring place at the edge of the mountains.

I practiced yoga and tai chi, took classes at Naropa University, participated in sweat lodges and Zen retreats, Sufi dances and past life regression workshops. In between, I read hundreds of books. Through it all grew the understanding that there was a lot more going on than the surface of life indicated.

A psychic told me I had come to Earth from Venus with the Kumaras long ago. I had always loved art and music and all things imbued with Venusian beauty, so the message resonated within my budding self-awareness. She also said that my interest in herbs, wild plants, and earthy crafts and rituals reflected many past lives as a Native American. In a workshop, I'd glimpsed a past life during which I left my body while traveling across the Great Plains in a blizzard with the little band that was my tribe. I had also participated in sweat lodges and pipe ceremonies, all of which had felt strangely familiar. My focus on such things would fall away, the psychic indicated, as my new expression in this life came forth.

"Once we have gathered in and honored the essence of past lives," she said, "we can move on."

She encouraged me to continue to investigate whatever had energy. Out of that open-ended exploration, she predicted, the deeper purpose of this life would emerge.

During this time, while my mother was still among us, my father was transferred to the Midwest. One day not long afterward, my mother called to share some news.

"You'll never guess who has bought our house!" she said.

It turned out Jane Roberts and her husband, Robert Butts, had purchased our family's longtime home. Mom was well aware that Ruth, my former music teacher and first spiritual guide, had attended Jane's psychic development classes, and that I'd eagerly read each of the Seth books as it was released. When I visited our former town some time later, I stopped in at our old house. Jane welcomed me in and showed me where she did her writing. There was her desk, in the room that had been my bedroom!

It seemed there was some sort of mysterious cross-fertilization taking place between us. Just as the Seth books had profoundly affected my consciousness, was Jane now receiving an infusion of my energy as she wrote the subsequent volumes in my former bedroom? Perhaps our souls were blending across time and space in ways there were no words to describe. Maybe the exchange of essence was planting seeds that would prepare me to someday teach and write about spiritual evolution and awakening, just as Jane did. In my former bedroom in the "Hill House," as she referred to our erstwhile home in her later books, Jane's soul would continue to unfold in ways that I, too, would one day experience. It all seemed intriguing and highly significant, though I could not have explained how.

Karen: The Grouping

Now, three years later, I was still reeling in the aftermath of Mom's suicide and the end of my first real relationship. During this potent time, glimpses of new possibilities alternated with immersions in the suffering that continued to erupt from deep within. Sometimes, I felt so flattened by it all that I could barely make it through the day. At other moments, I sensed the first glimmerings of a place beyond this uncomfortable evolutionary crucible I found myself inhabiting.

In meditation, I began to experience myself as part of a vast network of beings, all of whom existed in the nonphysical realms but me. I felt their presence far above my earthly life, where they seemed to be watching me and cheering me on. They conveyed that I was their "Earth representative," and that they wished to work through me to the degree I was available for that. I often inwardly heard or sensed their communications -- making suggestions, guiding me, pointing out what I needed to see and know about situations and relationships. Sometimes the information seemed to pour in from the totality of this enormous collective presence. At others, it came through a particular individuated aspect of the group, most often a male presence with a puckish sense of humor.

I began to bring the ever-present multitude of questions that arose about my life to these presences. As soon as I'd ask, the response immediately arrived. When it came in as a wordless knowing, it seemed to originate from within the totality of the group. When I'd "hear" specific words, they were "spoken" by the male presence who apparently individuated to communicate with me more directly.

Once, I asked how I was to refer to this vast community of souls. Did they have a name? I received the answer that they really didn't have a name, but if I liked I could refer to them as the Grouping. The individual and collective presences of the Grouping continued to gently guide my evolution, spaciously allowing me to go my own way but always available should I decide to ask for their insight.

Karen: You are Being Prepared...

Throughout this time, I often recalled a cartoon that I'd tacked to the door of my dorm room in college. In it, a round-faced character sits, head in hands, asking *Why me? Why me?*

In the next frame the individual simply sits, looking dejected.

In the final frame, a voice from above says, *Why not you?*

At the time, this seemed to sum up the way my life felt. Now, it reminded me that, for whatever reason, dealing with Mom's suicide must be my lot in life, because it was what was happening. I might as well do the best I could with it.

From time to time, when the intensity seemed unbearable and the emotions felt overwhelming, I'd ask inwardly, *Why am I going through all of this? What is this about?* In response, I always heard the same message: *You are being prepared for a time when there will be large numbers of people in crisis.*

The import of these words felt prophetic and full of portent. Hearing them didn't mitigate the pain, but they intimated it had a purpose. Yet I couldn't imagine how this harrowing phase of my life could be preparing me for an even more challenging time to come. How could I possibly serve during such a time? I was barely making it through each day, overwhelmed with my own suffering and that of humanity as a whole. Far from feeling that I was on an ascent toward some eventual service, it seemed that I was being systematically dismantled down to the very bedrock of all I thought I was. In every respect, this current phase was the antithesis of everything I had ever dreamed my life could be.

I had no clue how the devastating experience of Mom's suicide could or would prepare me to assist others. Yet the newly present sense that there was a purpose in this suffering, perhaps even a measure of dignity in it, gave me courage to continue through the dark woods the landscape of my life had become. If all of this loss could somehow become the compost for a new way of being, maybe I would someday fulfill my destiny in a way that was far beyond any possibility I could now envision.

The way through the forest still seemed lonely and long, but I had received an indication that this path I was on went someplace. And there was somebody witnessing all that I was going through -- a presence that could see the meaning in it all, and know its eventual outcome. I couldn't tell if the message came from the Grouping, or an even vaster level. All I knew was that, despite the ominous future the message portended, I apparently had a meaningful place within it, a role that would allow me to somehow assist others and perhaps mitigate their suffering.

It remained to be seen how Life would carry me from where I now stood, shocked and shattered, to being utilized by larger forces during a time of collective crisis. I had no idea how this transformation would come to pass, but I was willing to undergo whatever preparation it entailed.

Reflection

~ ~ ~

Barry:

I look back on the evening that my ego and I collapsed on the floor of my condo with gratitude. Through grace, I had reached a degree of humility, and could finally admit that I had no idea how to live my life and needed help. The desire in my heart for assistance seemed to have no other place to be directed than to a God I hoped might really be there.

It didn't take the Divine long to respond, for, unbeknownst to me, it was already assuming dominion over my life. The seeds were sown during the TM meditation experience, when a channel opened between the soul's domain and my personality-identified sense of self. That evening in the parking lot in West L. A., the process of ego~personality death escalated as the pain became so intolerable that I pondered the possibility of giving up this life. As I dissolved more deeply than ever into the inky blackness within, a conception occurred. A vast presence descended from above and anchored a cord of itself within my being. That tendril would remain forever unbroken, providing a conduit for the oversoul's gradual descent.

My prayer for guidance had been more than answered, for now a presence was moving within, making itself known to my conscious awareness as a movement of energy in the area just above my heart. This was the beginning of consciously communing with the soul. The upwelling of the Divine from the core of my soul became the compelling dynamic that catalyzed realizing my true nature.

As I responded to the inner sensations and allowed the soul into my life, everything began to shift. Behind the newfound feeling, I sensed an intelligent presence that knew exactly how to guide me through life. It took me on a mysterious voyage, opening up possibilities and dimensions of consciousness that evoked feelings of gratitude and awe. The pain and suffering lessened, replaced by more and more peace, joy and happiness.

This ever-unfolding journey was more satisfying than anything I had ever experienced, and gave me hope for what was to come. It took me to Don and then Linda to continue the process of dissolving my limiting identities and bringing me into deeper communion with who I really was. Exploring and merging with this presence became the central focus of my life, the "everything" I had been waiting to discover.

But the path does not always take us on a straight, upward ascent. There were many downs following the ups, especially after being with Linda. Even as I was thrust into powerful expansions of consciousness, my awareness was also propelled into the unconscious realms to face yet another wounded, exiled aspect of the psyche that was ready to come home to the soul. For most of us, this seems to be the way the journey unfolds.

All the while, the soul was clearly guiding and orchestrating the process, increasing my faith and trust. Even when things felt shaky, chaotic and painful, that still, small voice within the center of my being let me know I was on the right track, despite all outer appearances. A new, vast, multidimensional sense of who and what I was continued to magically unfold as the old sense of "me" went on dissolving.

Karen:

Like so many awakening souls, I apparently needed to be taken apart and put back together again in an entirely new configuration. My egoic sense of self was clearly becoming an evolutionary limit, so it had to be dismantled in order for the larger Self to take dominion over my life. Just as when a building is demolished, the fallout and debris can be considerable, requiring many years to deal with.

Yet the beginnings of a spiritual foundation had been laid long before through the connection with Ruth, the music teacher that became my first guide to the new territory. Through her, I became familiar with Jane Roberts' books, which had a profound impact on my budding metaphysical awareness. When Jane and her husband later moved into my family's former home, a web was being woven in a way that seemed both very unusual and highly significant.

The Seth Material and Jane's subsequent books had opened me to the realization that we are all part of a vaster world than we have ever imagined. This spoke to the magical, transcendental self within me that I had sent underground when I lost my sparkly rocks and fireflies. Her writings reawakened things I knew, but couldn't have put into words. As I read Seth's statements -- for instance, that humans' thoughts and feelings and energies create the weather -- I didn't really understand the words themselves, yet deep down I knew they were true.

So, all the while I was trying to create a third-dimensional, material plane life, a deeper aspect of my being was galvanized toward reading Jane Roberts' books and contemplating the expansive, often startling messages they delivered. And strange, synchronous connections abounded: Jane and I lived in the same town in upstate New York (one of my high school teachers even lived in the same apartment building as Jane and her husband, and I often passed it on my way to school), my dear music teacher Ruth attended Jane's classes and told me about them in intriguing detail, and to top it all off, Jane and her husband then moved into my family's former house!

Back then, I never imagined I'd someday be writing books, but someone who had published several volumes was continuing her writing career in my former bedroom. Maybe, if I'd had eyes to see, the intriguing series of synchronicities involving Jane Roberts was hinting at the destiny path I would one day follow.

Years later, sitting in the women's group around that camp-fire, I made the powerful discovery that what I was going through had meaning for others. Some were deeply touched, weeping with shared feeling, while nearly everyone was moved in some way by what I expressed. Although I had no idea at the time, this experience set the tone for much of what was to follow in my life.

My inner knowing had always been strong, but during this time the oversoul presences beyond physicality that referred to themselves as the Grouping came into my awareness. The budding realizations that I was not alone here and that I was part of a vaster level of beingness gave me great comfort, as did asking any question and receiving clear, definite guidance from Beyond. While I continued to grapple with shock, grief, loneliness, and other painful emotions, I was simultaneously becoming aware that I could look to that vastness for solace and understanding. I didn't always remember to do it, but when I turned upward and asked for help, so much more than what was available in this dimension poured in.

As both of us were discovering, the breakdown of the personality is the breakthrough for the soul. When our egos let go and surrendered, the vaster dimensions of Self began to shine through, and our conscious connection with the indwelling divinity allowed it to more fully guide our lives.

During this phase of the journey, we begin to experience ourselves as far more than the small, human self with its vulnerability, limitation and pain. At first it may seem that we are being stretched beyond our capacity to survive, as one "death" after another is followed by a corresponding expansion of our self sense and experience of the world. Yet through it all, we discover that with each death, a birth must follow.

Even though the breakdown continues, breakthroughs occur with ever greater frequency, and the light of the soul begins to guide us through our lives. As we discover there is something within that we can trust more than anything we have previously relied on in the world, we find ourselves transported through a mysterious journey of unfoldment that is both joyous and, at times, terrifying. While our orientation gradually shifts from the outer world to the inner realms, our self sense morphs and alters, as ever more of who and what we thought we were dissolves into the greater truth of the Self.

At this stage in the journey, the soul -- the individuated spark of the One Great Being -- is awakening, shining its light and presence into and through the outer-acting personality. As awakening progresses, the ego-self rejoins the soul, while the soul re-unites with its vaster, overlighting oversoul. Residing eternally be-yond the human experience, the oversoul may have "extruded" many individual soul aspects incarnated on this and other planets. At the same time, the oversoul exists in eternal, conscious union with the Godhead or Source.

As we shift our identification from the human ego~person-ality to the vast, eternal soul and oversoul, the journey of awaken-ing gathers momentum. No longer is awareness as heavily veiled by the limited self sense of the ego-mind. The higher light of the soul and the transcendent oversoul now exert their influence and take ever more control over our consciousness. This fundamental shift may be punctuated by potent initiatory events, as Barry expe-rienced in the parking lot and when Karen "heard" her oversoul grouping break through with clear guidance and insight.

These peak experiences indelibly etch the truth of our larger nature onto the receptive surface of the mind. Such mo-ments serve as mile markers on the long, gradual journey as the ego loses ground and the soul takes dominion. This is the organic process through which a soul-awakened human is birthed into ex-istence.

6

A Pivotal Moment Arrives

Barry: The Point of No Return

One Monday morning, hung over and heartsick, I found myself driving to a business meeting. On top of everything else, over the weekend yet another relationship had come to an end. Groggily traveling the freeways across Los Angeles, I had no idea that this day would become one of the most pivotal turning points in this life.

The meeting was with a young entrepreneur I'll call Richard, who had built a mini-empire of small companies engaged in defense-related subcontracting. I entered a suite overlooking Newport Harbor, a picturesque paradise of water and colorful boats. The man across the desk, in his early forties, tan and fit, reached out to shake my hand. Photos of a beautiful wife and family adorned his credenza, along with snapshots of his yacht and other sailboats and a number of regatta trophies.

Here was the embodiment of the ultimate dream image for my life. Despite the glimpses of enlightenment I'd experienced in Linda's presence and all that Don had revealed about who I really was, Richard epitomized the idealized self my ego still strove to become. His world offered a jarring juxtapose to my current weary, heartbroken state.

As the meeting progressed, I learned that Richard wanted to buy an aluminum foundry, owned by an older man content to let it grow slowly and steadily. I had often financed such takeovers, and was used to seeing aggressive entrepreneurs gulp up small, docile companies for a fraction of their real value. It always both-ered me, but today, with the gaping heart wound, I felt the pain more than ever.

When I asked Richard how he intended to position this company in his defense contracting empire, he said that he planned to retool the aluminum foundry to make tail and nose assemblies for air-to-surface missiles. These weapons of war would be launched from the fighter planes being sold to governments of second- and third-world countries.

As Richard went on explaining the business plan, I began to have visions of F-16s firing missiles into nearly helpless guerrilla army bands attempting to resist the brutality of oppressive regimes that allowed multinationals to exploit their resources, thus keeping their countries in poverty. Some of those missiles would likely be fired into defenseless villages in outright acts of terrorism.

Something snapped inside. A massive delusion that I had adopted as me and my world came shattering down as I saw the truth of what I had been perpetrating. Here I was, sitting in the middle of the ultimate American dream as exemplified by the life of this young entrepreneur, who seemed to be everything I had hoped to become. Yet the oceanside mansion, the yachts and the beautiful life rested on a foundation of darkness, death and destruction.

And I would be a willing accomplice, just as culpable of murder, if I provided the millions necessary to buy this company that would soon be producing weapons of death. I had to face it -- every time one of those missiles exploded and body parts flew in all directions, my finger was equally on the trigger.

Driving home, I entered into a spontaneous life review. I considered my quick career ascent to become one of the most successful young executives in a major West Coast bank. I looked at what that achievement meant to me, and all that the future held. To my human self it all looked incredibly good, if not ideal. Then I thought of those above me on the corporate ladder. Some had been my friends, but over time I had watched them become almost soulless ghosts, having sold themselves to whatever scheming and lies would further their career rise, often over the bodies of those they betrayed along the way.

Suddenly, this was not a place I could go, nor was the dream of being a wealthy entrepreneur enticing anymore. It all seemed dark, empty, soulless, and deeply disturbed. The word *evil* danced in my mind.

Now, without a dream or vision for my life, a strange mixture of feeling totally lost yet free in a whole new way coursed through me. For a while longer, I existed in an in-between zone; the transition was not yet complete. I still worked for the bank, and I needed to complete what I had begun with the visit to Richard's office. I remained sufficiently entrained to the matrix of the banking world that in presenting the loan proposal to my superiors, I knew my moral concerns could not be allowed to be an issue. The unspoken code of professionalism prohibited any expression of the misgivings that now filled me.

An associate presented a funding proposal for a well-known soft porn magazine the same day I made the submission to the loan committee. My defense contracting deal went through in a matter of minutes. Everyone on the committee loved it. My associate's proposal was turned down for "moral" reasons. The irony of our cultural values and blindness came home with a resounding thud. It all felt deeply soul-sick to me. I had to find a whole new way, but what would it be?

A week later, a dear friend invited me to the premiere of the movie *Gandhi*. I walked out of the theater with tears streaming down my face and a feeling of hope and possibility in my soul. Finally -- a life I could honor and embrace, one of truth, love and integrity.

Thoughts of India, triggered by *Gandhi* and all the books I had read about this mystical, saint-producing land, stirred within. The feeling in the upper heart became like a fountain, pouring out spiritual energies that coursed through my being, bringing truth to the mind. The activation told me that I was being propelled into a whole new life and way of being.

One Sunday, after a Thanksgiving weekend of partying with friends, I arose feeling particularly bad. Driving home, the voice within made it clear that now was the time to stop drinking alcohol and cut down my marijuana use. I knew this was an important turning point that would have a massive impact on my future. There was no other option.

I had tried to stop drinking many times with little success, but it was different now -- the emerging presence from within was taking control of me and my life. I never drank again after that day, and it was easy; I no longer had any desire to do so.

One day it became absolutely clear that I was through with my career and this whole way of life. I didn't know where it would all go, but I knew I had to let go of it all and completely give my life over to God and the Mystery. When I told everyone at the bank I was leaving, I received two very distinct and opposite responses. One group thought I was absolutely crazy, and some even questioned whether I had lost my mind. These people saw me as an ideal of success, with my rapid career rise, six-figure income, full expense account, and company car -- all at age 32. I would be leaving more than $200,000 of earned commissions behind as well as a pension, lucrative stock options and bonuses, and an excellent heath care plan. A part of me could understand how they would think I had lost it.

The other group of people often spoke to me quietly when no one else was listening. They'd express their own desire to somehow break out of the stifling life they found themselves in, and commended my courage. They saw, in my act, the hope of a happier, more fulfilled life, even if they weren't ready to make the leap themselves.

In 1982, I sold most of my belongings and bought a backpack and a ticket to India. More than anything, I wanted to find myself and discover a new way of life. Most importantly, I yearned to come face to face with a living, God-realized being. Something in me knew that this was the key to the next phase of my life. With great enthusiasm and joy for the adventure, off I went to the East, not knowing when -- or even if -- I would ever come back.

Karen: A Heart Breaking Open

Gradually I lifted out of the morass of emotional pain that followed the crushing, simultaneous crises and began to extend back out into life. A couple of years after Mom's death, I received an aura balancing, which released deeper layers of trauma. That evening at the Dances of Universal Peace, a tall, thin man I'd never seen before came over to me, looked into my eyes, and quietly exclaimed, "You're so radiant!" Clearly, the aura balancing had left my soul shining forth after the veils of density had been cleared away.

That was how I met Kurt, who would later become my husband. As we began to spend time together, there seemed to be an easy, natural harmony between us. I'd never thought that I would marry in this life until one day when we were hiking high in the mountains and a blizzard began. As I watched Kurt purposefully striding back down the mountain through the heavy snow, the thought suddenly and surprisingly arose: *This is someone I could spend the rest of my life with.*

But all was not smooth and easy in our connection. One evening, after a big snowstorm, I was inspired to cross-country ski across town to Kurt's apartment and surprise him with a visit. When a woman answered the door, it's hard to say who was more taken aback. I stammered a goodbye and numbly skied back home, chilled to the bone by what had just been revealed.

Determined to get to the bottom of this newest heartbreak, I lit candles and sat down to meditate, wrapping a shawl around my shell-shocked form. Layer after layer of feeling arose and moved through -- shock, disbelief, sadness, grief, and hopeless-ness.

Familiar thoughts surfaced: *There will never be anyone who loves me the most. I'll always be replaced by someone better, more alluring, more of **something**. Will I ever find true love in this life? How much more tragedy and loss can I take?*

Hours went by as everything emptied out. Finally, in the middle of the night, a deep peace overcame me. Nothing remained but the comforting solace of this inner stillness. And then it happened: I saw, and knew, with every fiber of my being, that I was blessed beyond measure, *because I loved*. In that moment, it didn't matter at all if the love was returned. It was enough -- more than enough -- that I loved, that I was capable of loving! Such immense joy arose that, if my housemate hadn't been sleeping in the next room, I would have shouted with glee.

I loved. And that was enough.

The realization stunned me with its simplicity. There was nothing else to know, nothing else that mattered. Exhausted and deeply fulfilled, I fell into sleep.

During yoga the next morning, I heard a knock at the door. It was Kurt. He told me he felt we were to be together, and he didn't want to see any other women. Although I had felt we were to be together since that fateful hike through the mountain blizzard, I had let Kurt and our relationship go when it seemed he did not feel the same.

Now, we were united in our sense of a shared future. After living in Germany for six months, we returned to the U.S. During the autumn of 1983, we were married. We moved to Montana and began to establish a new life together.

Reflection

≈ ≈ ≈

Barry:

It was time for a dream to end. There was much I liked about the identity I had assumed; I enjoyed the money, privilege, power, and respect. All of this had become who I thought I was and what I believed life was about. Yet it was nonetheless a dream, one that I had osmosed through decades of cultural conditioning. The dream crashed on the day I met my idealized image of who I wanted to be and the perfect life I wanted to live. The life of the entrepreneur building a defense contracting empire rested on a basis of death. This was certainly not the path my soul wanted to pursue.

When I looked at where my previous life was headed, the energetic signature in my heart and soul felt dead. The heaviness of that life felt like a restrictive, old overcoat. What had once held and comforted me had become a deadening weight. Conversely, as I looked ahead, I felt as though I was walking out into an endless vista full of potential and light. At the thought of heading off to Asia with a backpack and no certainty of what my life would become, the soul energy raced with joy.

The ego-self saw leaving the bank as crazy, a viewpoint that was mirrored back to me by many of my coworkers. Yet from the perspective of the soul, leaving the bank was one of the sanest things I had ever done. The only choice was to follow my inner knowing. It had proven to be infallible, and following it had become the core focus of my spiritual journey. That made it easy to step into the Mystery, leaving safety, security and all the ego~personality goodies behind.

The soullessness of my dream and the years spent pursuing it had now been revealed. Yet even that, I later realized, had been a necessary part of my soul journey. This passage not only freed me from a great deal of attachment and identification, but also forced me to face where the path of personal will, power, privilege and greed leads.

Yet the sculpting of a strong ego also had a positive side. I was no longer an unformed adolescent unable to cope with the world. A stronger ego~personality had been forged, sturdy enough to one day be utilized by the soul for its larger purposes. But now I was no longer identified with it and all of its cultural and familial conditioning.

Karen:

There had always been so much emotional suffering around my relationships -- so many ups and downs, so much attachment to having love returned, such a yearning for the ideal relationship. Deep within, I carried an image of perfection in which our feelings for one another would be reciprocal, we would share a deep, harmonious rapport, and basically live happily ever after. So far, my relationships just hadn't gone that way; the idealized possibility seemed to exist in a different realm from my actual, Earthplane life.

And there was a shadow side to this dream of perfection: If the man in my life was drawn to or actually with someone else, it meant I was not OK. The mind interpreted the situation as proof that I was not attractive enough, not interesting enough, not *whatever* enough. A lot of suffering had resulted from these ideas that the mind was sure were The Truth.

It was an enormous breakthrough to ski home from that unexpected encounter at the door and get to the bottom of all that pain. Through the willingness to be with the suffering and not go to sleep, have a drink, turn on the TV, or in any way attempt to escape, avoid or deny it, I was catapulted into the realization that *I loved, and that was enough.* It didn't say anything about me if the love wasn't returned. This may have been my first glimpse of real love, far different from the attachment of hoping for something in return. The middle-of-the-night epiphany also provided the first hint that my true nature, like the essence of each one of us, is none other than love.

For Barry, it was leaving the business world, the world he thought was everything to him, that propelled him toward everything he was looking for, and who he truly was. Just as his journey followed an archetypal masculine path, for me the process occurred within the quintessentially feminine realm of relationship. I was shedding the identity that had formed around the core belief that *if you love, you will be loved in return, and everything will unfold happily ever after.* Leaving behind this conditional reality, I discovered that what really mattered was *that I loved.*

As we awaken, our former sense of ourselves and the world progressively passes away. Within that gradual process, we may encounter pivotal moments when the most cherished aspects of ourselves, the ones with which we are most identified, must be relinquished. Barry's idealized image was the successful executive, fed by money, power and the adulation of others. Karen held the archetypal feminine dream of the perfect loving relationship.

The idealized image arises out of the familial and cultural conditioning with which we unconsciously identified as we grew up, and forms the foundation of the false sense of self we have tried to become. These idealized images fill popular media, permeate advertising, and are perpetuated through the institutions of our culture. Starting in childhood, we focus our life energy on sculpting a false self sense, or ego, that encompasses the identities we particularly glorify. According to the ego-mind, *If I have the perfect relationship, career, amount of money, health, place to live* -- or whatever the ideal is -- *everything will fall into place, and I will finally be the person I hoped I might be.*

Inevitably, as awakening progresses, our culturally defined, egoic self sense becomes a binding, confining limitation for the soul. While we adopted this identity as part of our individualization, now the soul needs to assert itself more fully. This may ask us to leave behind some or all of the support structures we took for granted as fixtures of our lives. Now we are asked to go forward without them.

During these pivotal moments, the apparent driving force of our life, from an ego~personality standpoint, shatters. We see the emptiness and falseness of it all, and know we cannot continue in the old way. We are left with the all-important questions: *What really matters to me? What is a worthy vision for my life?*

Like Barry, we may reach a point of no return, when it suddenly becomes clear that we can no longer participate in actions that harm or kill other beings or destroy our planet. We must make a clean break from that which is not of the soul, for our own soul energy is coming forth so strongly now that we can no longer ignore it. We cannot go on pretending we do not know the consequences of our actions. We must step forth as souls to do what is right, beyond all egoic considerations.

As we write during early 2011, millions of people in the Mideast have reached such a decisive moment in their collective soul-unfoldment. They are rising up as one to claim the freedom and self-determination that are their birthright as souls. Repressive regimes may quash these rebellions for a while longer, but the people's soul-needs for sovereignty and dignity will ultimately prevail. This is yet another wave in the unstoppable tsunami of awakening that has rippled through one group of souls after another, bringing an end to slavery, giving women and blacks the vote, and protecting the rights of all human beings. Over the centuries, many standing up for freedom have said they would rather die than continue to live as subjects of cruel tyranny. Once we glimpse what lies beyond oppression, we can never go back.

The further we travel in the journey of the soul, the more deeply we are carried into the Mystery. This soul passage asks us to leave behind the seeming safety and security of the idealized self and life that we thought were what we really wanted. Aware of its shadows, we cannot go on believing the illusions that propped up our former life pattern. We may have no idea what we are moving toward, but we know we cannot go back to what was.

7

Leaving the Known World

Barry: A Trip to India to Meet God in the Flesh

As I walked out of the Calcutta airport and saw rickshaws at the curb and a grass field with cows grazing just beyond, I knew I was not in "Kansas" anymore. The story of my yearlong adventure in India would fill a book in and of itself. I was blessed to meet many masters and saints. Sacred ash was materialized into my hand. I watched a yogi balance a searing-hot frying pan on his outstretched palm while he calmly cooked me a meal that instantly cured a critical case of amoebic dysentery. A stigmatist showed me her fresh wounds and described how Christ descended into her every Friday to heal the local villagers of their diseases. India was truly a land of magic and mystery.

It was equally transformative to simply live life with the Indian people. I stayed in simple hotel rooms and ashrams and spent a few weeks in a remote village where only one person spoke English. Throughout all my travels, I found a deeply soulful people and way of life.

Based on the stories I'd heard about the poverty and disease, I went to India with certain minor trepidations. The horrendous conditions I'd been warned about were not what I found. With a simple, human-scale way of life that nourished the soul, most Indians seemed more physically, emotionally, and mentally healthy than the average American. They got up early and worked all day with boundless energy and smiles on their faces.

I walked everywhere in India, through even the big cities, without the fear I feel in large American cities. The warm, openhearted people seemed delighted to share life with me. Their culture floats on a sea of spiritual energy, for the Divine lives at the center of their lives. In India temples are everywhere, and they are *living* temples, not the more or less spiritually dead churches I grew up with in America. Even the smallest temples are alive, with a palpable spiritual energy, and they are not reserved for special services one or two hours a week -- people come and go at all hours of the day and night.

I felt more at home in India than I ever had in the U.S. My soul was at deep peace. As Mother Teresa once said, while there is definitely physical poverty and suffering in India, a far deeper, more pervasive and tragic kind of poverty and suffering are found in America: a poverty of the soul. Based on my experiences in the two countries, I could not agree more.

Toward the end of the India sojourn, I found myself living in Rishikesh, in the foothills of the Himalayas. In the small ashram where I secured lodging, the sounds of strange musical instruments often emanated from the room next door. Upon investigating, I met a beautiful young German woman with a shaved head, wearing the exotic, flowing clothes of the East. Ilse and I became friends and began to spend a lot of time together.

I was drawn to a photograph of a yogi on the altar in her room. When I inquired who this was, Ilse responded, "Babaji," and added that he was also known as Hairakhan Baba. Instantly I recalled a yogi from Yuma, Arizona commenting, before I left the U.S., that maybe I would meet Babaji during my journey. The familiar, powerful feeling and knowing in my heart area told me I needed to go meet this Babaji. I had a strong sense this might be the same Babaji, the Yogi Christ of India, that Paramhansa Yogananda wrote about in *Autobiography of a Yogi*.

I was about to meet who and what had called me to India. And this alluring young German woman would take me there!

When we got off the bus eight miles from his ashram, I immediately felt Babaji's presence. The trip up through the jungle along the Gautama Ganga in the Garhwal Himalayas was an adventure of a lifetime. As Ilse and I walked along with a Swedish couple, the entire experience felt surreal, as if we were in a different dimension of reality.

We should have been at the ashram within a few hours, but mysteriously we never arrived at all that day, although everyone but me had visited the ashram on numerous occasions. They were completely puzzled about why we weren't finding our way. It grew dark and we were forced to sleep on the trail. Among the four of us we had only two blankets, which forced Ilse and me to sleep together under one of them. This created some awkwardness, for although I felt drawn to her, Ilse was in a relationship with a man who was currently the doctor at the ashram.

The next morning I attended the first darshan, a group worship ceremony with Babaji. Looking into his eyes, I was immediately lost in his presence. I remember him saying in English, "Very good young man" -- the perfect thing to say to someone who held a thin veneer of self-confidence over a deep chasm of self-doubt and unworthiness. Then Babaji asked with a chuckle how my stay on the trail last night had been. In a flash I knew he had arranged the whole affair to bring Ilse and me together.

In this darshan I had finally come face to face with God in the flesh. I now knew this was not a story relegated to books; I had experienced it for myself. Having gone to India to find out what a God-realized being was like, in Babaji I saw this and more -- God incarnate, a being who knew everything and held immense power over all reality. Many miracles happened during the stay at the ashram, and it was astounding how much evolution being there catalyzed. With no way to numb out and sleepwalk, I was continuously thrown back onto myself. There was a surreal quality to the psychic atmosphere, in which every experience was intensified and magnified. Even the smallest distraction of ego and mind could instantly become a painful experience.

Babaji demonstrated the unlimitedness and love that are possible for us all. I witnessed him speaking many languages, though to my knowledge he had never learned them or traveled out of India. He seemed to appear and disappear out of nowhere in the most natural way, yet it was also a complete mystery. Many people commented that he had demonstrated he knew everything about them. While he had a human form and presence, Babaji seemed devoid of even the slightest ego or personality. Looking into his eyes was like merging with infinity.

Being at Babaji's ashram constantly challenged all of us to go beyond our unconscious limitations. Each day began with a bath in ice-cold water at 4 a.m., followed by an hour at a fire ceremony, then off to aarti, a sacred ritual honoring Babaji as divinity, which was followed by breakfast. Then we went down to the Gautama Ganga in 100 degree heat for karma yoga, which consisted of carrying rocks to build walls. While to the mind the schedule sounded overwhelming, it all flowed with little effort.

One day I noticed that we were carrying rocks from the remains of one wall across the riverbed to build a new wall. Upon considering the purpose of it all, it finally dawned on me there was none. I felt like rebelling and dropping the whole thing when I began to laugh.

I suddenly saw it all as a spiritual metaphor for human life. We come here and spend our lives doing this and that, bestowing profound meaning and significance on our earthly "accomplishments," which in turn make us feel worthwhile and important. We build careers, homes, and businesses, all the while feeling we are leaving a lasting mark on the world. In the end, we come here with nothing and we leave with nothing, and for most of us everything we have done will be erased from existence and memory, usually within a very short time after we leave. When I saw how bound up I had been in a false sense of self-important striving to make a name for myself, there was simply nothing to do but laugh.

Day after day as I continued to carry stones, I noticed that everyone developed their own stone-carrying personas. Some piled the rocks onto big platters and heroically carried them across the river, struggling all the while -- a sure sign of their strength, perseverance and commitment. Others twirled a colorful sarong into padding, which they used to cushion the platters full of rocks resting on their heads, giving things a bit of style and flair. Many developed interesting gaits or body movements that communicated various personal themes of self-image. I particularly liked the hip swivels of the young women and realized I was still a long way from being a celibate yogi.

What a profound comedy! Here in this stark riverbed full of nothing but rocks, which were being moved in sweltering heat for no real purpose, we human beings turned it all into a display of our idealized self-images. I enjoyed laughing silently about it all, feeling slightly superior.

Then one day the local barber came to the ashram. Babaji ordered many people to get their heads shaved. Being who he was, he could tell exactly which of us that would push over the edge, causing a safe but precipitous collapse of our mask persona.

I had very long hair at the time, and really didn't want to experience shedding it all. Secretly I was too attached and vain to lose all my hair. I felt a great relief when Babaji didn't send me off for "mundam," as they called it, and reassured myself that he saw I was above that trick and didn't need the humbling.

Being extremely hot from carrying stones all day, I decided I would go get a haircut that would suit me. I gave the "barber," who was armed with a straight-edge razor, old, rusty scissors and a comb missing quite a few teeth, clear, careful instructions on the designer haircut I wanted. I was talking to a friend during the process and halfway through it he began to laugh -- at me. Suddenly I realized that I had virtually no hair left anywhere below a line about an inch above the tops of my ears. In fact, the "barber" was now beginning to shave me bald from this imaginary line downward.

Demanding the mirror, I stared horrified at my reflection. I looked like a strange Christian monk with an inverted tonsure; a big shock of hair on top resembled a bird nest, with bare, shiny skin below it. I felt angry, flabbergasted and embarrassed.

What to do next? I couldn't imagine going to dinner looking like this. I contemplated having him cut the rest of it off and at least being completely bald like everyone else. With this bizarre mop with white skin showing all around the sides, all I wanted to do was hide.

Then it hit me, and I burst out laughing. This was Baba's work at its best! He had literally played with my head as no one else could have. *Checkmate, Babaji, ego busted.* I humbly realized this was the best medicine for my prideful self and willingly surrendered to its purification.

The stay at Hairakhan became one of the most profound and magical times in my life. The last thing Babaji told me was to go back to my own country. Today, as I write this, I once again recognize the absolute rightness of this statement, and the ways its message echoes across time.

I wanted to stay in India forever. After I came back I never again felt totally at home in America, yet Babaji had told me that this is where I belong and where my service is. This has been one of the most difficult things for me to accept, and one of the greatest hurdles in my spiritual development. So many times since then I have wished I could leave the U.S. for good and go somewhere else that resonates more strongly with my soul. Yet in those moments Babaji's words return, and I know this is where I belong.

Karen: Launching Out into the Unknown

That pivotal night in Boulder was the first time I had ever deeply investigated what I was experiencing. Through meeting it fully, a life-changing realization emerged: The most important thing was *that I loved,* not that the love was returned. This direct revelation of truth fueled the next outward step in my life. It gave me the spiritual confidence to leave my familiar, secure world behind to cross an ocean and join Kurt in Germany.

Our relationship history had forced me to confront one of the challenges I feared most, the specter of "another woman." Yet a strong intuitive feeling indicated that going to Europe to be with Kurt was the right thing to do. There was no guarantee that it would work out well, but the inner knowing made it clear that this leap into the unknown was my next evolutionary step.

Until now, my nature -- and, by extension, my life -- had not been particularly adventurous. Leaving my tenured teaching job and moving out West had been a radical departure, but it was made easier by the presence of a definite goal. Being accepted into graduate school with a full scholarship assured that I would be on firm ground, financially, and I assumed all else would fall into place. Having visited Boulder, I felt a magical resonance with the town and its surroundings. A strong inner feeling that this was the next step emboldened me to leap into the unknown, half a continent away from my familiar world.

I'd established a comfortable life in Boulder, full of friends and many avenues of creative expression. I loved living at the edge of the Rockies, and often hiked, skied, and backpacked in the mountains. I'd frequently had the sense that the only reason I'd ever leave Boulder was for a relationship. And now, here I was, planning to move to a foreign country where I knew no one except the man I was moving to join there.

The uncanny certainty I felt about doing that amazed and worried more than a few of my friends. Nonetheless, buoyed by the inner sense of rightness that did not go away, I went on preparing to leave all that I knew behind. Although I felt quite attached to my belongings, I got rid of all but what would fit into a small closet. I got on the plane with about a thousand dollars to my name, and launched into my new life.

I'd never visited Europe before; my only forays out of the country had been to Canada. Arriving in Germany, I felt awkward and out of place. The insecurities and inadequacies I'd always been prone to arose yet again, and the harsh inner critic that seemed to be a family legacy found lots of opportunities to pester me. These Europeans seemed so much more articulate, cultured, and creative than I would ever be -- and they were communicating in a second or third language! I felt ashamed that my high school German was not at all adequate to carry on even the simplest conversation. When our housemate, an old friend of Kurt's, announced one day, "All my friends are beautiful," I immediately concluded she was indirectly conveying I should never expect to be included in her circle. On my way to meet Kurt at his office one afternoon, I passed a stunning woman descending the stairs from his floor. Instantly I knew she must be one of his bodywork clients. Again the voices of self-condemnation threatened to overtake me.

Yet in spite of the self-judgments and ever-present awkwardness in this foreign culture, somehow my life gained traction and new developments began to unfold. Kurt helped me to write little signs offering polarity sessions, and we put them up in the natural food shops. To my great surprise, people came. I did astrology readings for many of Kurt's bodywork clients, using a combination of English and German. Sometimes, a person who knew absolutely no English arrived, and I had no choice but to do the best I could in German. I felt nervous enough just to be doing my first professional readings, let alone in another language!

An enthusiastic polarity client invited me to meet his family, and over time I taught him how to do polarity sessions with his pregnant wife to ease her back pain. When I drew up astrology charts for the family, we discussed the ways each member's energies complemented the qualities of the others. I taught them the symbolism of the Tarot, and we did many readings together. Dieter and his wife cooked for me, taught me their favorite recipes, and warmly welcomed me into their lives. Did they know what a great gift this was to someone starved for human connection in an unfamiliar and often alienating land?

Reflection

Barry:

Everything had changed with the trip to the East. I had been with many highly evolved beings, and Babaji, who was God incarnate. A whole new level of possibility had opened -- God-realization. The thought of finding fulfillment as a banker or businessman now seemed ludicrous.

When I left the bank, I really left the world. That "world" was nothing more than my idealized image of who I thought I was and what my life was about. Now, I knew what I didn't want to do or be; the life that I had known seemed empty and without meaning. There had to be more! Without a sense of meaning or purpose for my life, I fell into a vast, open space, a vacuum Life filled by evoking deeper, hidden aspects of existence during my time in the East.

Launching out that day from Seattle to Asia, I knew I was looking for something very new and altogether different from that life I had been living, but I had no idea what that would be or how to find it. The only thing I could do was follow the song of the soul.

By this time, I had come to know the impeccable trustworthiness of the inner voice. Always it asked me to trust more, to take yet another step into the void. In one way going to India was just another step, but in another it was *the* step, the one I knew would change my life forever. It was clear there would be no return to what had been.

What unfolded was more than a new world; I found myself in an entirely new universe, one that manifested and expanded from within. India, a strange and magical land far from anything I had known, became a stage upon which this new universe could unfold. Removed from my familiar context, I melted into this parallel reality of thoughts, feelings, and experiences. I saw a people living according to a different version of what life was about, and in many ways it suited me more than what I had left behind. The materialistic lure that had briefly ensnared me had lost its attraction. My path was now spiritual; I knew that God was the only important thing, and that all material concerns would be taken care of as a result of putting the Divine first.

Life knew what I was looking for -- the only vision worthy of the consecration of our life energy, the true purpose of the soul's journey. In meeting Babaji, I experienced the ultimate possibility, a being who had realized and embodied his true nature. While, at the time, I wasn't able to consciously embrace this for myself, I had received the vision that would inform and drive my search. There were attachments left to face, but now I was standing directly in front of the doorway home to the true Self.

Karen:

The six months in Germany were challenging, and it never got much easier to be there. Yet everything I was experiencing conspired to build my self-confidence. By the time I left, it didn't even bother me that the market vendor whose stall I frequented every week chose my last visit to sternly inform me that I really needed to learn better German.

While Barry was off in India finding out he was far more than the human self he saw in the mirror, I needed to go to Germany to become more comfortable in my own skin. The tests and challenges I encountered there forced me deeper into self-acceptance and even the beginnings of self-love. Being able to laugh about the vegetable vendor's punitive remark was a victory over the forces of self-annihilation that still taunted at the edges of my psyche.

As I pursued a version of the archetypal feminine journey, the quest for relationship and love, little did I know that it would ultimately carry me deeper into the core essence of my own self. Immersing myself in a foreign culture taught me that when we feel at home within, we are at home wherever we go. I did not feel this way most of the time in Germany, but the time there helped me to settle more deeply into who I am. I was beginning to find out that when I feel safe within myself, the whole world becomes a safe place to be.

While Barry's consciousness soared upward, I was being taken down, deep into the realms of the dark feminine. During this time, I devoured books on Jungian depth psychology, the descent of Inanna into the underworld, and related themes. These writings helped me to understand the nature of my own journey into the depths of all that remained unresolved and unhealed within. Like Inanna, I was engaged in the task of peeling off the veils that shrouded me from knowing my true identity as a soul in the human experience, a radiant being of light. Before I was ready to directly experience that illumination, I needed to get to know the darkness.

If I could just love and accept myself through it all, I knew I would survive the descent. Thus far, my journey had been marked by so much self-judgment, self-hatred and condemnation, so much comparing and finding fault with myself and the way my life was, that being able to simply love and accept myself sounded miraculous.

During this time, both of us were prompted to launch out beyond our once-familiar worlds into the Mystery. With no scripts or plans, we followed our only source of guidance, the soul's inner voice. While Barry took off to Asia with nothing but a backpack, Karen moved to Germany, into a life that, like Barry's, contained far more unknowns than certainties.

Both of us were seeking a whole new way of being by jumping into the mysterious journey the soul laid out before us. Barry was looking for a new identity through his quest to experience a God-realized being. Karen's identity transformed through surrendering into a relationship that offered little of the ego-reinforcement or security her idealized image of partnership had contained.

This passage in soul-awakening takes us out of our familiar, predictable life context and into altogether unfamiliar lands -- whether literal, as in our cases, or figurative -- in which the support of cultural conditioning and previous ego-identities is largely absent. We may face challenges that develop soul qualities we will put to use in times to come. Through being completely present in each moment without our familiar mental, emotional and physical props, we discover a newfound freedom. Our experiences teach us that life is not only safe beyond the edge of our comfort zone, it is more expansive, magical, and soulful.

People experience this passage in as many ways as there are souls, but the keynote is that a whole new life pattern emerges that would have been beyond our ability to imagine, let alone plan and control. Living from the soul more than ever before, we are open and available to the experiences the Divine sculpts to evoke deeper aspects of our essential nature. In India, Barry discovered a way of being that resonated with his soul more than anything he'd ever experienced. As he internalized vital aspects of that new template, they became his, and he carried them within when he returned to America. Never again would he find his old way of being remotely enjoyable. In Germany, as Karen overcame challenges such as finding her way solo around a big European city and doing astrology readings in a second language, she was brought into a level of self-confidence and trust in Life she had never known.

8

All the Way Up,
All the Way Down

Barry: Levels Upon Levels of Being

After living with Ilse in Germany for a short time, in 1984 we married and settled in Santa Barbara, California. The communion with Babaji provided an ongoing source of spiritual sustenance, but much of my life didn't feel resonant with what was going on spiritually. Not knowing what else to do to generate income, I had gone back into banking, and it felt even less fulfilling than before. Living in the US again felt strange and empty after the colorful life of India. Nothing felt right anymore. I was treading water, losing my joy and passion. I knew I had to find a new way to live that harmonized with what had awakened within me.

As always, Life responded to my soul's desire, and I was drawn to study *A Course in Miracles*. As I meditated one evening after reading the day's lesson, a presence filled the room, emanating divine love and a deep peace that felt like an elixir for my troubled soul. In an instant, the suffering and turmoil vanished.

As I wondered who or what this presence was, the answer came from within: *The Christ*. I did not see anything; Jesus did not appear to me in a vision. Yet from the powerfully loving and peaceful energy that filled the room, I knew the Christ was with me.

I hadn't thought about Jesus since those boring childhood Sundays at church. Even then, I had no real connection with Christ Jesus. But this was real, and it had nothing to do with Christianity. It didn't even seem exclusively related to the being Jesus. This was a vast, radiant, divine presence that was beyond words. Nothing I had ever heard about during all those church services even approached what I was experiencing. This was the most magnificent inner experience I had ever encountered.

My childhood minister often referred to "that peace which passeth all understanding." This feeling of peace gave meaning to his long-ago words. I felt held by God, and knew that everything was fine. Even though my second marriage was already rocky and my job unsatisfying, somehow, none of that mattered.

As I sat immersed in this deep peace, my awareness shifted to a quartz crystal I was holding. My consciousness entered into the crystal and fully merged with it. I began to spiral out of my body, through the roof of the house, and upward into space. I looked back and saw my body far below me in the house as I spiraled up, up and up. A silver cord attached me to that resting body far below. Seeing it, I knew it was safe to continue on; the fear that I might not know how to get back vanished.

Below me were the lights of Santa Barbara and the outline of the California coast. To the west I saw the curvature of the Earth, and over the seemingly endless Pacific Ocean glowed the faint orange of the setting sun.

I surrendered deeper into the experience and turned to face the onrushing stars. Deep space opened before me, and soaring through star fields, I knew, without knowing how I knew, that I was going to a place I had been before -- a place that was home.

In a matter of moments, a bright star appeared off to the right, a sun I knew and remembered. Turning toward the star, I entered its planetary system, and saw, for the first time in perhaps millions of years, a very familiar planet. Gliding down toward its surface, I noticed that its atmosphere was thin compared to that of Earth. How different from our globe this place was, yet I immediately felt more at home here than I have ever felt on Earth.

Looking down at the planet's surface, I saw a familiar mountain range alongside a vast desert. This was the place; this was home at some other level. Descending to the area where the mountains met the desert, there were the trees, unlike anything I had ever seen on Earth, yet so familiar.

At last I touched down beside the range of mountains, seen with these earthly eyes for the first time, yet eternally known to my soul. Gazing down at myself, I noticed tanned feet and legs standing in golden sandals, with thongs wrapped around the ankles and calves. I realized that these were not the feet and legs of Barry, but they were definitely the feet and legs of the form I now occupied! The arms were much more defined than my earthly arms, with gold bracelets encircling the biceps.

I felt intuitively drawn to the mouth of a nearby cave. Walking in, I realized I was at the entrance to an underground city. Looking down the long tunnel that stretched out before me, I glimpsed an enormous domed chamber, where diffused light poured down on fountains surrounded with greenery. People in tunics serenely strolled through the idyllic scene. As I looked into the full-length mirrors adorning the walls of the tunnel, I saw a being with long, golden hair and a perfectly proportioned body clothed in a light blue tunic. This being, seen through human consciousness, resembled ancient sculptures of the Greek gods.

Into my mind flashed the painting that hung on Don's wall, the image of Martin, and I knew that the being in the mirror was the being in the painting, and that, at this level of reality, I *was* that being, Martin. This being had a countenance and presence unlike anything I had ever experienced. It was vast and divine and similar to the Christ presence that had entered the room at the beginning of the experience.

As I gazed into the mirror, the knowing arose that it was time to go back to my earthly life. I found myself rising up from this world and retracing my journey through the vast reaches of space until the blue orb I always thought was my only home appeared before me again.

Life on the Earth plane resumed, with one important difference: I now knew with certainty of the existence of Martin, my higher-dimensional self. His presence was with me constantly. Often, I felt his energy or saw his face, and knew he was present. It became clear that the source of the energetic guidance that I felt in my heart area was him. I also realized that Martin was the presence I had felt entering "me" in the drugstore parking lot years before.

I now lived with a strange but oddly comfortable dichotomy. I knew that at one level, I was Martin; at another, I was Barry. This paradox confused me for years. *How can I be two different beings at the same time?*

Barry: A Greater Love

Ilse and I held weekly kirtans (spiritual chanting sessions) and performed fire ceremonies, or pujas, in our temple room, which became charged with the power of these rituals in honor of Babaji. I will never forget placing some pale blue hydrangea flowers on the altar and watching them stay fresh and fragrant for weeks. One day I noticed that the blossoms on the hydrangea bush outside had wilted, while the cut flowers on the altar were still very fresh and alive. They lasted for another week or so before they faded and dried. *Wow,* I thought. *If this spiritual power is having a supernatural effect on the hydrangeas, what is it doing to me?*

I had thought I would be with Ilse forever; after all, Babaji had brought us together. A mystical seer in India, consulting wooden tablets thousands of years old, had told me I would soon meet my spiritual partner and we would have two children. I felt certain this was Ilse when I met her. She was my idealized woman, the one I wanted to be with for the rest of my life. My heart had completely opened to her, and that had never occurred with anyone before.

One evening, a man we had not met before came for kirtan. He would later become Ilse's new husband. As the two came together, I was torn open from within. I learned a lot about dealing with off-the-scale suffering, as I found myself barely able to function much of the time. I began to explore Rebirthing, an emotional release technique that uses prolonged deep, circular breathing to dislodge blockages. It was really effective, but something told me it wasn't necessary to huff and puff for an hour or more to blow obstructions out of my energy system. With some experimenting I found that if I coupled the deep breathing with a concentrated focus on feeling whatever was present within, the energetic congestion released more gently and easily.

Over the following months, I spent many hours during many days breathing and feeling the pain and then letting it go. This became my inner practice, and with time I became more proficient at it. As difficult emotions arose, I brought my awareness directly to them, instead of avoiding them or getting involved in all the thoughts that went with them. If I could just stay with the feelings and fully experience them, whatever they wanted to communicate in terms of understandings or insights into the source and nature of the pain manifested in my awareness. Breathing, feeling and releasing became, in time, almost a programmed mechanism I automatically fell into. I couldn't have made it through the avalanche of feelings in any other way.

During a workshop with Leonard Orr, the founder of Rebirthing, the pain again arose. As the intensity built, I felt most of the contraction in my chest area. When the release came, I found myself getting up on my knees and thrusting my hands skyward as a sharp pain exploded from the heart. As it issued forth from my throat, it became an ancient, unfathomably deep, grief-filled cry: "Father!!"

Sobbing, I repeated this call for help again and again. Never had I felt the depth of my desire for union with God. It was all that I wanted. ALL!!

As always, the sincere call from the heart and soul was answered. Or is the prayer a precognition of what the soul is already ushering in? In a bookstore, I came upon a pamphlet about Heart Master Da Free John, later known as Adi Da. The little booklet radiated a deep heart-warmth of love, and led me to *The Dawn Horse Testament.* Every time I meditated on his teachings, I strongly felt Da Free John's presence. Da seemed to be leading me on a new spiritual path into another dimension of the journey.

Da's teachings focused on the opening of the Transcendental Heart. I intuitively knew this was directly related to the space just above the heart that had become the core of my spiritual journey. Da's presence, together with what I was reading in *The Dawn Horse Testament* and a meditation process he taught, catalyzed a profound opening in my consciousness.

By this time, Ilse had moved out and I rarely saw her. It was time to move on. One evening, I found myself standing on a beach, tossing my wedding ring into the Pacific, and saying goodbye to a life that I had thought would continue until the end of this embodiment. I felt done with it all -- the marriage, the suffering, the banking career -- as the desire for absolute freedom and union with God welled up in my soul.

As my heart opened through the trauma of the separation and all the spiritual practices, I realized that what I had sought in the love with Ilse would only be obtained through union with God. Personal, romantic love seemed like a dim substitute in comparison. The deep desire for union with God that had surfaced during the Rebirthing session was nearly all I thought about.

Barry: Divine Union -- the Lotus of the Soul Blooms

When I was offered a consulting job on Maui, off I went to Hawai'i to start a new life. After finishing the project, I felt called to move to Kaua'i, which I had heard was the ashram of the Hawaiian Islands. Kaua'i was said to be the third eye of the chain of islands that begins with the Big Island as the base chakra and continues up to Ni'ihau, the "forbidden island," as the crown chakra.

On Kaua'i, I began to spend hours each day doing Babaji's pujas and Da Free John's kundalini-raising yoga. Da had a sanctuary on Kaua'i, so his presence was particularly strong on the island. As I continued to read his teachings, the relationship between the space above the heart and the process of awakening became clearer. Da referred to the place where the Transcendental Heart resides as the lotus of the soul. According to Da, when the Transcendental Heart is awakened the vast, nonphysical levels of Self unfold. Without really knowing what I had been doing, my practice had already been all about merging with the presence of God within.

The passion for divine union that burned in my heart had become the single-pointed focus and purpose of my life. Through this profound consecration, I had unconsciously opened a new portal of possibility, leaving the previous life plan behind. A whole new reality was about to unfold, resulting in a life that even the seer in India couldn't have known about, because it hadn't existed.

Slowly at first, the kundalini began to move up the spine through each chakra. As it gradually rose, the soul center just above the heart opened more fully, and love poured forth, engulfing my being. The warmth of this love, coupled with the bliss and ecstasy rising up from my base chakra, engulfed the ego-knots in each of the chakras, resulting in ever more surrender. After a few months of melting through all the smaller energy blocks, the kundalini energy, together with the soul-love, began to dissolve the primal knot in the heart. As the heart opened, kundalini rose up the spine and emerged like a fountain of bliss from the crown of the head. I had always yearned to experience this kind of ecstasy, but had never known how to get there. As I continued the practice for many hours each day, all I wanted was to dissolve in the bliss.

One day, from the depths of the darkness within, a beautiful, voluptuous Hindu goddess arose. Dressed only in a belt of silver beads and ankle bracelets, she undulated in a dance of pure ecstasy. Desire arose within me, as did a deepening of the bliss. Slowly I was drawn into sexual/cosmic union with the feminine presence I now know as Shakti. As I entered her vagina, the bliss and ecstasy meter began to go off the scale. Slowly my entire body was drawn into her.

While there was no greater compulsion than to surrender to the intense ecstasy, a corresponding wave of fear arose, the primal male fear of being engulfed by the feminine. But the draw of the ecstasy overpowered the fear. As the thought *What a way to die* arose, I let go and completely disappeared into her womb. The ecstasy went off the scale, and all resistance dissolved in the intensity of the feelings.

Then everything emptied into a quiet but immensely powerful and totally pervasive hum. The ecstasy floated in a void that was also a plenum. There was no sense of me, no other, no-thing, only the presence of something that was the foundation of everything. How long I remained in this state I know not, for time no longer existed. Then, in an instant, my soul lotus exploded outward into everything. I was the one being whose omnipresent nature was pure love. I now had manifest existence, and my being was the fabric of the universe. All the planets, stars and galaxies were suspended within the fabric of my being. Like the Egyptian goddess Nut, who arches over the universe, I experienced all of Creation as residing within my infinite body.

During the following months I lived in a state of absolute love and bliss. In one way, nothing had changed; outer events and circumstances went on as before. Yet everything had profoundly altered. The source of the shift was the living, radiant presence of God that was now alive within me as me, and simultaneously had no bounds, interpenetrating all of Creation. The experience continued to deepen as I spent many hours, sometimes most of a day, absorbed in this state.

The world had been totally transformed. Everywhere was a softness and a sense of communion. The colors of nature were vibrant; sounds resonated on levels beyond normal hearing range. Everything was alive, sensual and One. The happiness I had sought for so long had become an integral part of all experiencing, not related to anything in particular that I might "like."

Karen: Emptying, emptying...

After six months in Germany, Kurt and I moved back to the U.S. Before leaving, we had spread a big map of America across the floor and used a pendulum to dowse possible places to live. Kansas came up strong, but we felt no desire to move there. Rugged, untamed Montana seemed a better fit for our energies.

We lived in the mountains, and it was clear that the strengthening program that had begun in Europe had entered its next phase. Hauling firewood in from the shed and frequent trips up and down the stairs to keep the wood stove going formed the core of my strength training. During the winter, laundry and groceries had to be carried to and from my car, of necessity parked a quarter mile down the hill. Visitors inevitably got stuck in snow banks; only when we couldn't dig them out would the tow truck be called. For recreation, we hiked and skied in the mountains that surrounded our small town.

I sold my beadwork jewelry at craft fairs and lettered names on thousands of diplomas. My study of tarot had led me to an in-depth exploration of astrology. Here, at last, I discovered what I'd hoped to find in graduate school: a way to support people to love, accept, and understand themselves and one another. The sense of not feeling seen as a child drove me to seek out ways of working with people that would help them to honor their unique divine pattern and purpose. Astrology, in particular, gave me the ability to see deeply into who each client was, and reflect this magnificence back to each person who came for a reading. Each birth chart also revealed the evolutionary issues and challenges the client had set up for this lifetime, as well as the gifts and talents s/he had come in to develop more fully. As I became increasingly proficient at reading each person's divine pattern, my understanding of my own mandala of challenges and gifts became ever more clearly defined. Gradually, over many years, the confidence that I had meaningful insights to share with others was annealed.

During this time, I longed to experience the glamorous parts of the spiritual journey. I'd met people with psychic abilities, and others whose presence brought about healing. Some exuded joy, while others seemed as vast and deep as the inky night sky. A rare few seemed imperturbable, established in a steady state of inner peace. All of this seemed to be the culmination of the spiritual quest. Would I ever get beyond the emotional turmoil that continued to plague me and be capable of experiencing such things?

Years before, during a psychic reading, I'd asked about my spiritual abilities, hoping to be told they were on the verge of coming forth in some major, life-changing way. Instead, I was firmly advised to focus on building emotional strength; the rest would follow. It was encouraging to hear that I might evolve into a new place in myself, but disappointing to be told that the time for that to happen was not imminent. I felt ashamed and embarrassed, and judged myself as less evolved than others. Part of me wanted so much to go for the light, to experience the upper chakra explosions of awakening I'd read about. Yet I knew there was truth in the recommendation to focus on getting stabilized emotionally. That calm steadiness had eluded me for as long as I could remember.

But what if it took the rest of this lifetime to work through the tangled web of feelings and thoughts that so often consumed my awareness, and I never experienced higher states of consciousness? What if my emotional healing process remained so overwhelmingly all-consuming that I was never able to truly serve others? That would be an unbearable disappointment.

There was something bigger I felt I was here to bring forth, even if I had no idea what it was. I longed to get started, but the psychic was right; there was still a lot of emotional work to be done. Close relationships seemed fraught with challenge. Even the simplest of interactions often unearthed knots of feelings I seemed incapable of sorting out. I continued to struggle with the suicidal hopelessness that had not only claimed my mother, but her father as well.

During my childhood, Mom's unresolved emotional turmoil often boiled over in anger and resentment. At times she threatened suicide, but Dad, my brother and I never took it seriously. We assumed her dark mood would blow over; hadn't it always before? Dad sought solace in nightly martinis, and drinking was central to the business lunches, bridge games, and cocktail parties of mid-century corporate life.

During the years of intensely facing all that lay within me, using mind-altering substances fell away around the time I got the message it was time to stop drinking. Like my parents, I had been a heavy social drinker. Now, I inwardly heard, *It's in your way*. In that moment, I understood that the spiritual upliftment and evolutionary breakthroughs I longed to experience would never happen if I continued to muddle my consciousness with alcohol and substances. It was clear they only increased my emotional instability.

In the moment this internal message arrived, I was blessedly freed of the compulsion to consume alcohol. Other than an occasional champagne toast at a wedding, I have never had another drink. Breaking free of the family pattern of addiction undoubtedly helped my emotions to calm down, and living in the mountains imbued me with a sturdiness I had never known. Clients seemed to appreciate their astrology readings, and the long hoped-for sense that I might have something useful to offer others slowly grew.

Kurt and I embarked upon a three-year-long chakra clearing process. During the months it took to clear the second chakra, all the issues and patterns around relationships, nurturing, sexuality, and my femininity roared to the surface. And once again another woman entered into our lives.

It became clear that this was not just about Kurt. I had to go beyond blaming him for the problems in our connection, beyond making him the "bad guy," and dive even deeper within to find and heal my part of this dynamic. Here I was again, facing the outer mirror of what lived within me. Layer after layer of fear, insecurity, unworthiness, and hopelessness arose. Would I ever get to the bottom of it all?

Our chakra-clearing facilitator felt sure the rupture in our connection could be mended, so we stayed with the process. Slowly, healing occurred in us both. By the time we went to Kaua'i for Kurt's advanced bodywork training in early 1987, we felt warmer and closer than we had in a long time.

While Kurt was in class each day, I explored this magical paradise that daily revealed ever more facets of her beauty. I hiked, swam in the warm ocean, and visited farmers' markets all over the island. At Secret Beach, I spent whole days free of clothing, and the surf crashing against the black volcanic rocks was as powerfully dramatic as my emotions had so often been.

Reflection

~ ~ ~

Barry:

After many years of living with the sense that there was a higher being or presence with me, I met the being Don had referred to as Martin when I ascended far beyond my earthly abode into the higher realms that felt like my true home. There, I met the perfect divine being I instantly realized was my oversoul Self. I knew that this was the larger beingness of which "Barry" was but a small part.

While Karen had experienced her oversoul as the Grouping many years earlier, consciously connecting with this level of existence happened later for me. Conversely, while I had been led to the seat of the soul above the heart early in my journey, this would not occur for Karen until much later. There is no linear path or sequence of events that determines when these openings will unfold. The soul and oversoul progressively make their presence known in ways that are perfectly choreographed for each of us.

After meeting Babaji, I had a new vision or possibility -- to become as he was, a God-realized being. There was no forethought of what that meant or what would be asked of me. I meditated, did the empowered rituals Babaji taught, and prayed to him. In my heart, a small flame began to burn with the desire for God communion. I didn't realize the path would lead right to and through yet another unconscious idealized image and attachment, which would be brought to the surface to be immolated in the hot fire of awakening.

Ilse's personality and physical appearance ignited a passion and desire for union that I hadn't experienced with any other woman. She was my idealized woman incarnate. The immense attraction I experienced allowed the heart to open as never before. But this was a romantic and erotic love, based in personality infatuation. While I experienced love as never before, it did not have the pure, unconditional nature of agape. I had harbored a deep desire for romantic union with the perfect woman, right alongside the soul's deeper desire for God-realization. The path through the relationship with Ilse was also the way to the true, deeper desire. The immense pain and suffering of having, and then losing, my idealized woman plunged me deeper into my heart and soul in the quest to find out what my greatest love really was.

When the inner fire begins to burn more brightly, it brings everything that is in the way of full union to the surface. That was certainly true in my relationship with Ilse. When the pain of loss severed the attachment to my earthly love, what erupted from the core of my being was a deep cry for that which was more important than all else -- experiencing union with God. A fire had been ignited by God in my heart, a burning passion for union with the Divine. I look back with awe and gratitude for the way that perfectly scripted segment of my life propelled me into a deeper realization of who and what I truly am.

As I saw it, what keeps us from realizing our oneness with God is that which we love more than the Divine, that which we hold more important than reuniting with the One. Whatever we are un-willing to die to, whatever we believe we cannot surrender, is what shrouds us in veils of separation from Source. Full, ultimate unity with God demands everything; we are asked to give all of our-selves and everything in our lives to God. When we do this, the doors open. It is that simple. We don't experience divine union be-cause we are consciously or unconsciously holding other things more sacred than God.

When I arrived in Hawai'i, I completely focused my life on realizing the Divine. With this consecration, the doors were des-tined to open, and the soul's unquenchable thirst for its Source was at last satisfied. I had experienced union with God, the greatest gift possible, the only thing that ultimately mattered. I had been trans-ported back to the Garden, never to leave again. As Rumi so elo-quently put it, "A star exploded in my heart and the seven skies are lost in it."

Karen:

Barry's journey of awakening during this time included sub-lime encounters with awakened beings that resulted in potent inner experiences and dramatic shifts in consciousness. While his awareness soared up and out, my evolutionary sojourn took me down and in, to the lower chakras and all that remained unresolved there. The changes that occurred were often subtle and went largely unnoticed in daily life, yet deep within a stable foundation was slowly forming that would provide a sturdy energetic platform for the openings in consciousness that would one day occur. I was also building a sense of self that included a strong, capable will. As spiritual texts remind us, many of us must first focus on developing a clear, definite sense of who we are before that identity can be relinquished.

While Barry was pursuing the classic male spiritual path of seeking the transcendent light, I needed to dive deep into the darkness. He was shedding the identity of the seeker of worldly satisfactions, while I felt compelled to overcome the family patterns of self-destruction and addiction that had become incorporated into who I believed I was. This entailed confronting the emotional recesses within that were the hardest to face -- the underpinnings of guilt, shame, unworthiness and self-hatred that drive self-annihilating behaviors.

This inner work received little immediate outer reinforcement, and its subtle, gradual effects remained largely invisible, even to myself. During these years, I often wished I were experiencing the more "glamorous" aspects of the spiritual journey. I longed to be lifted into exalted meditation states and excursions into the higher realms, things I had heard about but had no idea how to actually experience.

Perhaps my biggest challenge during this time was to accept myself just as I was. Having read about others' spiritual experiences, I judged myself as dense and unevolved, seemingly incapable of reaching those places in consciousness. In contrast to friends whose emotional lives seemed blissfully serene and uncomplicated, my inner world overflowed with turmoil and self-defeating perfectionism. Comparisons and self-judgments persisted, alternating with a slowly growing faith that everything I was going through must be necessary, or it wouldn't be happening.

In the absence of outer evidence, I had to trust that all of this deep, hard emotional work would one day result in a strong, confident sense of self. I looked forward to the day when I would easily accept myself and my journey exactly as they were, and finally be truly, lastingly happy. There were still plenty of moments when I wondered if that day would ever arrive.

We awaken to our true nature in as many ways as there are beings who are awakening, and the journey has as many chapters as the best adventure story. Some phases of soul-evolution, like Barry's year in India and the awakenings on Kaua'i, are full of spiritual fireworks. During quieter times, as Karen experienced, a lot may be changing on the inside, even though not much appears to be happening from without.

As we awaken to the soul, our core divinity unfolds through the expansion of consciousness up into the transcendental, superconscious realms and down into the depths of the subconscious. All along the way, our awareness of both vectors -- that which exists above our existing state of consciousness and that which lies below -- is enlarged. We are transported up into the light of our higher nature, which then descends into the deep, dark realms of unresolved shadow material. As the transcendental, oversoul aspects of our being land deep within us, they purge and purify all that is unlike our vast, true nature while planting seeds of consciousness that will grow and flourish over time.

Years may be devoted to expanding in one direction, while the other patiently awaits our discovery. Karen spent many years in descent, diving into the depths of the subconscious to heal the wounds from this and previous lifetimes. This ongoing, deep inner work built a sturdy emotional base capable of supporting the spiritual openings that would one day occur. Barry's journey was primarily moving in the opposite direction as he sought union with the transcendent Divine, which he saw manifest in the being called Babaji. Although we had not yet met, both of us were experiencing complementary expansions of consciousness.

Riding either vector, whether up into the superconscious or down into the subconscious, expands our conscious sense of who and what we are. This is how we stretch our awareness and transcend our limited sense of self. When consciousness lifts into the transcendent realms, we realize our celestial nature, which is always beyond and untouched by the human experience. Descending brings us in touch with aspects of the human psyche that have been fragmented from our original wholeness. As we reintegrate these parts, we realize the totality of what we are as embodied souls.

The end of the journey on this level of Creation occurs as we wake up to our transcendent nature and incarnate it within a healed, whole and complete human nature. For this to occur, consciousness must travel all the way up and all the way down. The many paths, practices and approaches present within the spiritual landscape today testify to the evolutionary need to integrate both vectors. At one point we may find ourselves focusing on deep psychological work such as healing core childhood wounding, only to become fascinated by ascended master teachings or channeling higher energies during the next cycle of unfoldment.

Many of us tend to glamorize and overvalue the sparkle and light of transcendent awakenings, while diminishing and even dreading the deep descents that are equally necessary for our full flowering. A complete path views conscious evolution as a dynamic, integrated interplay of ascent and descent, orchestrated by the infinite wisdom at the core of our being.

It's helpful to remember that whichever vector our journey is currently highlighting, we are peeling away the veils of identity that have kept our self-sense limited and small. They drop away whether we are soaring into the ethereal realms of light or diving deep into the murky domain of the shadow. Within a paradigm of wholeness and inclusivity, neither represents the totality of who and what we truly are.

Eventually, we arrive at a point when our being has expanded sufficiently through the weaving together of our multidimensional vastness and the fertile ground of our deep human nature that the higher Self or oversoul can fully descend, anchor, and take dominion. This is what occurred during Barry's kundalini awakenings. As consciousness expands infinitely to encompass All That Is, we are illumined, transfigured, and reborn. Now, we are finally back home, as awareness rests in the true, eternal Self.

9

Meeting our Divine Counterpart

Karen: A Mysterious Encounter

My husband and I had traveled to the island of Kaua'i for his advanced bodywork training. Although this course was the farthest from our home, my intuition had insisted that this was the one he was to take -- and I was to go with him. Neither of us had ever felt drawn to visit Hawai'i. Yet somehow, it seemed important that we both go there now.

While Kurt was in class each day, I explored the island. Kaua'i revealed her magical, beautiful essence more fully with each day. In some ways it felt like a foreign country, with its people of many nationalities and its undulating music reaching out to caress everyone from the loudspeakers in the tourist shops. Yet to my soul this new and unfamiliar place felt like home. Its essence resonated with my own more than any other place I'd visited. Deep within, I felt as though I had known this island forever.

Every day on Kaua'i was a new adventure. My awareness was being stretched open through encounters with new people, the freedom to follow my energy each moment of the day, and most of all the energetic atmosphere of this unique place on the planet. Something about this island filled me with a feeling unlike anything I'd ever experienced anywhere else on Earth. Each day here was a blessing, that much was clear, although I had no idea the blessings were just beginning.

One day, Kurt mentioned that he thought I'd enjoy meeting one of his bodywork clients.

"Why don't you invite him over for dinner?" I offered. But that was not to be.

A few days later, I had stopped off at Ambrose's little natural foods store when I suddenly saw a brilliant flash of light out of the corner of my eye. I turned to see a man walking toward me. Somehow, in a way I didn't at all understand, this man and the flash of light I'd just seen were one and the same.

"You're Kurt's wife, aren't you?" he half-asked, half-stated.

I stammered a surprised affirmative, and he went on to say, "My name is Barry. I've been seeing Kurt for bodywork."

Oh, I realized, *this is the man Kurt thought I'd enjoy meeting.*

We talked a bit, and Barry asked if I'd do an astrology reading for him. We set up a session and said goodbye.

There was clearly something unusual going on, but I had no idea what it was. I had definitely never experienced a meeting like this before. It wasn't at all like the sexual or romantic attractions I'd felt in the past. If anyone had told me that within a couple of years I would be embarking on an entirely new chapter of my life with this person, I would have been incredulous!

A few days later during the astrology reading, Barry exclaimed, "I feel as if you're reading my soul!" Since self-doubt still often arose, I felt happy to hear that the reading resonated with him. It was gratifying to learn that our session was having a meaningful impact on my new client, but I didn't think more of his remark than that.

Back in Montana, we occasionally received a postcard from Barry. When I'd extract them from the post office box, each one glowed with the same brilliant light that had emanated from Barry at our first meeting. This was mysterious and powerful and very intriguing. I had no idea what it meant.

Strange synchronicities began to occur. When Kurt and I traveled to Boulder, Barry, who was now living in New Mexico, turned up in the motel room next door. Months later, back home in Montana, I looked out one wintry day to see a vehicle barreling up our steep driveway. Astounded, I watched Barry get out, holding the boogie board I'd lent him in Hawai'i!

I didn't feel a romantic attraction to him, or any sexual chemistry. To be honest, I wasn't even sure how much I liked this person. Kurt and I agreed that Barry seemed somewhat arrogant and full of himself. Yet the way he kept showing up was unusual enough to make me wonder. Whatever our connection was, it wasn't like anything else I'd ever experienced. But, immersed in my life, I didn't give it very much thought.

Barry: I Meet Myself

The trade winds gently rustled the palm fronds overhead as I pulled up to the small natural foods store and emerged from the "great white boat," as I jokingly called my aging Chevy Impala. The vehicle was a perfect island cruiser, a laid-back means of transportation that was totally out of character for the person I had so recently been. It matched the rest of my new existence, which was far beyond the edge of all that I had previously thought of as "me."

Ambrose, who owned the little store, embodied the relaxed aloha spirit of the islands. When he wasn't surfing, he could be found in the tiny wooden building painted a bright yellow that instantly announced his eccentric aliveness. The surfboards for sale by the door told the story of his greater love. If the surf was up, you could be sure the doors would be closed.

On that afternoon the ocean was flat, so I felt certain I would be able to get something to eat. Shuffling into the shadowy interior, I was met by an ear-to-ear smile and a warm greeting from Ambrose. After we talked story for a while, I set about finding something quick and easy for dinner.

Standing in front of the frozen food case, my reverie was shattered by a blinding flash of white light that filled the store with a luminosity so bright it had a blue tinge. Startled, I turned to look around, expecting to see someone with a camera. Instead, my eyes came to rest on a woman standing by the front counter. She was the only other customer in the store, and she didn't have a camera. She had long, sandy-brown hair and a tan that let me know she'd been in the islands for more than a few days.

I immediately knew there was something very different about this woman, although I couldn't have described it in words. The magnetic attraction was instantaneous, and dissolved all of my normal hesitancy and insecurity in such situations. Without thought, my body walked me across the store, stopping directly in front of her.

As I came to within a few feet of her, I became aware of a very powerful energy. Just being near her transported me into a heightened state. The nature of the attraction was completely unfamiliar; although she was attractive, the pull was beyond normal male-female magnetism. I felt as if I knew this woman quite intimately, even though I knew nothing about her.

What came out of my mouth was a half-question, half-statement: "You're Kurt's wife, aren't you?" I had been seeing Kurt for a series of bodywork sessions.

Yet even this rather surprising awareness was only a surface-level manifestation of a deeper sense of knowing that seemed ancient. All I wanted was to get to know this woman as quickly and deeply as possible. The pull toward her was a compulsion from the depths of my soul.

With a surprised look, Karen responded that yes, she was Kurt's wife. As the conversation unfolded, she indicated that she was an astrologer. I immediately scheduled an appointment for a reading.

Karen's astrology reading was so profoundly insightful, I felt as if she had known me forever. But what struck me the most was that I felt the same energetic signature with her that I experienced in the deepest communion with my inner divinity. It wasn't that there was a *similarity* in the energetic signature of my indwelling presence and Karen's essence -- the two were *identical*. Whenever I came near her, the area above the heart, which I now knew was esoterically called the soul lotus, instantly became so energized that my whole body vibrated, making it difficult to stay grounded.

It was obvious there was something profound about this relationship, something I had not even remotely experienced with any other human being. While I felt attracted to Karen as a woman, that was a secondary level of the energetic resonance I felt. I had no context for what was happening, but the indwelling divinity knew that it was something to pursue further. The feeling was so vast, so primal, so deep, and so totally transporting into a dimension of communion that I only wanted more. It was far beyond a romantic impulse, or feelings for Karen as a woman. The attraction was the same that I felt for the Divine within myself. For the first time, I experienced the presence of God within the core of another in the same way I did within myself. There was no difference; the two felt identical -- one -- the same divine presence existing within two seemingly separate bodies.

I took the astrology chart home and hung it on my bedroom wall alongside the copy of Karen's chart she had given me. I was mesmerized by her beautiful, hand-lettered and colored astrological mandala. One day I decided to throw the coins for an I Ching reading about our connection, and for the first time ever, hexagram number one, The Creative, with all six yang lines, emerged. In essence, this symbolizes the first movement of the Tao, the primal emanation of the Godhead manifesting its creative impulse. I was struck by the power of this, and by the fact that I had never before received this hexagram. Nor have I ever again.

I felt deeply that Karen was my divine complement, but she was married, and I didn't feel the impulse to go any further with it.

We did spend a day together with her husband and my housemate, and I managed to take a picture of her to have after she went back home to Montana. Whenever I gazed at it, a strong upwelling of energy caused me to vibrate and almost become short of breath.

I stayed in touch with Karen by mail, and occasionally we met up in ways that just seemed to serendipitously occur. With each meeting, the knowing grew that this was my divine complement and that we were inextricably bound, married eternally in an even more divine way than she was with her husband. Yet there was no guidance to broach the subject with her, and I did not sense she knew what I knew. The knowing indicated, though, that somehow the force drawing us together would not be denied.

Reflection
~ ~ ~

Barry:

The flash of light that electrified our physical eyes provided unmistakable testimony to the spiritual lightning that struck in the moment Karen and I met. In Karen's presence, I was instantly transported into a vaster state of consciousness. The connection with her was unlike anything I'd ever experienced. I had been in the presence of other soul mates, beings I had known for lifetimes with whom I felt a deep, eternal communion. The feeling was similar with Karen, yet also very different, as our connection transcended even the most potent soul mate experiences I'd known.

Not until years later would it become clear that the flash of light we both experienced in Ambrose's natural foods store on Kaua'i occurred at the moment when Source energy descended and arced between us and into the physical plane. In that instant, a new level of the unfoldment of our soul purpose began, and our journey home accelerated. From that moment forward, I have felt the powerful nature of our connection as the primal ground of my/ our being -- which it is, for our souls are one.

After my marriage to Ilse ended, I wasn't looking for a relationship. My connection with God seemed more than sufficient. Yet every time I was in Karen's presence, I felt a deep communion with the Divine. Looking into her eyes, I saw myself. This wasn't about romance or even the joys of intimate, human connection. Little did I know at the time how potently catalytic and foundational this communion would be in the unfolding of my soul. Walking out of Ambrose's that day, I had no idea that the flash of brilliant blue-white light marked a beginning. Really, it was The Beginning. In many ways, the life of my true Self was only now about to commence.

Through spiritual study and inner reflection I had come to understand that although we may meet and have relationships with many soul mates, we each have only one divine counterpart, or twin soul. Often twins do not meet until the souls are well-established on the path of Self-realization. At the point during the journey of lifetimes when the two are ready to reunite as one, we are brought together with the sole being in all the world who is central to our process, as we are central to theirs. This person becomes as much the path as anything that has ever been encountered, and the relationship provides more evolutionary stimulation than either has ever experienced with anyone else.

Karen:

When that flash of light occurred in Ambrose's little shop, I wasn't at all looking for a relationship. After the challenges we had faced, the connection with Kurt had transformed and stabilized, and I had reached a point of relative peace with my own internal issues. Yet although neither Barry nor I was hoping to meet a new partner, Life had something else in mind. It would take some time, though, to find out just what that was.

Twin souls are two faces of one presence that emerges out of the Godhead and divides into two beings. Paradoxically, they are two souls that are also one, forever united in the most fundamental way possible, for their core essential nature is identical and indivisible. The journey begins as the one becomes two, and it will end as the two once again realize their essential unity.

As part of the process of planetary awakening, twin flames are coming together as never before. Twin souls often reunite during their last earthly lifetime as a natural part of the completion of their journey as souls in the human experience. Their reuniting also serves a larger, planetary function, for the energy of two such souls joining provides a powerful catalyst to every other soul completing the journey of earthly embodiment.

The Source or Godhead level of being is synonymous with the unmanifest Absolute, prior to all creative manifestation. All levels of being flow forth from this ultimate Divine Wellspring. When twin flames join, the connection to Source is immediately catalyzed for both beings. Their coming together activates their reunification with the highest, vastest level it is possible for them to access. The heavenly realms of illumination in which our oversoul presences exist manifested for both of us as the brilliant flash of white light we each saw when we met.

Neither of our souls could have invited down that level of light and divine presence on its own. The vessel created when the two join is far stronger than a single soul's presence. That's why the reunion of twins souls is such a powerful catalyst for awakening, not only for themselves but for the Earth and humanity. The pillar of light they continually ground increases the vibrational rate of their physical and subtle bodies as well as that of the planet.

The union of twin souls also powerfully catalyzes the inner marriage that is central to birthing the Luminous Self, a process synonymous with liberation or ascension. As Christ Jesus expressed this in verse 22 of the Gospel of Thomas, to complete our spiritual journey the inner and outer, higher and lower, and left and right must become one. All polarities will eventually be unified -- the soul and the personality, the spiritual and human aspects, and the dominant and receptive or masculine and feminine parts of our nature.

Each of the two "twins" carries the mental, emotional and spiritual patterns that complement those of the other, for they have mirrored one another throughout their many lives. As the Balinese understand, the fundamental law of duality or polarity maintains the precise balance of the universe. Ceremonies are nearly continuously performed on that island to appease all aspects of the Whole -- the good and the evil, the profound and the ridiculous. All must be included and kept in a happy balance.

When twin souls separate and each soul embarks on its own journey, it sculpts its being with certain divine qualities and ego~personality characteristics that are complementary to those its "other half" is engaged in developing. For instance, Karen devoted years to the archetypal feminine descent into the underworld of the psyche, while Barry was focusing on the equally important and energetically opposite ascent into the transcendental realms. Barry's personality focus had been in the masculine-dominated world of business, while Karen had developed the feminine ability of providing an emotionally safe and nurturing environment for her students, and later for her clients. These diametric explorations would later enrich their partnership and their service in ways neither could have accessed individually.

10

A New Octave of Soul Life Begins

Karen: A Door Opening onto an Empty Sky

Usually, as fall approached, I'd be gearing up for another season of teaching astrology and tarot classes and selling jewelry at holiday craft shows. But as the autumn of 1988 neared, I felt absolutely no energy arising to set up anything. And when I looked within, all I saw was a door opening onto an empty sky. It was a striking image, as stark and potent as a Georgia O'Keeffe painting, and there was something mysteriously thrilling about the unknown future that lay within that vast, empty sky. But what did it mean?

Leaving my schedule empty, I headed south to Lama Foundation, high in the mountains of New Mexico, for a two-week workshop devoted to the Dances of Universal Peace. It had been years since I'd had the chance to join in the Dances -- not since my years in Boulder, when I'd met Kurt at one of the weekly dance gatherings there. Now, an immersion in the heart-opening uplift-ment of the Dances sounded wonderful.

A while ago, Barry had written that he'd relocated to Taos. When I let him know I'd soon be in his neighborhood, he wrote back with a question: Did I mind if he, too, came to the Dances workshop?

"Not at all," I had responded.

At Lama, under the deep blue New Mexico sky, I set up my tent and prepared for two weeks of nothing but circle dancing and being in this elevated, clear space.

One evening, Barry invited me for a walk. As the sun set and the stars began to twinkle, he told me that his inner knowing indicated we were to be together. Not only that -- we had some-thing important to bring to the planet. He acknowledged that I was married, and admitted that he had struggled with this internally for some time. Ever since we'd met a year and a half before, he'd been waiting for the right moment to tell me, and this, he felt, was it.

My mind immediately concluded that Barry was either de-luded, imagining things, or simply crazy. *This has nothing to do with me,* I thought. *He doesn't even know me!* I dismissed the en-tire matter and went off to sleep in my tent.

Yet Life was trying to get a message through, and if one way didn't work, there were plenty of others. Barry and I often sat together at meals, and people began to comment on the glow that surrounded us.

"There is such a beautiful light around you and your hus-band!" they would enthuse.

Taken aback, I'd respond, "He's not my husband!"

Many of my new friends had heard me mention a husband, so if this was not him, what was going on? They were as puzzled as I.

"If he's not your husband, you really do have a problem," one woman pointed out.

The remarks continued, and I remained mystified by the whole thing. Yet I began to surmise that Life was trying to tell me something through these reflections from virtual strangers of what I was too blind to see. I started to open up to the possibility that Barry was right. Maybe we *were* to be together, for some reason yet to be revealed.

I had always done my best to live according to the inner knowings that arose about life situations. These knowings didn't come often, but when they did, they were always about something important and possibly life-changing. One of them had led me to leave my tenured teaching job when that seemed foolish to the more security-minded part of me. Another had guided me to end the relationship with my boyfriend before my mother died, although my human self was deeply disappointed to hear the inner message that we did not have a future together. My mind and emotions didn't always easily adjust to what emerged from within, but these inner knowings had always proven to be right, and the rest of me learned to go along with them more quickly as the years passed.

At the moment, I wasn't totally sure what was going on with Barry, and my inner knowing was not saying anything definite, ei-ther. Yet all indications were that this relationship, should I choose to enter into it, presented an evolutionary possibility beyond any-thing I had ever encountered.

When I returned to Montana, I told Kurt, "I think maybe I'm supposed to be with Barry now." I still didn't know for sure, but I wanted to express what seemed to be coming into focus more clearly with each new day.

"That makes sense," was his initial reply. After all, he'd been the one to initially suggest that we meet! Kurt's affirmative response was yet another sign that perhaps Life *did* want me to leave my marriage and embark on a new chapter with Barry.

Still, this was not a move I took lightly. To be certain I wasn't making a colossal mistake, I consulted not one but two well-recommended psychics. I expressed my hesitation to leave a relationship that had arrived at a stable, positive place after all that we had been through. Kurt was a wonderful man, I went on, a gifted healer and a brilliant, unusual human being.

Both of the psychics felt my evolutionary direction lay in the new relationship.

"You could have a good life with Kurt, and you would be happy. But you'd grow more in one day with Barry than in a month with Kurt," one said.

I came away feeling the right thing to do was to begin again with Barry, and find out what it was we were to do together. In a strange way, it all felt very impersonal, as though I were simply fulfilling my role in a much bigger plan. Part of me would have preferred to remain with Kurt. I felt such love and respect for him, and knew I'd probably never again meet someone who was so extraordinary in so many ways. Yet I was being asked to go on, and I felt willing to answer the call.

Many in our community saw us as a model couple. When they heard Kurt and I were going apart, they were shocked, confused, and even heartbroken. Some later confessed they went home and cried. *If they can't make it, how will we?* they wondered.

But it wasn't that we weren't "making it." Life had a new assignment for each of us. Neither of us knew what it was yet, but we were willing to let go of this relationship and life pattern if it meant we would be brought more fully into our true purposes for this lifetime.

People we knew were baffled when they saw us walking around town holding hands. "I thought you were getting divorced..." they would venture, looking more than a little perplexed.

"We are."

"Then why are you holding hands?"

"We aren't going apart because we're angry with each other. Divorce doesn't have to mean the caring has stopped." Many clearly found this a new and unsettling concept.

Kurt and I took one last trip to the 45th Parallel hot springs in Yellowstone Park, a place we had often visited to soak in the soothing waters. We took off our matching handmade wedding rings and tossed them into the river. *Good-bye, marriage.*

I had thought I'd be with Kurt forever, but Life had other plans.

Barry: A Call To Service

In the summer of 1988, I found myself living outside of Taos, New Mexico, in a small, funky, wonderful home constructed of discarded tires, adobe, and chicken wire, appropriately nick-named the Tire House. Colorful bottles embedded in the walls provided a stained glass effect and added to its delightful eccentricity. The dirt floors assured me that I would never get overly fixated on neatness while living there.

It was a quiet time in my outer world. Every morning I walked across the arroyo to a hot spring, where I soaked until late morning. Afternoons, I often made gem or flower essences in crystal bowls, meditated in a big copper pyramid, and played with my cat, Ra. There was nothing I felt compelled to do.

Yet subtly moving within was a sense of wanting to do something about the suffering of humanity. As I looked at the state of the human race and the planet herself, I felt compassion and wanted to assist in any way I could. I had a strong feeling that the massive planetary initiation I knew was coming would be an intense passage for many. My awakening process had been seriously challenging at times, and I only wanted to see it be easier and faster for others. They wouldn't have the luxury of all the time I'd had, and outer conditions might become much more demanding.

One morning during meditation, I felt the presence of my higher Self, Martin, descending. The relationship with him had been shifting lately; I often found myself residing as Martin looking down at Barry, seeing the human aspect as a projection of my true nature. Barry and Martin were essentially the same presence focalizing at different levels of reality. The "I" sense was present in both in an undivided way, but it originated in the being of Martin.

As consciousness shifted into this larger dimension, another familiar energy joined it -- the presence of the Christ that I had first felt in Santa Barbara. Although it had come and gone during the intervening years, today it was very strong. It was distinctly different this time in that there was a strong sense of a being associated with it. Slowly the face of Christ Jesus appeared, reminding me of the image created from the Shroud of Turin by an Italian painter that I had come upon while living in Germany.

Jesus and Martin began to speak with me through direct, mind-to-mind communication. They discussed what was occurring upon the Earth, and what lay ahead for humanity. We had entered the time, they conveyed, during which humanity and the Earth would make the largest evolutionary leap in history. Together, we and our planet were about to shift into a new, higher-dimensional reality in which a fully awakened, God- or Self-realized species would eventually emerge. This was the time foretold in prophesies, when "a new heaven and a new earth" would be born.

Christ Jesus asked me if I would serve him and those who worked with him. I intuitively knew this to mean the Office of the Christ, which was often mentioned in *The Keys of Enoch* by Dr. J. J. Hurtak, a book that had powerfully impacted my consciousness. As described by Hurtak, the Office of the Christ consists of ascended masters, brotherhoods of light, and extraterrestrials working together to awaken humanity and shepherd the planet through its dimensional shift process.

My first response was joy and expectancy, mixed with fear and doubt. The mind echoed the latter: *Why me? What do I have to offer the Christ?*

Jesus gazed at me with such love and compassion that I instantly melted. He said there was no mistake they had come to me. It wasn't about who or what I was as a person. No great spiritual demonstrations were expected of me. In essence, they needed human beings on the planet through whom they could work, and they were always happy to locate someone who was available. I was assured that I was prepared and capable of doing what was asked of me, for they would always guide me, step by step.

Everything he said felt easy and comfortable. I felt a deep sense of brotherhood with Jesus, and began to call him Yeshua, the name a close friend always called him. For me, the name Yeshua resonated more deeply with the essence of the being most people call Jesus. Over the years I have found myself referring to him as Jesus in some cases and as Yeshua in others, depending on the nature of the connection. When it feels more personal, he feels like a brother and I call him Yeshua. At times his vast, powerful presence instills such a state of awe that I refer to him as Christ Jesus or simply the Christ.

Yeshua dissolved away as quietly as he had come and I was left to consider his proposal. Over the next few days, many feelings passed through. I intuitively knew that to say yes to the request would forever change my entire existence. I noticed some fear of losing control over my life, doubt that I'd live up to what was asked, and unworthiness because I saw myself as a very imperfect human being. Every time I thought of Yeshua it all dissolved away, and I was engulfed in a larger sense of joy, happiness and awe at the new adventure the request portended, one in which I could truly assist humanity.

I felt guided to accept Yeshua's summons, with a couple of important caveats. First, I realized I didn't have a clue about what I had to offer, so I would ask that they oversee everything I do and take full karmic responsibility for the outcome. Second, I wanted whatever they gave me to share with humanity to be solid, tangible and beyond question, demonstrating its divine origin beyond all doubt.

A few days later Yeshua and Martin returned. When Yeshua's presence descended into the adobe, all remaining questions dissolved in the knowing that saying "Yes" was not only the right thing to do, but also the greatest opportunity I had ever been given, one that was integral to the fulfillment of my soul destiny. Little did I know that before I had completely digested this momentous shift, I would face another of similar proportions.

Barry: A Moment Of Truth

One late-summer afternoon, a postcard arrived with a poem called "The Garden" printed on its front. Karen wrote that she would soon be coming to Lama Foundation for a Sufi dancing retreat. I had never felt a major attraction to circle dancing, yet had recently noticed myself contemplating going to the very same retreat.

The card vibrated with energy. As I held it, my spiritual heart center began to amp up with a great excitation. It was time to return to the Garden, the Edenic state from which our species had inadvertently wandered long ago, and reunion with Karen was the path home. The inner message was very clear: It was time to speak the truth to Karen about our relationship, to tell her I felt we were to be together.

Soon I was on my way to Lama to begin what would become "the dance" of my life. One evening, I found myself inviting Karen on a walk, and knew that this was the moment. As I laid it all out, Karen took it in with very little response. That night as I drove home, fear and doubt coursed through my mind. Was my guidance clear, or was it all fantasy?

In the dark silence of the Tire House, I prayed for clarity. The Christ presence descended, the lotus of the soul just above the heart opened, and I knew the truth of it all. I realized that since we were one, if I held that truth, so, too, would she be brought into it. This was all I needed to know to come to peace.

I returned to Lama and finished the dance camp feeling deeply aligned. Karen and I connected at times, and the energy was always strong. When the dance retreat ended, Karen went back to Montana and her husband and life there, but everything had changed for me. More than ever, I knew I was to be with her and that we had significant things to do together. A process was going on deep within my soul as a primal desire for union with my twin aspect grew stronger by the day.

The warmth of summer gave way to autumn as the aspens' golden hues ran like rivers of light down the mountain canyons of northern New Mexico. As the cold began to bite, I felt the call to return to the warmth of Kaua'i and the next step in the adventure. The Christ had given me a new task -- to engineer an energetic space in which people would more rapidly awaken and prepare for the dimensional shift.

I invited a newfound friend, Robin, to assist with this project, and she agreed to journey with me to Kaua'i to get started. Then it was time to pack my things and leave the Tire House. I gave my dear feline friend, Ra, to Drunvalo Melchizedek, who had taught me much about sacred geometry and was an icon of someone fulfilling his divine purpose. When all was complete, I left for the islands.

Reflection

~ ~ ~

Barry:

When Christ Jesus came to me, I knew it was a momentous turning point in my life. As he told me that the Earth and humanity were ascending into a new dimension of reality, the magnitude of what lay before us all was brought home. The desire to serve gained a new sense of importance and urgency. Yet when Christ asked me to be of service, I struggled initially to take in his request as I subconsciously felt so unworthy.

The same gratitude, awe, humility and devotion that welled up then, more than two decades ago, are still present today. But what also arises is the knowing that I am not "special" or unique, and neither is what happened to me. I have met others who have been asked to provide some type of similar service. As the Earth's dimensional shift progresses, divine beings are increasingly making their presence known, showering grace and assistance wherever an opening exists. Many on Earth are being asked to be of service at this all-important time.

Often, when people wonder aloud why this happened to me, I jokingly find myself responding, "I'm just the one who answered the phone." In some simple way, that sums it up. I am grateful that I was listening for the divine phone to ring, and I pray that all who have come to serve during this great awakening are also listening at this crucial time.

Coming together with Karen was a vital part of the divine plan. The service I was to embark upon was inextricably woven together with reconnecting with her. For both of us, a whole new dimension of life and being was about to open. Our coming together would set the stage for the final chapters of our journey and service.

Karen:

It was hard for me to believe what Barry was telling me during that fateful evening walk at Lama Foundation. Could I really have a part to play in a larger plan when so much insecurity and turmoil still persisted within my psyche? My mind did its best to convince me that Barry's message was mistaken, if not ridiculous, but when people exclaimed about the light they saw around us, I knew something significant was going on -- something I needed to pay attention to.

More than anything, I had always dreamed of being able to help others to go beyond their trauma and pain into freer, happier places in consciousness. The astrology readings I had begun to do gave me an opportunity to reflect back to clients the beauty and meaning in their divine patterns of energy. Perhaps because I had suffered from such low self-esteem for most of my life, I hoped to bolster others' self-regard and reveal the magnificence that lay just beneath their egoic predicaments. Little did I guess that during the long years of diving into my own unresolved suffering, I was being prepared to join with Barry in a new level of service.

~ ~ ~

One of the most significant passages in the journey of the soul occurs when we have become sufficiently awakened to be placed into service of the Light. Many of us have known for some time that we came to this planet to help usher in a new age. Serving as part of a multidimensional team of beings and presences, we learn that the ramifications of our actions are of far greater magnitude than when our own will and energy have impelled us to act. Now, a powerful field of energy is moving through us, and our efforts will affect many. Whatever we do impacts the larger endeavor, so we must be ready to surrender our personal desires to the direction of divine will.

Until we are ready for this level of surrender, we can't serve in this larger way. Our souls must be in strong dominion over our outer-acting personalities, so that we can follow guidance clearly and perform our function. Our particular role is part of a larger outworking that will be compromised if we don't do our part in the divine plan.

Making ourselves available for planetary service also means higher energies will be poured through us. These multidimensional frequencies must enter the Earth's domain through relatively pure vessels, or they can create misaligned outcomes. Any egoic distortions tend to be magnified by the inpouring energies, which can multiply their effects and lead to results that are the opposite of the intended goals of our service. The level to which we can be used as conduits of divine grace has everything to do with how fully and clearly the higher-frequency energies are able to pour through us.

As the soul enters into planetary service, our life focus radically shifts from serving ourselves and our personal desires to serving the Divine. Our inner drive and passion are on fire as never before, but now they are consecrated to serving God. Fulfilling our soul purpose becomes the central focus of life, right alongside the ongoing process of awakening. This accelerates the dissolution of the egoic self sense and the emergence and realization of the true, eternal Self.

11

The Evolutionary Crucible
of Sacred Relationship

Barry: The Christ in Dyadic Union

As Robin and I finished constructing the energetic matrix that would come to be called the Chrysalis, I began to get inner messages that it was time to come together with Karen. For some time now I had been told that our union had a larger purpose in the planetary awakening process, and that the next step was about to begin with the completion of the Chrysalis.

After my awakening, beneath whatever was going on in the mind, emotions and personality, a deep, ongoing communion with the inner presence that I knew to be the real Self was ever-present. Nothing felt more fundamental and precious than being at one with this true, eternal Self. And nothing attracted me more than deepening into the luminous core at the center of my being.

As a result of this ever-deepening communion, my relationships with others became much clearer. Soul connections were perceived as different from mere acquaintances. I met several soul mates, members of the same soul grouping that I had known well during many lifetimes, and although some thought we were to be together, my inner knowing indicated I was to live with none of them.

But something radically different happened when I met Karen. The moment I looked into her eyes, I did not sense the presence of her soul as I did with others. Instead, my experience was that I was literally looking at my Self. It was uncanny -- I could tell no difference between looking into a mirror at my own eyes and looking into hers. When our souls joined, it was as though a primal circuit between my outer human self and God was finally made and would never again be broken.

At first I could only maintain full, eye-to-eye soul communion with Karen for a moment or two. In the transcendent bliss and oneness, the illusion of separation collapsed and all ego~personality orientation dissolved. I was not at all ready for that potent influx of energy at the time, and the ego often rebelled and separated as it struggled to retain control.

It quickly became clear that our connection was far beyond a relationship of human personalities. Since our essences were one, the Divine was able to flow through us very powerfully. I witnessed that when we were together, a pillar of light went straight upward into Source and grounded down into the Earth. I felt strongly that the larger divine plan was to bring us together, as this would allow far greater levels of grace to be poured down through us to the planet.

It all felt much vaster than me and my little life, and yet the personal considerations were many. Seeing Karen's marriage and rather wonderful life in Montana be dissolved put a lot of pressure on the situation for me. On top of that, I barely knew her, and I had never entered into a relationship without a strong romantic connection, which we didn't have. I was very happy living alone and had essentially renounced seeking anything through a personal relationship. I also wasn't sure how it would all work out financially. I had traveled extensively and invested a lot of money into developing the Chrysalis, and now the inheritance I had received when my grandfather died was running out. How would I support the two of us and the work?

Once again flying on faith, I knew there was nothing to do but surrender into the Mystery, even though fear and apprehension sometimes surfaced. I also felt a deep commitment to doing God's will and serving the Office of the Christ. These higher considerations made it easy to trust that all would be taken care of and to put aside any personal desires and preferences that ran counter to what I knew was asked. In the end, there was really no decision. Divine will was moving like a great river to the sea, bringing us back together.

On Valentine's Day in 1989, Karen deplaned on the Garden Island of Kaua'i. The promise of her postcard of the previous summer seemed to be nearing fulfillment. But far from a return to the Garden, our initial connection turned out to be a roller coaster ride of ascents into divine bliss followed by almost hellish descents into the most intense psychic pain and ego-annihilation either of us had ever experienced. As great as the sense of love and union with God felt when we were aligned, the polar opposite became just as strong when our egos clashed. This was a whole new dimension of relationship, a realm beyond anything I knew existed. I had no idea a connection could be so intense, a word that is woefully inadequate to describe what I was experiencing.

At times during those early days, all I wanted was to run away. The pain was so strong it felt like I might die from the intensity. I felt drained, dismantled, and nonfunctional a lot of the time. Many a day I considered leaving, but the inner knowing was always to stay. Deep within, that sense of union with Karen's essence never went away, and its uplifting effect transcended all the pain and suffering. When I communed with her at that level, nothing but the presence of God existed. That knowing was always there, residing beneath and beyond everything going on at the other levels. Without that, it would have been impossible to continue on together.

Whenever we asked our souls about what we were going through, we heard the same message: We were experiencing a massive cleansing and purification of our egos. This was comforting, for at least there was a larger purpose. But at the day-to-day level it did little to lessen the severe psychic pain, which was often more than I could bear. Occasionally it even felt like a sentence from God, far, far from the expected return to the Garden I had envisioned. I seemed to be perpetually caught under a psychic rototiller stuck in high gear, set to maximum depth and seemingly never running out of gas. If a garden was going to sprout, I was definitely being churned into the compost for it.

Our connection seemed even more difficult since it was so often in stark contrast to the blissful, ecstatic heaven on Earth I had been living in since my awakening. I had come to think I was free of all my "stuff," but this relationship was making me abundantly aware that that was far from true. The depth of the well of unfinished business was overwhelming! It seemed a lot bigger than I could address on my own, and for good reason.

One day in meditation it was revealed that we were processing not just the contents of our personal subconscious, but also the collective unconscious. It was a great relief to see this, as I had been fighting self-criticism and depression, thinking what I faced was all my personal stuff. The challenging feelings were further eased with the realization that everything we worked through lifted some of the density from the collective karmic load and made it that much easier for others to find their way through similar issues and separation.

Through all the difficulties, there was great comfort in knowing that all we were going through had a larger purpose. Still, there were times when fear and doubt nearly took command. We would find ourselves wondering what the point of it all was, and whether it was healthy to stay together. Our level of dysfunction seemed off the scale!

Every time things got tough and we felt we couldn't take it anymore, we prayed for guidance. The message was always to stay together, and that being together would get easier as our egos surrendered to the annihilation process underway. We had no choice but to let go of all personal dreams of an idyllic relationship and surrender into the larger purposes for our being brought together, whatever they would turn out to be.

Our connection, though, was not only about the painful process of ego-death. There were also moments when we lifted out of the fog and saw each other as we really were. The joy and exaltation of these times helped us remember the larger truth. Yet the shattering was often more than either of us could bear, and we wondered at times whether it was right to continue.

For me, it was all settled one day during a practice session, when the powers above decided to help us come into alignment. I was lying down and Karen was sitting at my side facilitating, when I sensed a presence behind her. I opened my eyes to see the faint, almost-physical presence of three beings. Jesus was the only one I recognized, but the inner knowing indicated that Moses and Elijah were the beings standing with him, shoulder to shoulder.

Elijah stepped forth and announced to the two of us, "You are here to experience the Christ in Dyadic Union." He then stepped back and the three of them disappeared.

With that one statement, a holographic packet of information had been dropped into my being. Over time, through outer experiences and inner revelation, that packet unfolded and revealed the evolutionary possibilities now manifesting through divine, soul-to-soul relationship.

I came to understand that each of us is an individualized aspect, a holographic fractal, of God/One/Source. In esoteric literature this aspect is often called the I AM or Monad. A Christ-conscious being has fully awakened to and embodied the I AM or monadic level of being. When two beings that have completely realized their God or monadic nature unite, the two wholes become a dyad, a larger oneness.

Although the two of us were far from being established in it, I intuitively sensed the power of reunited twin flames who exist in the Self-realized or Christ conscious state. Their contribution to raising the planetary frequency would be immense. I repeatedly heard within that one of the things that made this time so unique and powerful was that the Divine would now incarnate through relationships that would catalyze the planetary ascension process. A primal schism between the masculine and feminine was being unified, and this needed to occur for the planet to shift to its next octave of evolution. Twin souls and soul mates had and would continue to incarnate together specifically to fulfill this promise.

Seeing all this made the intense transformation we were going through not only more understandable, but easy to align with. There couldn't be a higher purpose in the nonstop ego-shredding we were experiencing. What else would I rather be doing, even if it meant that I would be dying daily?

The ever-present vast, deep and powerful energy between us never waned, despite the frequent states of separation we struggled through. Like the steady hum of Creation underlying all things, our fundamental soul-oneness always eventually reminded us that something larger was going on, and held us together no matter what our egos were doing.

The nature of our connection continued to be confirmed by countless synchronicities that were obviously far more than happenstance. Life seemed to be using whatever means were available to get the point across that yes, we belonged together. Even during the times we felt most separate, we had to admit we had never witnessed such an amazing number of "coincidences" in the lives of anyone we knew of, much less our own. When we enumerated them for others, they nearly always agreed that something unusual definitely seemed to be going on.

Here's a partial list. Karen has only one brother, and his name is also Barry. His birthday is on December 6th -- one day after mine. Her mother's birthday was December 5th, the same as mine. We grew up within two hundred miles of one another, and both of us felt a strong pull to go to Cornell University. Although we were each accepted there, we both decided not to go, mostly because of the financial burden it would have placed on our parents. Instead, we each attended state universities, which not only saved our parents money but allowed us to be close to our romantic interests at the time.

Having grown up on the East Coast, we were both prompted to move west in our mid-twenties. Karen landed in Boulder, Colorado and I lived in Southern California. We each married tall, slender Germans who became doctors; both of us lived in Germany for six months in the early 1980s. It was our job to provide the doorway for our partners to emigrate to America, where, instead of practicing medicine, they pursued careers in alternative healing and transpersonal psychology. Karen's husband was a Capricorn with a Gemini moon; my wife was a Gemini with a Capricorn moon. We sensed a resonance between their energies, and often wondered what would happen if they met.

Along with all of these synchronicities, we seemed to be wired into one another in a unique way. We always instantly knew what the other was thinking and feeling. There wasn't one millimeter of space to go into denial or hide anything in our connection. The truth was always present like a neon billboard, 24/7. This was as wonderful for our souls as it was brutal to our egos.

When things got really difficult, if I remembered to look into Karen's eyes -- if I softened my focus and dropped into my core -- I always found that I was looking into my own eyes. This never failed to bring me back into conscious communion with myself and, of course, Karen, for the truth is oneness. I often forgot to do this, especially when the separation was most extreme. When I remembered, looking into Karen's eyes always magically reminded me of the truth.

Karen: What Have I Done?!?

On Valentine's Day of 1989, I left my former life behind and journeyed to Kaua'i, where Barry was again living. The day before I flew across the ocean, I wrote in my journal that I had never felt clearer or stronger. Within 24 hours, I wondered whether I had ever felt more confused and clueless.

Until now, Barry and I had spent a total of about two weeks together. We had not "dated" or "courted" -- we simply began living together, with no idea whether we were compatible in any of the usual ways people evaluate relationships. I had never made such an enormous change so quickly in my life, but most of my doubts and hesitations were overcome by Barry's certainty that we were meant to be together, along with the psychics' guidance and my own budding sense that there was something about our connection that put it in a different category altogether from any relationship I'd known. So off I went to Hawai'i to begin a new life.

From the literal moment I got off the plane, Barry and I were confronted with the most intense mirroring of egoic patterning we had ever experienced. It seemed there was not one area of our connection that felt easy and harmonious. In every way, we appeared to be exact opposites.

Years later, a friend would say, "You two seem to be coming toward each other from opposite ends of the universe." This perspective might have helped us get through those first few months more gracefully. As it was, we were on our own.

We seemed to alienate one another on a regular basis, and over just about anything. I liked to sit down to meals, while Barry and his assistant, Robin, ate snacks on the fly. I wanted to enjoy beautiful Kaua'i; Barry was so focused on his mission that he felt we should break only for a daily half-hour swim in the ocean. Then it was back to work!

During the following weeks, the romantic fantasy about what it would be like to move to Hawai'i and live with Barry was thoroughly shredded. It was too late to change my mind; I could not go back to my old life, for that life no longer existed. I had to go forward, though I wondered with varying levels of panic what I had gotten myself into.

Barry continued to insist that we were twin flames, whatever that was, and that we had something important to bring to the world together. Everything he was involved with seemed to be coming from another galaxy. With my limited understanding of sacred geometry and multidimensional physics, most of it was incomprehensible. Barry did his best to explain things to me, but my diffuse, feminine awareness found little overlap with what I termed his "mad scientist" projects.

The invention Barry was currently working on was an energetic space in which a person's subtle anatomy would balance, align, and open to experience the multidimensional realms of the true Self. This space incorporated many technologies that Barry and Robin were busy constructing out of crystals, copper wire, and an assortment of other materials. The Chrysalis contained a magnetic blanket, Flower of Life patterns inscribed in gold, devices Barry called transducers, gold pyramids, and much more.

I had no real idea how any of this worked or what my role with it was to be. None of it connected in any way with my previous life or the abilities I had cultivated. I wondered if somehow Barry had gotten it wrong. In so many ways I did not seem to be the woman he imagined me to be, the woman of his dreams, at all. And I was not finding it easy to live with him, either.

If we truly were twin souls, why were things so difficult between us? Why did we find it so hard to connect, to share intimacy, and to enjoy life together? Where was the joy?

What am I doing in this picture? I often asked myself. I missed the gentle harmony I'd known with Kurt. I missed my friends, and being part of a community where I was known and appreciated. Now all of that was gone, and this new life often seemed strange and incomprehensible.

Reflection

When the two of us were finally brought together, the crystal-clear, uncompromisingly revealing mirror we each provided for the other would turn out to be both the greatest gift and most difficult challenge either of us had ever experienced. When we look back on this time, we are still astounded that we managed to stay together. In all the intervening years, we've never met another couple who has endured such a thorough ego-drubbing, which the simplest aspects of everyday life continually provided during these early days.

Before now, most human beings needed to embark on a monastic path to attain liberation. Many traditional spiritual disciplines have long required that aspirants disconnect from intimate human relationships and put all their energy into their inner journeys. Over many millennia, the planet's vibrational frequency level has risen so much, and so much grace and divine assistance are showering us all, that it is now possible to stay focused on one's spiritual path while entering into divine relationship. That is why so many more souls are reuniting with their divine complements during this time. In the past, it was enough of a challenge to experience divine communion in solitude. Now, the evolutionary task for many souls is to fully realize and embody their God nature within the context of intimate relationship.

As part of this process, the various primary soul relationships can now be reactivated so their participants can enter into full awakening together. As these unions occur in awakened states of consciousness, ascension-level frequencies integrate into the planetary grid. Together, the masculine and feminine aspects of the dyad can hold a sufficiently vast field of energy~consciousness to allow the energies to fully ground. This amazing possibility is a key element in the planetary ascension process -- but not one that necessarily comes easily, as we were finding out.

Couples who are not soul mates or twin flames can also have a powerful transformative impact, for at the largest level we are all one. The level of love and oneness a couple can enter into and sustain over time is what really matters. Two beings who are not soul mates, deeply communing in love, might have a different but just as powerful effect as those who are but haven't united. Any two beings who live their lives immersed in the ocean of the Divine and ground their communion with Source through intimate relationship can have a profound impact on planetary evolution.

Finding our twin flame or soul mates is way beyond anything we can personally will or make happen. That remains a matter of destiny, although our inner state of consciousness can expedite or delay its occurrence. It is important to remember that every relationship offers fertile ground for more fully embodying the divine qualities we are cultivating in a given life. We can utilize any relationship as a catalyst toward greater self-awareness and the ability to feel and express love and compassion. And when it is no longer soul-nurturing to remain in a relationship, our inner guidance will make that abundantly clear.

12

A Vision, a Mission, a Purpose

Karen: Learning to Facilitate Sessions

I had always relied on a strong sense of inner guidance to lead me through life. The Grouping had stepped back over the years, which I took as an indication that it was time to develop greater spiritual maturity by finding my own way through whatever arose. Now, the sudden transformation of every aspect of my life pattern had unsettled my inner connection with the higher sources of guidance I'd always counted on. So much change had occurred so quickly that I felt lost and adrift on a strange sea, with all previous bearings rendered obsolete. When Barry began to teach me how to facilitate sessions in the Chrysalis, I felt in over my head, clueless about what to do or say, and fearful I would negatively impact someone's process. None of what I'd learned so far in my spiritual quest seemed to be useful here.

I was coming to understand that sessions in the Chrysalis were intended to bring the energy and consciousness of the higher-dimensional oversoul into full union with the human self. Since I had not yet experienced that blending, I was in uncharted territory. Barry began to facilitate a series of sessions with me, which started to open up my higher awareness. A great deal of shadow material also arose, and sometimes I felt flooded by it all.

As the long-ago psychic had advised, my journey thus far had focused on emotional healing. The years in Montana had instilled a certain grounding, and I'd begun to develop some skill and depth with astrology and tarot. Yet lack of confidence still plagued me, particularly when faced with learning new things.

Barry was not only trying to teach me how to facilitate sessions, but also how to use a computer. Our tutorials brought up the deepest primal fear I'd ever felt. I would freeze, terrified to do the wrong thing, petrified with anxiety that I'd somehow destroy the computer or lose all the files. Caught in a mental vise-grip, I could barely follow Barry's instructions.

Slowly, over time, Barry's patient tutelage, along with his faith in my abilities, won out over my deep fears. I began to co-facilitate sessions, and gradually started to find my way through the mysterious, unknown trajectory of each inner experience. Occasionally I'd even feel prompted to say something or move my hands to a particular place over the person's body. Each time, I felt relieved when what resulted didn't turn out to be a disaster. Sessions actually seemed to go well with our combined facilitation, although Barry, more able to see my readiness than I was, continually pushed me to step in more fully than I felt ready to do.

Just about anything could turn out to serve as an evolutionary catalyst. On one occasion, a rat came into the room during a session we were facilitating. It scurried across the floor behind Barry toward the kitchen. I watched with horror, unable to say anything for fear of interrupting the client's inner journey.

I've always felt repulsed by rats more than any other life form, and here was one scuttling across the very floor I was sitting upon, just a few yards away! What would I do if it came toward me? To my great relief, it eventually left the same way it had entered, beneath the door. But in my own next session, I was taken back to a lifetime in which I died in a dungeon, eaten alive by...you guessed it.

As the session unfolded, I dove into the utter horror of the situation as though it were right here, right now -- which it was, in my consciousness. My body felt sick with revulsion. I breathed into and felt layer after layer of helplessness, hopelessness, and self-pity, and faced my complete inability to change my fate.

As the overwhelming charge of emotion dissipated through feeling each layer of it to the bottom, I found myself in a place I could never have imagined. Having survived the process of fully facing an utterly repugnant situation, I was shocked to feel at peace with what had happened. I saw that on this planet, all kinds of things can and do occur. There was some comfort in the realization that although my body had been ravaged, my soul was not touched by the horrific way that lifetime had ended.

My sessions were rarely lightweight; this one least of all. But through the willingness to go into even the most frightening places in consciousness, I learned to be with whatever arose, feeling it fully, and then tasting the freedom on the other side of the emotional intensity. This direct, personal experience would later allow me to be totally present and hold a strong, secure sacred space as clients dove into traumatic memories, fears and pain.

Together, Barry and I were taken through all sorts of experiences to build our capacity to be with whatever presented itself during sessions. Once, a client seemed to be possessed by entities that had her shrieking at the top of her lungs. As the screams went on and on, I worried that a neighbor might conclude we were axe-murdering someone. Would the police show up next?

Having no idea what to do, I joined Barry in calling to God and the Christ: *Please take over here! Banish any entities that are controlling this woman's consciousness. Lead us through this as only You can.* Fervently, we made the calls, asking for divine help with every fiber of our beings.

After a time the screaming stopped and the woman reported that she felt lighter and freer than she'd felt in ages. Wrung out, we gratefully registered this news and the session ended. Although this may have been the most dramatic example in our training program, there were many others. Over and over we were humbled as it was brought home that our little human selves really weren't "doing" anything during sessions; they were acting as conduits for the Divine to pour through the energy, wisdom and guidance needed.

When we'd suggest what seemed to be a skillful, "therapeutic" way to proceed, it rarely turned out to be appropriate. Usually, the client immediately corrected us: "No, it doesn't want to go that way; something else is happening." Over time, we learned to say or do something only if it had the right inner energetic signature. The impulse to speak or act had to originate somewhere beyond the mind. We learned to wait for that inner feeling before we opened our mouths or moved our hands.

Our centering in the soul would be repeatedly tested in the years to come. Like steel, we were being tempered, annealed into our full strength and courage and brought into complete trust in the Divine. Each session carried us a little further into the faith that became increasingly unquestioning over time.

Karen: Taking Off our Overcoats

One Sunday morning, Robin and I journeyed toward the center of the island to the Hindu temple. Its setting was as close to an Edenic paradise as anything I'd ever seen. In the valley below the temple, a waterfall cascaded into a natural pond surrounded by lush foliage. All was pristine, undisturbed, and sublimely gorgeous.

We joined others sitting on the floor inside the beautiful structure. As we waited for the service to begin, I had no idea that a pivotal teaching was about to enter my life. Gurudev, the head teacher of the temple, was most often either away or in seclusion. But during this morning's service, it was announced, he would give a discourse! Immense gratitude arose for the hand of the Divine that had moved me to come here on this exact day.

After much singing and chanting and reading of scripture, Gurudev entered the hall. With his long white hair and beard, worldly-wise, smile-creased face, and rotund, robed form, he resembled a delightful cross between an old hippie and a Hindu Santa Claus. A hush fell over the room as we all prepared ourselves to receive this holy man's blessings.

Gurudev's talk was utterly simple. Our essence is light, he began -- the limitless light of God. Our only problem, he went on, is that we have covered up our light with so many overcoats that our true nature cannot shine through. The overcoats are the thoughts and feelings and ways of being that prevent us from remembering the divine radiance that is always shining within us.

We don't need to fix ourselves, Gurudev said, for we were never broken. There is nothing to change, and nothing to add to who we are, for as parts of God, our beingness is already enough.

Gurudev paused to let this sink in before delivering the stunningly simple truth: Our only task in this life is *to take off our overcoats.*

A thrill of joy arose as I absorbed the simplicity of Gurudev's message. *That's it!* I realized. *I'm here to help people take off their overcoats!*

Instantly it became obvious that in order to assist others in that way, I would need to remove as many of my own overcoats as possible. And I would have to become proficient in this task, so that I could pass on what I'd learned and make it easier for others to shed all that obscured their inner radiance.

I considered the seemingly endless challenges of the last few weeks, since I'd moved to Kauai to be with Barry. *Ah, so that's what has been going on -- I've been busy taking off overcoats!* Somehow, this realization put everything into perspective.

When I shared Gurudev's teaching with Barry later that day, he was as touched by its pithy, profound simplicity as I had been. We realized that the sessions we facilitated had two main components. The first, "taking off the overcoats," happened as people became aware of the limiting beliefs and patterns they had mistakenly thought were real. As they released their identification with and attachment to the "not-self," the true Self shone forth in all its glory. This was the second aspect of sessions -- directly experiencing the limitless light, love, and power of the eternal Self.

We realized that in every moment of a session, just as in life, one or the other of these two primary activities was occurring. We were either in the process of removing an overcoat, or basking in the grandeur of the Self. Each time an overcoat fell away, more of the radiance of the Divine could shine through. And the light of the true Self would, in turn, naturally illuminate the next layer of not-self -- the next overcoat -- ready to be brought into awareness and then shed.

It was clear that both of these aspects were essential to the process of awakening. Neither was "better" or "more spiritual" than the other; nor could either be skipped over or left out. As sessions had repeatedly demonstrated, one led to the other in a beautiful, endlessly cyclical dance of alternation.

In the past, when a session began with removing overcoat after overcoat, we had sometimes waited impatiently for the person to "get to the good stuff." Now we knew how important this part of the process was! How could anyone see or experience their inner light when so much obscured it? Once again we surrendered more deeply to the impeccable wisdom of the Self. It knew exactly what needed to happen, and in what order, at each moment in the awakening process.

Anna's Life-changing Session

Anna had experienced several sessions in the Chrysalis over a moth or two. During previous sessions, Anna had demonstrated her willingness to journey into the deepest of places and face the most intense emotional pain. Today, Anna once again dove into the trauma that remained from childhood sexual abuse, opening her heart to embrace herself and her experience. Wave after wave of anger, resentment, sadness, grief, and helplessness passed through, accompanied by copious crying.

As the emotional intensity was fully allowed to be as it needed to be, it eventually subsided. The session emptied into a sea of peace and Divine Presence even more powerful than the storms of emotion had been just a short time before.

As we all basked in the stillness, the beauty and power of the Presence continued to deepen beyond anything we had previously experienced. During the timeless silence that ensued, Anna's countenance began to transform, as her auric field lit up in an almost palpable glow of golden light. The room filled with a very refined energy of divine love.

An ecstatic smile suffused Anna's face. In awe and wonder she murmured that she was seeing a beautiful golden star shining within, just above her heart. She felt the star was her true essence, her real Self, which she had for so long yearned to contact.

A long silence followed, as a sublime energy of grace filled the room. The entire experience seemed to be held within a profoundly loving divine Presence. The radiance of the golden star was so strong that we, along with Anna, perceived it with our inner vision.

The rich, full stillness continued to deepen, leaving no doubt that Anna was communing with her inner divinity. We were all in the presence of the radiance of her true Self, fully revealed. The Light of God in Anna shone forth, revealed as her true nature, its luminous magnificence beyond words.

Gently and quietly, Anna began to express a whole new perception of the traumatic experiences she had endured. She could now see them in a new light, bathed in love and forgiveness. The anger and resentment were gone, replaced with gratitude for everything she had gone through. All that remained was the experience of love, peace, and an essential wholeness and perfection. She was beyond it all, free at last.

Anna's outer appearance was transfigured by the radiance of the luminous Presence that lived within her as her true Self. She glowed with an ethereal beauty that reminded us of images of holy beings. The remainder of the session passed quietly as Anna's new, living awareness of her Luminous Self integrated within all levels of her being.

After Anna left, the two of us sat together in speechless awe. As we walked to the beach for a swim, the magnitude of what had occurred began to fully land. We had just witnessed the most profound event either of us had ever experienced.

The space above the heart that Barry had often sensed guiding him through life had taken on a new significance. Unmistakably revealed to us all, Anna had experienced that the Divine lived within her there as her true, essential nature. Her eternal Self did not reside somewhere above and beyond her bodily form, in a distant, inaccessible dimension. It radiated within the very core of her physicality!

Reflection

༄ ༄ ༄

In the evolution of any creative unfoldment, at a pivotal moment it becomes absolutely clear what the mission and purpose of the endeavor are all about. Whenever and however it occurs, this initiation ignites the fire in the hearts and souls of those involved so profoundly that it galvanizes a commitment to bringing forth the vision into manifest reality. For us, this happened that sunny day in 1990, when Anna came for a session. The impact of this experience would forever change the course of our work and our lives.

In sessions, it had often seemed that some people had been waiting their entire lives to find a safe space in which they could dive into their deepest suffering. Others had spontaneously soared up into the exalted realms of spirit, as if they had always yearned to do just that. But this was the first time we had witnessed someone discovering, through direct experience, that *the presence of God lay within*. What a profound revelation -- and what a liberation to find the real truth of who and what we are, not somewhere far above the physical form, but right here, at the core of our being! What could be more important for anyone to know?

Discovering this, we surmised, must be the primary, the most fundamental, the only goal of human existence -- the answer to all human conflict, suffering and dis-ease. Yes, what all the saints, sages, mystics, and gurus have always said was true -- there is only one ultimate solution, only one final goal: to come into a direct experience of our true nature. From the beginning of time, the answer to all human suffering has always been right within us, waiting for us to discover it. Through grace, expanded perception reveals that God is no longer a transcendent presence somewhere up there, juxtaposed against our dark and flawed humanness; the Divine resides within and as the soul of every human being.

Direct experience had now revealed the absolute truth of Adi Da's teachings. When the soul lotus opens, the Transcendental Heart, the primary locus of God within us, awakens. This had happened to Barry on Kauai, as the presence of God unfolded from the place above the heart. At the time, it seemed to be a natural unfolding of the journey he had been on for years. The full significance of his experience wasn't revealed, though, until he saw it happen to Anna; this helped to objectify and validate his inner, subjective experience. The similarities in Anna's and Barry's experiences underscored the significance of what had occurred for them both. Seeing Anna transfigured into a luminous presence with infinite love and wisdom pouring forth made it abundantly clear that this was a pivotal experience in realizing the true Self.

What more could any human being want than to know that God lives within us as our true nature? The endless struggle to fix and change ourselves, to seek something "out there" to make ourselves whole, comes to an end as this revelation is integrated and embodied. We felt sure that once anyone truly "got it" that all they had ever wanted was and always would be right within themselves, their strongest desire would be for complete union with their indwelling divinity. It was becoming clear that this would resolve their suffering as nothing else possibly could, as their inner magnificence became their outer, manifest reality.

Anna's session brought home Gurudev's message in an unforgettable way. The golden star at her heart's core was nothing other than the Divine, shining within. And what had catapulted Anna into this profound, fully felt realization? The utterly determined willingness to shed overcoat after overcoat of some of the deepest pain and suffering we had ever witnessed.

The path to experiencing her inner divinity took Anna through the darkest passageways of fear, guilt, shame and hopelessness, everything that seemed the very opposite of "divine." But underlying it all was the light of the spiritual sun, shining within the core of her being: the pure, holy divinity that is who and what each of us really is.

This pivotal session brought the two of us together in a way that nothing else could have done. We were now united in our focus and purpose. More than anything else, we wanted to facilitate the life-changing experience of the holy, interior Presence that Anna had discovered in her heart of hearts with as many beings as we were meant to encounter.

What would we rather do with the rest of our lives than support people in coming to know, through their own direct experience, that they are radiant aspects of the One, here on Earth to shine forth and bless all of Creation through their very Presence?

PART TWO

✣ ✣ ✣

The University of the Soul

✣ ✣ ✣

13

All Roads Lead to the Soul

The image of Anna's luminous, transfigured presence had been engraved on our minds and hearts, leading us to consecrate our lives to assisting as many others as possible to realize their true, divine nature. Shortly after Anna's pivotal session, we left Hawaii and traveled with the Chrysalis throughout the western U.S. While our outer travels took us to many communities along the spine of the Rockies, the real journey unfolded in the inner worlds. During the hundreds of hours we spent within the higher-dimensional energy field of the Chrysalis, it became our evolutionary crucible. Each session served as yet another "class" in the University of the Soul, and the Chrysalis became the living laboratory in which the alchemical process of awakening was revealed.

Often, the journey to the soul passed through the darkest places in clients' inner landscapes. Within the catalytic energetic environment of the Chrysalis, feelings and issues that had long waited to be acknowledged rose to the surface. We relied on our souls to guide our facilitation, asking for assistance from the higher beings overlighting the planetary awakening and inviting their wise, loving power to inform all that we did and said. Knowing that we weren't the ones making anything happen gave us the faith and trust to enter the Chrysalis for each session.

An amazing cross-section of humanity walked through the door of the converted garage apartment that housed the Chrysalis. We never knew whether we would greet a business owner, a stay-at-home mom, an artist, or an alternative healing practitioner. Our humble digs provided the perfect setting for clients to let their masks down and drop into where they really were. To further ease performance anxieties, we made it clear the entire session process was about being with whatever arose, not what any of us thought should be happening. Then, we'd ask what brought each person to the session. Most people came because they had some kind of problem -- an issue or "dis-ease," be it mental, emotional, physical or spiritual -- that they saw as core to their suffering.

In those early days, we called our work "Beyond Healing," because we knew that at an absolute level, there is nothing to heal or fix -- all we really need to do is return to the state that lies beyond all symptoms and suffering. As Gurudev had reminded us, we can simply take off the "overcoats" of limitation so that the true Self shines forth in all its glory. In sessions, we focused on helping people to reframe their suffering, to see their "problems" as reflections of disconnection from the soul. Instead of striving to solve or get rid of them, we simply came back home to the truth of who each of us really is. As layer after layer of mental, emotional and physical distortion fell away, people were brought into the peace, joy, love, wisdom and perfection of the true, eternal Self.

When it was time to begin, the client lay down on the massage table in the center of the Chrysalis. We joined in a prayer to consecrate our time together and ask for divine assistance. Together, we offered up the session and the life challenges that had prompted it, asking God and the person's soul and oversoul to overlight and guide the process.

Then it was time for the client to turn attention away from the outer world and venture inward. Having worked with the breath for years, Barry had discovered that it offers a potent assist in shifting awareness out of the busy arena of thoughts and into the inner realms. The breath provides a focus for awareness that can easily be sensed and felt. This palpable, kinesthetic awareness has a very different quality from the mental chatter of the mind.

When we suggested that people focus on their breathing, we stressed the importance of paying attention to the sensations that accompanied each inbreath and outbreath. "Notice the feelings that are present as the breath comes in through the nostrils and goes down into the body," we'd recommend. "Become aware of all the subtle sensations."

Bringing awareness to the breath is very different from attempting to make the breath respond in a particular way. "Let the breath breathe you," we'd emphasize. "Let yourself be breathed exactly as it wants to happen, breath by breath." One breath might be long and deep; the next, short and shallow. Each breath was just as it needed to be. Many people seemed to feel relieved that since they were not doing the breathing, there was no way to do it wrong or fail at this initial step in the session.

As the client focused on feeling each breath coming in and going out, we all dropped into an energetic space of non-doing and stillness. If the mind continued to buzz, we'd suggest gently bringing awareness back to the breath and the sensations in the body.

"Invite the breath to go wherever it wants to go," we'd recommend. Nearly always, the breath moved toward areas of tension and tightness. This might be felt as discomfort or pain, a stuck or heavy feeling, or other bodily sensations. Since we had all turned the session over to the person's soul, we knew that whatever was surfacing must be part of the process of unwinding all that was not of the soul so the true Self could be revealed. We trusted that this unwrapping process was directed by a higher intelligence and power that knew exactly where we needed to go next.

We'd then suggest inviting the breath into the part of the body where the sensation was arising, and continuing to breathe into it while feeling everything that presented itself. As the client deepened into breathing and feeling whatever arose, the sensation often spontaneously changed. When s/he felt the sensations on each inbreath and then released them with the outbreath, the pain or blockage usually lessened and then disappeared. As this occurred, a visible sense of relaxation and release often came over the client's face. Soon, another sensation would arise somewhere else in the body and we'd address it in the same way. After a few breaths it, too, would melt away. Since virtually everyone carries at least some bodily tension, we devoted the first part of each session to this process of breathing and feeling, which nearly always dissolved energetic knots and tightness. We liked to call this the "meltdown" phase of the session.

But sometimes the breathing and feeling process didn't release the tension; instead, it seemed to make it worse. A mild ache in an arm might become a throbbing, painful knot. Most of us instinctively move away from uncomfortable sensations, but experience had taught us to do the opposite. Charles, an old friend of Barry's, had passed along what he called the 100% rule. If we feel 75% or even 95% of the discomfort, Charles said, we experience resistance and suffering. But when we commit ourselves to feeling 100% of whatever is going on, the pain dissolves into complete relaxation and even bliss.

Session after session proved Charles to be right. Just when clients didn't think they could deal with the pain for one more moment, if they fully opened to the feeling and felt it 100%, it shifted. For virtually everyone, this was a potent revelation.

There was usually a reason the body had cramped up so thoroughly. As the intense pain released, the deeper layers of energy that had held it in place arose. They usually consisted of emotions such as anger, fear, sadness or grief, coupled with discordant thoughts and mental images. Most often, all of this was related to a traumatic past experience. The body had contracted long ago as a result of the unconscious decision that it was not safe to experience these feelings at the time.

When clients experienced this intensification of sensation, we proceeded as we always did. We encouraged them to continue breathing and feeling whatever was arising, simply witnessing any thoughts and mental images on the screen of the mind without engaging with them in any way. By not going along with the ego's strategic attempts to analyze, categorize, fix, change, or get rid of whatever arose, clients discovered a new way to be with their thoughts and feelings. They could simply be present to them, feeling what was there to be felt, and observing the thoughts without giving them any power or credence. After they had fully met what needed to be felt and witnessed, the inner journey continued on to another arising sensation or emotion someplace else in the body. All we needed to do was follow the "trail of crumbs," as Karen began to call it, the path laid down by the person's soul that would take us all home to the true Self.

Following the Trail of Crumbs

Late one sunny afternoon, Barbara arrived for her session, still dressed in her business attire and clearly carrying the tensions of a hectic day. The first part of her session unfolded as a meandering inner journey, following the "trail of crumbs" through her inner landscape of energetic knots and contractions:

> As Barbara settles into her inner world and invites her awareness to focus on her breathing, she becomes aware of energies moving in her body. She remarks, "There are two sharp pains on the right side of my back, near my heart." As she continues breathing, feeling, and releasing the pains, they soon dissipate.
>
> Barbara then experiences a flood of sensations moving throughout her body. As each is fully experienced, it opens into the next. "Now it feels like [there are] little currents in my feet and legs, like acupuncture...Now I'm feeling pulsing in my right mid-back...It's changing to aching all over my body..."

> *As each of these sensations is met and felt, it segues into the next, bringing Barbara into new levels of awareness:*
>> *"Now I feel fear...I'm feeling how I haven't been able to go inside my body; I see it's an open vastness. Instead, I have been going up above it, someplace else...There's a pain at the top of my head, like a volcano ready to go off...Now I'm seeing flashbacks of uncomfortable situations I've forgotten..."*

This first part of Barbara's session typifies the process of melting down through the layers of tension, pain, and unfelt emotion that keep us out of touch with our bodies and souls. As facilitators, we came to understand that all we and our clients needed to do was surrender into the mysterious journey that unfolded, being present with and fully experiencing whatever arose. Facilitating hundreds of sessions taught us to fully trust the journey, no matter where it went or how difficult or painful it temporarily became. We knew that each person's higher Self was orchestrating every bit of it, knowing precisely what needed to happen.

Facing Fear

Decades ago, when Karen felt an inner prompting to leave her comfortable, secure teaching job and move a thousand miles away to begin a new life, she hit a wall of fear. Pallas, her therapist, responded, "The fear is a good sign. We only feel fear when we're thinking of doing something truly new. The bigger the leap, the greater the fear that is likely to arise. If there's no fear present when we're considering a new step, it probably isn't really new, but just another version of what we've already done." Pallas added that the people who succeed in life are the ones who don't let the fear stop them. They just feel it and keep on moving toward their dreams.

So when we bring our awareness into the realm of the soul, it's only natural that fears may arise, because we are venturing into places within ourselves that we have probably never visited before. Nearly every one of us discovers at least some minor trepidation or anxiety as we travel toward the soul space.

When fears and limiting beliefs arise in sessions, we do not give them any power, since we know they are ultimately not true. Instead, we suggest that, like all other emotions, the fear be witnessed, fully felt, and then turned over to the soul. The truth revealed and the way the soul resolves the situation invariably astonish us all, as the next three session excerpts demonstrate.

> *As his session gets underway, Nathan seems agitated. When he begins to breathe and feel whatever is present within himself, he immediately becomes aware of a knot in his stomach. Barry, his facilitator, asks if he feels open to exploring what the knot is about and if it has anything to impart to him. Nathan replies in the affirmative.*
>
> *When Nathan directs his awareness and breath to the knot in his upper belly, fear begins to emerge. Barry suggests he continue to breathe and feel the fear, allowing it to move as it wants to. With each inhalation, Nathan brings the energy of the breath into the fear, and on the exhale he releases it out of his body.*
>
> *As the fear starts to move, Nathan's face becomes etched with stress. He says, "I can't just let go and trust life completely. That's just a metaphysical concept. It doesn't apply to real life, especially one as busy as mine. With so many things I'm responsible for, I have to stay focused and on top of things, at least to a degree. If I don't, things will completely fall apart."*
>
> *Barry asks Nathan to simply observe the thoughts and continue to feel and release the fear. As he does so, Nathan's face relaxes and a subtle smile emerges. He says, "It's OK to let go. What I've been doing hasn't been working anyway. I see that if I let go and trust, life will work far better. I'll know in my heart what I need to do."*

Nathan had been carrying a lot of stress and tension in his body, centered in his solar plexus. When he allowed himself to fully experience the contraction in the knot, fear turned out to be the deeper layer behind it. Nathan's fear of losing control is a common one in our busy world. It's what keeps us pushing and driving ourselves through life. When Nathan saw what his mind believed, it became clear that all of his struggling with life wasn't necessary. In fact, he was shown that if he could let go and trust life, things would go much better.

Jane's soul communicated through vivid imagery, as the following session excerpt illustrates:

As she becomes aware of her breathing and feels whatever is present within, Jane encounters a pool of fear deep in her pelvis. "I can see a little snake. It's coming up from deep inside, telling me I'm not good enough to be doing this."

The facilitator asks, "Is the snake right?"

"No," Jane replies. "I'm thanking it for its protection all this time, and now I can let it go. Now it's turning blue. I'm seeing dolphins swimming around in shimmering gold."

Once the fear/snake is simply acknowledged, it transforms into pure life energy, beautifully represented by the dolphins swimming within exquisite golden light.

When Christine first ventured into the soul center above the heart, she encountered a fear of dissolution, which segued into a surprising outcome:

I'm seeing a lotus blossom, full and open. I'm afraid I'll be lost in it. But when I surrender into it, it infuses me, making me more of the whole that I am.

Just as so many others have discovered during their sessions, Christine and Nathan learned that the truth is exactly the opposite of the fear. This realization has tremendous power to deactivate the ego, for the truth of the soul is actually diametric to everything the ego-mind insists we should believe.

Many people experience fear of merging with their inner divinity. As Christine found, the subconscious fear that we will lose ourselves has no basis in reality. We are not lost, but found, in the soul.

Approaching the Inner Sanctum of the Soul

After following the "trail of crumbs" through the inner landscape of feelings and sensations, most people eventually arrived at a point where everything emptied out. In this quietude, nothing new was arising; all had come to a standstill. What remained was stillness and peace, which are often the first qualities of the soul we experience.

Now, it was time to move toward a deeper communion with the luminous, essential Self, the spark of the Divine that is who each of us truly is. The radiant golden star in her chest that emerged during Anna's session, along with Barry's years of merging with the wise, all-knowing divinity at his core, had made it clear that the indwelling divine Presence has a specific focus within the body, a few inches above the heart and heart chakra. During sessions, we often found ourselves referring to this sacred space as the altar of our being, the abode of the divine Self. These phrases spoke to a deep truth: The most holy of holies is not found in an outer temple, but within.

As we approached this sacred space, many people wondered, whether aloud or silently, "How do I get through the temple doors and approach the altar of my being?" For some, the doors simply opened as the next natural unfoldment in their soul-awakening journey. These clients had been brought into a place of total surrender as they were led by their higher Self through the layers of ego-distortion and resistance they met along the way. Through being present to all that arose, no matter how scary or intense it got, they were led right into their sacred core.

Others found that resistance arose when we introduced the possibility of directly connecting with the soul. As always, we suggested being with their experience -- in this case, by inviting the breath into the soul center above the heart and feeling the sensations present there. This often brought deeper layers of emotion to the surface, along with judgments such as *I am unworthy to experience the soul* and other layers of mental and emotional suffering.

A few people even wondered, "What if I find out I don't have a soul?" We hastened to reassure them that not one human being among us is without a soul. It may be covered over with layers of pain and forgetting, but it is there within each one of us, or the body would not be alive.

Although John had let go of a lot of tension and contraction in his body-mind during a series of sessions, each time he invited his breath into the soul center above the heart, nothing much happened. His disappointment finally bubbled to the surface:

> *I'm feeling really frustrated. I'm not getting anywhere with this process. I don't know what to do next. What should I do?*

Breathing and feeling were not enough; something else was needed. Barry found himself saying, "You can't do it! You cannot make this happen. Let go and ask God for help."

Within a few moments, John's tension dissipated. He was then taken on a gentle inner journey through various past experiences during which his propensity to control things with his Type A behavior had caused himself and others a lot of suffering. As the session ended, he found himself bathed in a peace he couldn't recall ever having experienced.

The profound understanding imparted through that experience imbued our session facilitating from that day forward. Awakening requires assistance from beyond -- we cannot do it on our own! If we could simply make ourselves wake up, we wouldn't have spiritual paths and tales of epic quests such as Buddha's sitting eight years under the bodhi tree. Yes, we can prepare the ground within ourselves, as Buddha and many others have taught, but in the end it is the movement of divine grace that reveals our true, eternal nature. Now, more than ever, we understood that none of us needed to **do** anything during a session, or throughout the awakening process as a whole. The only thing any of us can truly "do" is allow ourselves to be led home by the soul, oversoul and God.

We often use these three terms somewhat interchangeably, since they refer to differentiated aspects of the same One Being. For instance, while the soul is a microcosm of God, it is just as true that God is a macrocosm of the soul. When the oversoul descends and is embodied, it is experienced as one with the soul. What we call the true Self is the unification of all aspects and levels, realized as our true nature.

The Deepest Yearning of All

Some people who came for sessions were so ready to experience their true Self that they were almost immediately catapulted into an immersion in the soul. When she arrived and sat down with us, Gisele seemed impatient. Her countenance had an aura of rare intensity and determination. As we began to discuss the nature of our work, her agitation escalated. Gisele assured us she understood the purpose of our work; that had brought her to the session. She wanted to connect with her true Self more than anything.

Gisele briefly described the problems and suffering that had pervaded her life, and all the ways she had tried to heal herself emotionally, mentally and physically. Her efforts having borne little fruit, frustration had reached the breaking point. She simply wanted to be free of all the pain and limitation.

In her quest for the core cause of it all, Gisele had intuited that the only answer was to get connected with who she really was. Frustration dissolved into excited anticipation as Gisele described what had clearly become the central dream in her life. The focus of her existence had shifted from healing her self to coming home to her Self.

"I really don't want to talk anymore," she admitted. All she wanted was to go into the Chrysalis and begin her session.

> As soon as Gisele lies down, a huge back-log of emotional and mental pain begins to release. Gisele says she has no need to understand what any of it is about. She only wants to connect with her true nature. After some time, the psychic storm passes and Gisele's countenance rapidly shifts. The same beatific smile we had seen on Anna's face emerges, while we sense an emanation of divine love pouring forth from the area just above her heart.
>
> Gisele's happiness bubbles over: "Thank you, thank you, God!" she exclaims, laughing and crying with joy.
>
> After lying in this state for a timeless interval, her eyes slowly open and we all know the session is over. It is clear that Gisele has connected with her true Self. The room is now suffused with the same love and bliss that beam from her face.
>
> Before leaving, Gisele thanks us profusely. Through one humbling, awe-inspiring experience after another, we have absorbed the truth of Jesus Christ's statement: "Of myself, I can do nothing." Knowing that all gratitude rightfully goes to the Divine, we join Gisele in thanking God and her own soul, the Divine within that has led her Home.
>
> What, we wonder, could be more gratifying than watching this woman walk out the door in her radiant, love-filled, soul-connected state? We can't imagine that her life will ever be the same.

Sincerity, Humility, and Desire

As we facilitated sessions, we were always on the lookout for what helped people to connect with their inner divinity. Over and over we noticed that the presence of three inner qualities made it much easier to access the soul realms. They are sincerity, humility and desire. Gisele's session made it clear how important these inner alignments are, for she had them all in abundance, and the soul could therefore easily reveal itself.

As sessions began, we started to suggest that clients check within themselves to see if these inner alignments were present. They could ask themselves: *How sincere am I about this? Do I feel I have Life all figured out, or do I need the soul's perspective to guide me? Are there things that are more important to me than connecting with my true Self, or is this the overriding desire of my life?*

We also asked clients how willing they felt to surrender into the inner journey. Did some part of them want to control it? Like Gisele, many admitted that suffering still permeated their daily experience despite all they had attempted to ameliorate it. Those who intuitively knew that reunion with their true nature was the only answer easily accessed the sincere desire and humility to fully surrender into the journey that would take them there.

Even when sincerity, humility, and desire were present, not everyone experienced the powerful revelations of their divine nature that Anna and Gisele were blessed with. Some clients and workshop participants felt frustrated and disappointed and blamed themselves or us. Once again we had to admit that despite our best intentions, we aren't the ones in charge. Each journey of soul awakening is held within a larger divine process whose timing remains a mystery to the human mind. We could create conducive circumstances and check for the inner alignments we knew to be helpful, but awakening to the soul would only occur when the right moment in the soul's earthly journey had arrived.

That said, a pivotal experience during a soul-awakening workshop led to the discovery of a way to expedite the process. After we led the group through a soul-connecting inner journey, Caitlin felt deeply disappointed that nothing had happened for her. Her sadness only escalated as she listened to others describe their glowing, luminous inner experiences. As Caitlin talked, we felt sad, too; the last thing we wanted was to set up performance expectations that would result in disappointment and self-doubt.

After the workshop, we went home and prayed for help. Meditating on the issue revealed some simple realizations that refined our approach to facilitating soul awakening. The first thing we saw was that every one of us, no matter how ego-identified we may have become, has experienced the soul, for the soul is who we really are. These living experiences can take many forms, but all are united by the ineffable essence that is present. The soul might, for instance, emerge during a moment late at night, when the house is quiet and we slip into a deep reverie that lifts us beyond the cares of everyday life. Or looking into the eyes of a newborn, we are drawn into the luminous vastness in those clear orbs, and remember that we are so much more than the form we see in the mirror. An inexpressible love for this new little being wells up, and we cannot control the flow of tears. Gazing out at the ocean, the sense of being a person watching the sunset dissolves into a state of oneness with the numinous beauty of life. During such profound experiences, aspects of our divine essence emerge into our conscious awareness.

Although these times of soul-communion come and go, in truth there is never a moment when the soul is not present. When the ego~personality becomes consumed by outer events and the focus of consciousness turns away from our inner world, it is easy to forget that we are the soul. But since it is our true identity, the soul is always there at our core, hidden beneath layers of veiling. Just as on a rainy day the sun still shines behind the clouds, the soul's radiance glows within us no matter how many years or lifetimes go by in forgetting.

When we suggested recalling a time when the soul was present in their awareness, most people had no trouble remembering sacred moments when the soul's light shone brightly or its love poured forth from within their heart of hearts. We suggested they invite their awareness to revisit such special times. As they dropped into the experience, they got in touch with the feelings and sensations that were present at the time. These gave them a window into the ways their souls revealed themselves. Many people felt immensely reassured to discover that *yes, the soul lives within me.* They saw that the soul was never truly absent -- it was they who had wandered away from its constant presence within.

When people asked their souls to bring them back to a time when soul-awareness was clearly present, we suggested paying attention to the feeling-tone of their experience. "Notice the feelings and sensations that are there, just above the heart and the heart chakra," we advised. When people described the qualities that had colored the experience, they included deep peace, immense love, and a clarity they had rarely known. As they realized they had already felt the presence of the true Self, the prevailing belief that the soul was inaccessible was revealed as just another figment of the mind's imagination.

Reflection

~ ~ ~

Anna's session had taught us that if we could all stay present with whatever unfolded in the journey toward the soul space, the inner sanctum would eventually reveal itself. It often seemed we were being taken in the exact opposite direction, as uncomfortable bodily sensations and feelings arose. Yet hundreds of session experiences left no doubt that all roads led to the soul. Remembering this made it easier to surrender into the process and let it take us where we needed to go.

Over and over, we found that being fully present with What Is kept the flow flowing -- both in sessions and in life. This couldn't be approached, though, as a strategy to make things move through so we could get to someplace else more desirable; it had to be held in the spirit of honoring every aspect of our experience by letting it fully be. When thoughts, feelings, and bodily sensations were totally allowed to be present, the tension and tightness wrapped around them released. Then, they could simply be what they were, free of additional layers of resistance or judgment. Holding an attitude of being neither for nor against anything created an open spaciousness that invited buried mental-emotional content to emerge. When thoughts and feelings were fully met, they no longer vied for our attention and eventually emptied out, revealing the peace of the soul.

In contrast, if the feelings that arose weren't fully felt, the soul remained elusive. The knots of mental-emotional and energetic contraction didn't dissolve or move through; they just stayed there in a muddle of distracting thoughts and unfelt feelings. It seemed almost as though the soul was communicating, *You need to say "YES!" to everything you meet along the way to my inner sanctum, to show me you are ready to say "YES!" to me.*

It became obvious that there is never any point in trying to escape, avoid, or run from the pain of egoic existence. Avoidance is a primary strategy of the ego, for it knows that if we face our feelings and go into our suffering instead of avoiding it, we will eventually be led right through it into the freedom and peace we have always yearned to experience. And then the ego will be out of a job.

When we have faced the impotence of our own personal will, when it has been brought to our attention that we do not have what it takes to control what happens in our lives, we understand that surrender to the Divine lies at the heart of the journey of awakening. Clients who could admit they were suffering and didn't know how to get to the peace and happiness they so much wanted found that their humility opened the door to surrender. Others were interested in opening spiritually, but had reservations about how much of themselves and their lives they were willing to surrender. If their level of sincerity and desire to awaken weren't strong enough to impel them to press on through fear, doubt and vulnerability, the awakening process slowed or stopped, at least for a while.

Those who stayed with the process found that the journey toward the soul inevitably catalyzes ongoing, repeated ego-shreddings. As we venture ever farther into the soul realms, all that we are not is brought to the surface. All along the way, aspects of the shadow self arise, and some of them can be very hard to face. As we meet each one, see it for what it is, and realize it is not who or what we truly are, it melts into the all-loving embrace of the soul. From time to time it may still arise, but now we know it is not our true identity. We can witness it, send it love, and wish it well on its way into wholeness.

In spiritual circles there is a lot of talk about doing battle with the ego, and even "killing" it. But such violent metaphors do not accurately describe the process of evolution as we have experienced it. As we and our clients discovered together, the ego is not harshly destroyed, but loved into dissolution. All that we thought we were is not banished into oblivion, but absorbed into the limitlessness of the true Self. We do not need to try to get rid of whatever lies within us that the spiritual ego judges as unlovable, for the soul can love it all.

The physical, mental and emotional "stuff" our spiritual egos think we should be beyond is not *in* the way, it *is* the way. Being willing to fully meet whatever arises plants our feet firmly on the path homeward to the true Self. By feeling and embracing all aspects of our experience, by saying "Yes" to every layer of what is present, we open the way for our divine essence to come forth. Through the willingness to meet whatever presents itself, no matter how painful, we are led through our suffering into the love, peace and joy we have endlessly sought out in the world.

14

Soul Communion:
A Guided Induction

Now that you've read about the journey toward the inner sanctum of the soul, you may feel ready to venture inward yourself. This chapter includes a distillation of the soul-awakening induction process we have used in sessions and groups for two decades. Here, it has been divided into several parts. We suggest you work with each segment for a while before moving on to the next. How will you know when you're ready? Let the inner feeling that is the signature of your soul be your guide.

Although all the experiences in the previous chapter took place within the highly coherent energetic environment of the Chrysalis, that is not necessary for an experience of the soul to occur. Many people have been graced with immersions into the soul realm in living rooms and workshop spaces, and during tele-conferences and telephone sessions. Some people are so ready to consciously commune with the true Self that all they have to do is hear about the possibility and it begins to unfold.

If reading the following induction process to yourself seems awkward, you might find our *Conscious Soul Communion* CD helpful. The CD contains a version of the induction into the core of the soul that appears below. On the CD, the induction is not divided into segments, as it is here, but is delivered in one smooth flow. The *Conscious Soul Communion* CD contains and transmits the field of awareness of two beings who, over the past twenty years, have become ever more rooted in the true Self. As with tuning forks, when one is vibrating at a particular frequency, the other soon comes into sympathetic resonance. For information on how to obtain the *Conscious Soul Communion* CD, please refer to the Resources section at the back of the book.

If you would like to experience the entire process as it is on the CD, simply read the indented, italicized sections below. You might also take turns reading the induction aloud with a friend. In the sections below, ellipses (three periods in a row) are used to signify a short break to allow the experience to deepen before going on to the next stage in the process.

Before beginning, create a sacred space for your inner journey. A quiet environment is extremely helpful, so turn off the TV, radio, and music player. Choose a comfortable place to sit or lie down where you will not be disturbed for some time. Lying down seems to help most people surrender into the process and drop into the inner world more easily than sitting upright. But if you feel guided to sit up, please do so.

Prelude: Checking the Inner Alignments

The most important thing to remember about connecting with the soul is that *you aren't doing it*. You're creating an intention for the connection to happen, and focusing on the inner alignments that will help it to happen. But you can't *make* it happen, so now is a good time to drop all identification with the egoic "doer" and simply surrender into being, releasing all doing, efforting, and trying.

You don't need to find the soul; simply feel your yearning to commune with the soul and let the soul find you. The intelligent, loving true Self, the God in you, will do everything. All you really need to do is be present and invite a conscious connection to occur. Your willingness to surrender into the process, no matter where it may take you, will carry you right into the sacred domain of the soul.

> *It's helpful to check inside for the presence of the three divine qualities that facilitate a conscious connection with the soul. They are **sincerity**, **humility** and **desire**.*

> *How sincere are you about this? What is your motivation? Is it curiosity, or an attempt to get more, better, or different things from the outer world? How does connecting with your inherent divinity rank in importance in your life? Take a few moments to contemplate that. ...*

> *The second quality is humility.*

Are you willing to drop everything you think you know about who and what you are, and humbly rest in the state of not knowing? Are you ready to let go of all ideas about what communing with the soul should be like, and instead ask to be shown the way into the soul that is right for you? Allow a few moments to consider this. ...

The third divine quality is desire.

How much do you really want to know the true Self? Are you mildly curious, or is a strong fire burning in you to know and live from the soul? Ask yourself, "What would it be like if I lived in communion with my true Self?" What are you willing to do or surrender to help bring this about? Be honest with yourself here. ...

As in all things, God will respond to the depth and strength of your sincerity, humility, and desire. So communicate your heartfelt intention to the One who knows how to activate your conscious communion with the true Self.

Step One: Becoming Aware of the Breath

Begin by letting your body find a comfortable position, either sitting or lying down -- a position that can easily be sustained for a while. Invite your eyes to close. As you feel the body settling in, become aware of the breath as it travels in and out of your physical form. Allow the breath to breathe you, exactly as it likes. ...

One breath may be big and deep, and the next shorter and shallower. ... Relax into simply enjoying the sensations of the breath coming in and going out, and with each breath feel the body settling in even more deeply. ...

This is all you have to do, and you really aren't even doing it. You are simply lying down and breathing, and since you aren't even doing the breathing, there's no way you can do this wrong!

Being with the breath is a foundational practice in most meditation techniques. If this is a new experience, you might start by devoting a few minutes at a time to dropping into your inner world of feeling and simply being with the breath as it comes in and goes back out. Stay with this until you feel an inner prompting to go on to the next step in the process. If inner exploration is new to you, you might choose to stay with this first segment for as many experiences as it takes until being with the breath feels natural and comfortable. If being with the breath is very familiar, you might feel ready to go on right away.

Step Two: Breathing and Feeling Body-Sensations

Allow your body to come into a comfortable position, either sitting or lying down.

With your eyes closed, focus your attention on feeling the breath as it comes in and leaves the body, just as in the first step above. If you become aware of an area of tension or tightness, invite the breath into it. Feel the inhale moving into the tension, and fully feel whatever sensations are present. ... Then, on the exhale, release all sensation, letting it ride out of the body on the breath. ... As you feel the breath carrying the sensation out of the body, release your hold on it and turn it over to Life.

You can do this with the innocence of a little child: "Here, God (or whatever name for the Divine you prefer), I'm giving this to You. I don't know what to do with it, but with your Infinite Intelligence, You do." As you turn it over, feel the freedom that comes with letting go.

Continue to breathe into whatever sensations are present in the body, fully feeling each layer, and then releasing it on the exhale. Layer by layer, turn it over to Life, God, the One ... Breathing, feeling whatever is present, and turning it over ... experiencing layer after layer of sensation, letting each one be exactly what it is and then feeling it peel away as it is fully allowed and turned over to the Divine ... (Allow a longer pause here to be with your experience for as long as it feels meaningful.)

Sometimes a layer of sensation grows stronger and more intense before it releases. Discomfort and pain may temporarily increase. It may take more focused awareness to stay with the sensation, and something inside may want to move away from it. But staying right with it is the key. ... Again, focus on each layer of the bundle of sensations that are often labeled as pain or discomfort, investigating every aspect of whatever is present, and allowing it to reveal itself in its own ways. ...

Invite the sensation to spread out and take up more room, breath by breath. The antidote to the contraction of painful sensations is expansion, so let everything expand back out now. (Allow a long pause to let this occur.) If discomfort or pain is still present, you may want to give yourself more time to go deeper into this part of the journey. ...

It's never about forcing or pushing through anything. If at any time you feel you've gone far enough, let your eyes gently open and come back into normal waking consciousness. Still lying down, allow a few breaths to come and go as your awareness returns to the outer world.

Work with this practice of breathing into and feeling whatever is present until you gain facility and ease in being with the ever-changing landscape of bodily sensations. If being present with what is alive within you is a new experience, give yourself plenty of time to sink into it. Short, experiential immersions on a regular basis build confidence that you are capable of being with whatever arises. You might choose to lie down and breathe and feel bodily sensations until the body becomes at least relatively peaceful inside. Just after awakening and right before falling asleep are also natural times to engage in this practice.

You may find that not every sensation completely dissolves as you breathe into it and turn it over to the Divine. Persistent tension and long-term conditions may require regular attention over time. If the sensation does not completely release, you might send love and compassionate acceptance into the area of the body

133

where deep-seated contraction exists. This lets it know you are there with it and willing to stay with it over time. Bringing love into the process transmits the larger message that you are there for yourself, which offers great comfort to the parts of your being that are hurting.

Staying with things doesn't mean trying to push through uncomfortable sensations with force, nor does it mean to continue when you feel you've gone far enough for now. Play with the edge, but don't override a sense that to go further wouldn't be in your highest good.

Bodily sensations may also persist when there is associated emotional content held within them. Memories, stored experiences, trauma, and deep-seated feelings and fears may also want our attention. In the next step of the process, we will bring awareness to these layers of what is present.

Step Three: Being with Feelings and Thoughts

Once again, lie down or sit comfortably and invite your awareness to ride into your inner world on the breath. As body sensations arise, breathe into them, feeling the sensation and allowing it to spread out and take up more space, breath by breath. Then, once whatever is present has been fully felt, allow it to release on the outbreath.

> As you breathe and feel into deeper layers of bodily sensations, emotions and thoughts may arise. When you become aware of feelings, simply continue to breathe and feel whatever is present. Fully allow whatever is arising to be exactly what it is. ... Invite the breath to take you to the place or places in the body where those feelings are living. ... With the help of the breath, fully feel each layer of feeling and body sensation. ... Breathe into whatever is present, fully feeling it, completely allowing it to be what it is, and then, on the outbreath, turn it over to Life, God, or the One. ... Continue in this way through all the layers of feeling that arise, being fully present with each one. Allow some time for this now. ... (long pause)

> Each sensation and feeling is a "crumb" in the "trail of crumbs" the soul is laying down for you to follow. You cannot get lost, for the soul will inevi-

tably lead your awareness to the next crumb of body sensation or feeling. As you follow the trail of crumbs, you are letting the soul be your guide, and it will always take you into whatever is most important to be with -- now, and now, and now.

The trail of crumbs often goes back and forth between body sensations and feelings and fears. It may jump around the body and take you into many seemingly unrelated places in the psyche. The path may seem totally nonlinear, but the soul knows best how to unwind the layers of body-sensations and feelings so you can go free.

If sensations and feelings continue to arise, allow plenty of time for everything to be fully experienced and then turned over to the Divine. This is a gift you give yourself, a beautiful form of intimacy, which someone once pointed out really means into-me-see. Once feelings are fully allowed and felt, they never have the same control over our awareness.

Thoughts may also come and go. ... You may notice ideas about reality, concepts, theories, "shoulds" and judgments arising. ... As thoughts arise, simply notice them and return to the breath, your lifeline. ... Witness the mind's tendency to generate thoughts; nothing wrong here, this is what mind does. ... You probably won't succeed in stopping it, since this is the mind's natural function. ... Instead, simply notice each thought that arises, and then turn it over to the One who knows the truth. ...

"Ah, there's another one!" you might notice. With an attitude of Beginner's Mind, letting go of all previous concepts about what anything is about, remind yourself, "I don't know what this thought really means, and I don't know what to do with this idea, but You do." As you breathe into the thought, let the outbreath loosen it from the mind and turn it over to Infinite Intelligence. ...

Instead of hoping they will go away, invite all the thoughts that want attention to arise now, so they can be received, witnessed and turned over. Allow each one of them to simply be what it is. You might also ask the Divine if there is any truth to each of the thoughts. Imagine how your life would feel without them, and let yourself go free. Allow some time for this now. ... (long pause)

If thoughts continue to preoccupy your attention, continue to fully witness and observe each idea and judgment, and just as fully turn each one over to the Source of Infinite Wisdom. ... When everything is simply seen for what it is, it has no power over you or your consciousness. Let your awareness rest on the breath, and feel whatever is present within. Staying connected with the feeling-sensations in the body is tremendously helpful in deactivating a busy mind.

There may be more unfelt emotions wanting attention. As you breathe and feel, invite any feelings to come to the surface so they can be fully met and felt. Staying right with each one is the key. When it is completely allowed and felt, it will give way to the next. (long pause) In this way, we empty ourselves of all that has been stored within, simply waiting for us to be with it.

And into that open space the soul will inevitably emerge. ...

If you need more time for this, let the process continue for as long as it likes, until most of the thoughts and feelings have passed through and your inner world begins to feel quieter. ...

Many human beings have been run by their thoughts and feelings for a very long time. If there seems to be an endless stream of thoughts that want attention, or feelings wanting to be felt, consider focusing on this part of the process for a while longer before going on to the next. You might devote some time each day to this by either sitting or lying down, opening up a safe, sacred space, and being available to the thoughts and feelings that arise. The point of this is not to evaluate the feelings and thoughts, agree or disagree with them, or even to pay attention to what they say. Simply witness them, seeing them for what they are -- products of the ego-mind. Then turn each one over to Infinite Intelligence, with the awareness that although the mind is doing its best to persuade you to believe it, you do not know what this or any thought or feeling really means. Give it over to the level of Creation that can absorb it within its vastness so you can go free.

In the same way, feel the bodily sensations of each emotion, layer by layer, eventually feeling each one to the bottom. This may take time, and again, it can be beneficial to set aside a daily interval in which you can be with whatever is arising. Over time, you will become more comfortable with the process of being with feelings as they arise. You may also discover that each feeling is driven by a corresponding thought or belief. Seeing those concepts for what they are -- not believing them, but simply observing them as they appear -- is a key to freedom.

Learning to observe thoughts without giving them any power is the foundation of many meditation practices, for if adhered to faithfully over time, it brings a freedom we may have only rarely experienced. When we stop trying to quiet the mind or make the thoughts go away, we reverse our adversarial relationship with the mind. We are no longer resisting the mind or making it wrong; we accept that this is what mind does -- generate thoughts. When we witness thoughts without giving the content of the thoughts any attention, they eventually subside. Then we find ourselves naturally and inevitably falling into a deeper level of ourselves, the level below the mind.

Step Four: Entering the Soul Space

As you have done before, sit comfortably or lie down, close your eyes, and bring your awareness to your inner world and the breath. Breathe, feel, and be present with whatever is arising within, whether it is body sensations, feelings, thoughts, or a combination of things. Follow the "trail of crumbs" as the soul leads you through your inner landscape, fully being with whatever you encounter. Stay with this until everything empties out into a sensation of openness, a feeling of peace and inner quiet.

As you become aware of an overall sense of quiet peacefulness, it's time to go on to the next part of the journey. ... Enjoy the flow of the breath in and out of the body, and feel the sensations of inner harmony and spaciousness expanding with each breath. ...

Now, invite the breath to carry your attention into the area in the center of the chest, above your heart. ... This sacred space is the doorway to who you really are -- the true, eternal Self. ... You might like to place a hand over this area, to help anchor your awareness there. ... As you invite the breath to come into this space, let your attention simply ride in on the breath. (Allow a longer pause here so awareness can drop into experiencing the soul center.)

Continue breathing and feeling whatever is present in this space just above the heart that is often called the heart of hearts, the spiritual heart, or the soul lotus. We also call it the soul space. ... As you feel the breath opening up more spaciousness in this part of your being, notice the quality of energy that is present here. ... Beneath the ever-changing parade of sensations, feelings, and thoughts, feel the eternal undertone -- the subtle, quiet pulse of your true being. ... Continue to feel, noticing whatever is happening, letting it all be what it is, being fully present with whatever you're experiencing. ...

The soul space is the primary place in the body where the Eternal Essence of All focalizes itself within the form. For this reason, many people find that this place above the heart is where it's easiest to directly experience the eternal Self -- the Self that is, in fact, who we truly are. ... As you continue to rest your awareness on the breath, feel each breath opening up more space in the body, space in which the eternal Self can reveal itself. (Allow a long pause here.)

You are now at the altar of your being. ... Feel in your heart how much you want to experience deep union with your true nature. ... This is the answer to every question, the fountain of everything you want, the doorway to the end of your suffering. ... Remember, you don't have to know how to find your way into this union -- your true self already knows exactly how to find its way to you. ... Completely surrender and ask your true Self, right now, to lead you Home. ... Know that everything that arises is the path Home. You can trust that, knowing that the Divine is in charge. ... (Pause to allow the subtle sensations of the soul to continue to come forth.)

For most people, there is a special feeling here, a particular quality of energy and conscious-ness that is unique to you. ... Becoming aware of this unique feeling-tone lets you know that you are in touch with the true Self. ... As you continue to breathe and feel the quality of energy in this sa-cred space, invite it to spread out and take up more room there, in the center of the chest. It may want to spread out beyond the confines of the body. Allow it to expand as far as it wants to go. ...

You may be experiencing a sense of peace, a deep inner quiet, an empty fullness that is unlike your regular waking awareness, or an-other expression of the soul's true nature. ... (pause) Invite this unique signature of your soul to continue to grow stronger and more defined in your awareness. Invite the presence of the soul to expand and spread out. (longer pause)

As you become more aware of this sacred core of your being, your experience of its energetic signature grows stronger. For most of us, the unique feeling-tone of the soul is the most impor-tant way it manifests in our experience. So, right now, give yourself as much time as you like to sink more deeply into the soul's uniquely individual quality of presence. (long pause)

Because the soul is a spark of the One Great Light that has embodied to experience earthly life, the true Self reveals itself most often as some sort of light. ... This may take the form of a field of light, a glowing ball of light, a flame, a spark, or another form of radiance. ... The light may appear as a dim, small glow, a huge, burning fire, or anything in between. ...

Return your awareness to the breath, and let your inner vision ride into the soul space on the breath. ... Breathe open a space for the light of your true Self to come forth into your awareness. ... You may see the light, or sense its presence, or it may make itself known to you through a feeling of warmth or radiation. ... The light may be white, golden, or colored. ... Let it come forth in its own way, and enjoy your experience of it. ... (pause)

If you like, invite the breath to amplify the light of the soul. Breathe into the light, be present with all the sensations of the divine glow within yourself, and allow the breath to strengthen the radiance and carry it wherever it would like to go. You may sense the breath helping the light of the soul to grow in size or intensity, and to expand out from your heart of hearts. ...

Invite the light to go wherever it wants within the physical body. ... (pause) If you like, you can invite the light to completely fill the physical form. ... (pause) Once it fills the body, the light may want to radiate out to fill the energy-field around the body with the energetic frequencies of your true Self. (longer pause)

As your awareness rests in the soul space, you may also become aware of sounds, or the absence of all sound. ... Invite the breath to open up more space for all of these sensations to fully be what they are ... (longer pause)

You may also find that the true Self, the God in you, has a message for you, communicated simply through a few words or phrases. Listen with your inner ears to whatever the soul would like you to understand. ... Open to receive the gift of the soul's communication. (Allow a longer pause here to receive any soul-messages.)

Continue sinking deeper into the feeling, that particular quality of essence that makes you the unique facet of the Divine that you are on this planet. ...

At times the soul reveals itself in the form of a symbol, a particular configuration that expresses its essence in an unforgettable way. ... If you like, you can ask the soul to present itself to you through a symbol that will always evoke the divine Self for you. ...

The soul symbol may transport you on a journey of its own. ... Or the light may continue to reveal itself to you more fully. ... Allow some time now for your own unique soul journey to unfold. ... (Allow a long pause for the inner experience to continue as long as it likes.)

As your experience comes to its own natural conclusion, feel your gratitude for all that you have been shown. ... Notice how your gratefulness amplifies your experience of your Divine Essence ... Know that this rich inner world is always there within you, for this is who and what you really are.

Feel the sacred, vibrant presence of the soul realm within you, even as your eyes gently open and you begin to connect with the outer world once more. ... As you look about you, you can remain simultaneously aware of the precious presence of the soul, the Divine within, animating your physical form and guiding your life. ...

As today's experience gently completes itself, know that the more you consciously identify as the soul, the more you are inviting it to take dominion over all facets of your life. ... The more quickly you turn over anything that arises to the true Self, the more rapidly you will be led through the emotional turmoil into greater clarity and peace. This peace is your natural state, for it is the peace of the soul, the true Self. ...

All of Life responds when any one of us awakens to itself as the soul. When we come to know that the soul is our true identity, and live from the soul in more and more moments, the light that we are naturally and effortlessly ignites the spark of soul in all who are ready for that experience. So as you go out into the world, know that your presence here is a blessing to all of Life, and to the beautiful Earth herself.

Namaste -- I bow to the Divine Light within you, the Light that you are. When we know ourselves to be that Divine Light, there is only one of us.

After an immersion in the inner world, it's best to be gentle with yourself. Take some time to be quiet and allow your experience to settle in and integrate. Resist the temptation to get busy with outer activities. A cool glass of water, a walk in nature, or a rest in comfortable surroundings might sound appealing. You might enjoy journaling about your experiences, or expressing them through another creative avenue.

Once the doorway to the soul realm has opened, a never-ending journey of exploration has begun. You can invite the soul to take you on a journey any time you like, beginning by breathing into the soul space and feeling whatever is present, and then inviting the true Self to carry your awareness into the inner places that would be most helpful and resonant for you to be with right now. Each journey will be uniquely orchestrated by your own inner wisdom, which knows exactly what the next steps are in your evolution as a soul in the human experience.

Consciously connecting with the soul is a foundational element in the process of birthing the Luminous Self. We know of nothing more powerful in shifting our sense of who and what we are. When this becomes a cornerstone of our spiritual practice, we can trust that we will be shown, step by step, everything else that will serve to support the birthing of our radiant, divine Self. As we give our life over to the soul, its impeccable guidance will steer us toward what will be of most benefit in all areas of life, from diet and exercise to relationships and creative expression. There is no part of our existence the soul is unwilling to address, for the soul wants nothing more than to live through us, as us.

A practical way to incorporate the soul into everyday life is to commune with the soul each morning for at least a few minutes, inviting your consciousness to immerse in the frequencies of the true Self. Once awareness is ensconced within the comforting surround of the soul space, turn this day over to the Self, asking the soul to guide the way through whatever arises. If feelings, thoughts, concerns or issues are present, give them all to the soul; pour them into the ever-welcoming sacred space above the heart where the soul focalizes within the physical body. If a focused prayer would be helpful, it can be as simple as *Show me the Way*. Over time, bringing all earthly considerations into the soul space and turning them over to the One Who Knows becomes a spiritual habit of the best kind. The sooner we remember to let go of all striving to figure things out and call to the soul for help, the more quickly the divinity within us will respond.

The Door of Possibility is Wide Open

When the two of us first began to facilitate sessions in the Chrysalis, we, like most human beings, did not know that it was possible to directly experience the soul. We had no idea how easy it would be for people to consciously, volitionally experience their true nature. And we never dreamed the soul would come forth, over and over, in such palpable, unforgettable ways.

Now, ever-increasing numbers of sleeping souls are re-awakening to who and what they truly are. We are emphatically in the midst of the transition into a soul-awakened species. And each person reading this book is taking part in that collective awakening.

Our deepest gratitude goes out to all the pioneers who, as much as two decades ago, blazed the trail to the soul during their sessions and life experiences. Thank you for participating in the University of the Soul with us! Through your willingness to go where few had ever gone before, each of you made it easier for the many who would someday follow to come home to their true Self. Every direct experience of the soul serves not only ourselves, but all of humanity, for it expedites the birth of the Luminous Self in each of us, and in all of us.

The next chapter contains descriptions of many immersions in the soul realm. Some may echo your own experiences, while others might reveal as yet undiscovered aspects of the soul's domain. May these accounts inspire you to continue to go within and invite the magnificence of the true Self to come forth. The veils of forgetting and the traumas that remain unresolved may obscure the soul's light for a time, but all who persevere and ask the Divine to reveal the way to the soul will be brought in touch with their inner divinity. The soul is who we really are, and once we know the truth about ourselves, it cannot remain hidden for long.

15

The Soul Revealed

Outside many temples in Asia, large, stone dragons and demons guard the doorway. But once the fear has been faced and the threshold has been crossed into the cool, dark temple interior, serenity prevails. So it is with the journey into the soul. After passing through the gauntlet of egoic gargoyles and monsters, the first thing most people experience when the doors open to the realms of the soul is a deep peace unlike anything that can be found in the outer, ego-based world. The soul's peace resembles the intensely alive, hushed stillness we encounter when we leave the din of the world and enter a great cathedral. As a stillness not of this world washes over us, we know we are Home.

Lillian was blessed by the soul's peace during her first session. As surface tension released and she relaxed into a deeper space in consciousness, she said:

> I feel a warm, liquidy feeling. It's like everything is OK. There's nothing to worry about. Just accept it all. Everything seems to be perfectly OK in this space.

The soul's peace rests in the knowing that came to Lillian, that everything is "perfectly OK" in this space. Gone are the fears and worries of the ego-mind. Here at last is a place where we can find the rest we all deeply yearn to experience.

In sessions, many people spend long periods of time floating in the peace of the soul. What better healing balm could there be for the wounds of a world that is often anything but tranquil?

Soul Signature and Soul Symbols

People often ask us, "How do you know when you are connected to your soul?" The simplest answer to that question remains, "You'll know." To those who have not yet communed with their divine essence, this might sound vague and mysterious. But just as we all know how we feel when we see a spectacular sunset or a thrilling performance that moves us to our depths, we know the soul when we experience it. A particular quality of energy conveys the essence of who we really are, beyond all the transitory levels of thought and feeling. We like to call the unique nature of each person's soul essence the *soul signature*.

Those who have experienced soul signature know that it is all about feeling; a subtle but unmistakable felt-sense lets us know we are one with our core Self. Our soul signature beams out *This is who I AM*. We feel most ourselves, in touch with what makes us the unique facet of the Whole that we each are. There are few, if any, words for this feeling, though *numinous* and *divine* come close. When we are in touch with the soul, the quality of energy that is present leaves no doubt that our divine essence is what we are experiencing.

Soul signature is our unique energetic fingerprint. As we become more deeply rooted in the soul, its signature is not only increasingly present in our awareness, but also colors more and more of our outer expression. In each moment, we leave our one-of-a-kind imprint on the world through the particular nature of our soul signature.

Like fingerprints, no two soul signatures are exactly alike. Similar themes may be present, but each manifestation of soul signature is a unique expression of the Divine. In sessions, as people enter into the holy of holies within the upper part of the heart area, they often attempt to articulate their experience of returning home to the true Self. There is as much communicated between the words as in them, for words to express the inexpressible can be elusive.

Here is how Camille described her first immersion into the soul space above the heart:

> *I feel so peaceful...I can see inside of me -- it's bright, and there's such serenity...I can see it...there's a feeling of balance, of peace -- a calm feeling. It's expanding all throughout my body...(Camille drops into silence while she experiences this.)*

I'm so grateful that God has given me the ability to do this, that I'm feeling this...

While soul signature can feel like an energetic atmosphere that bathes us in a warm ocean of essence, the frequencies of the soul can also manifest as a distinct symbol. Anna's session took our work to a new level when her soul came forth as a golden star in the center of her chest. Far more than just an inner visual image, the living presence of that glowing star in Anna's soul center radiated her divine nature.

Jen shared what took place as the soul realm revealed itself to her:

I saw my soul as a bubbling spring. It went through various ways of being seen, depending on my involvement with it. It was either gushing or barely running. It is a place I will always go, to lean over and put my hands in it. I will remember to clear the weeds if I neglect it.

Jen's soul signature expressed through the symbol of the bubbling spring, a life-giving fountain of nurturance. How beautiful to discover this healing, nourishing place within herself, a sacred space she can visit whenever she likes.

Suzanne discovered a different kind of soul symbol:

There's a bell there (in the soul center)...a golden bell that rings and brings joy. It's musical...It resonates throughout my body and soul with vibrations. It can go through the entire spectrum...It can create golden light.

The magical, extraordinary qualities of the bell echo the soul's own multidimensional nature, which, like the bell, transcends all earthly limitations.

The Light of the Soul

At the core of all soul-experiences, the pure light of the One shines forth from the center of the soul. We may have read about the light within or intuited it was there, but directly experiencing it leaves no doubt that, as the *Astavakra Samhita* puts it, "Light is my very nature."

An immersion in the light at our core can surprise us with its transformative power, as Lucinda discovered during her first session:

> The light is pouring down, sparkly golden flecks all through it...Everywhere it touches seems to be healed...All the darkness is turning into blues and pinks and purples and greens...My pain is turning into light...

While pure light of various colors may manifest, the light of the soul appears within an inner landscape in which everything is luminous, imbued with a refined radiance that is not of this world. The most fundamental light in the inner realms is a clear light, the light of consciousness itself, which brings truth, insight, and clear understanding to everything it illuminates.

The soul symbol is often a focus of illumination, as Ben discovered:

> "The energy or presence I'm feeling has a lot of light coming through with it." A few moments pass as Ben drifts deeper into his journey.
> "I'm starting to see a focus of the light. It's a flame that's bright golden white. It's the light of God. It's my real nature, the original flame."

Within the core of the soul, in our heart of hearts, we discover the flame of the One. The inner divine fire has manifested during spiritual awakenings the world over for millennia. It often appears in religious iconography, including the flaming hearts of Jesus and Mary and the sacred fire Hindu gods and goddesses often carry. The central illumining source in each one of us is the spiritual fire that resides in the lotus of the soul.

The Soul's Love

When awareness deeply lands within the soul space, the soul's love may come forth, transforming our relationship to aspects of ourselves we have always judged and rejected. Through the eyes of the ego, we inevitably come up short. But seen through the eyes of the soul, we are completely worthy of its love, which is the love of God.

In the soul space, love embraces all. When we are blessed by the soul's unending love, we discover, through our own living experience, that love is the fabric of Creation, the "glue" that holds everything in all universes together. The love of the soul may present itself as the all-purpose solution to life issues and challenges that have eluded resolution.

Angelina's session began with exploring the feelings that arose as various challenging life situations came into her awareness. As she turned everything over to the true Self, Angelina's awareness dropped beneath it all, into the quiet depths of her soul. As the soul came forward, it communicated quite clearly:

> *It's saying, 'LOVE.' There's a lot of heat in my body now. 'LOVE, LOVE, LOVE.' ... All I have to do is love and be happy, and help other people to love and be happy.*

With one clear stroke, the soul swiftly, simply cut through the complexities that had occupied Angelina's mind. It was not necessary to seek solutions to each problem; all that was needed was love. When a soul-message comes forth with this kind of clarity, we have no trouble believing it originates within our divine core.

As Angelina learned, the essence of the soul is love. That love forms a continuous backdrop to our experience when we are living from the soul. Whenever clients wondered whether what they were sensing within originated in the ego or the soul, we shared a simple test: *Does the inner feeling or guidance contain an undercurrent of love?* Everyone can sense the answer to this question. If love permeates the transmission, it is of the soul. If not, the message is most likely yet another disguise of the ego-mind.

During sessions when the soul lotus opened, the entire room was flooded with the frequency of divine love. We all basked in it, feeling its healing balm going to the places within that most needed its comfort. As we sat with clients in the warm glow of this infinite love, we often asked that it stream out from the Chrysalis to bless all beings everywhere.

The Wisdom of the Soul

Ed was feeling overwhelmed. The sudden onset of serious neurological challenges had severely limited his mental functioning and curtailed his ability to cope with daily life. Because he had experienced seizures, his driver's license had been suspended. Pressing custody and settlement issues with two previous wives added to his sense of overwhelm. The complexity of the challenges

Ed faced, on top of his greatly diminished neurological functioning, resulted in considerable stress.

> During a session, Ed reaches an impasse. "I've been here many times before -- in this and previous lifetimes -- and I've never gotten through."
>
> The facilitator offers the possibility of giving the crises up to larger levels of beingness for assistance. The tension peaks as Ed's face contorts in the obvious release of his accumulated mental stress. He falls into silence.
>
> An extremely deep peace unfolds, and we all drop into it together. This silent communion is then followed by a stream of higher intelligence flowing in: "I need to let go of the children and my former wives...The way I have been conducting relationships doesn't work."
>
> During the next few minutes of silence, Ed receives further guidance. He comes out of the stillness to say, "I've been shown how to deal with all the different issues...I have the solutions I need."

Once Ed was able to release the idea that he needed to rely on his own mental capacities and asked the soul and oversoul for help, he tapped into universal levels of mind. During just a few minutes of Earth-time, he was shown, through inner pictures and instructions, exactly what he needed to do to resolve the situations with which he had been struggling for months.

The soul's wisdom often comes forth in this way as we deepen into the soul space. The messages and guidance we receive sound so simple the mind often dismisses them. But the inner feeling of rightness tells us all we need to know.

The Soul, the Gateway to our Vastness

Journeying toward the soul inevitably brings us face to face with the core wounds and scars sustained in this and possibly other lifetimes. Some underlying, foundational trauma often proves to be the root cause of many other issues. Recurring, painful patterns are usually related to the core issue, which may have been carried from one lifetime to the next.

Jeremy was told he needed to come for a session by his six-year-old son, Micah. Otherwise, he might never have met us.

Our first impression of Jeremy was that he seemed shut down and largely absent from his own life. He seemed nice enough, but much of his energy appeared to have been locked up in the emotional pain reflected in his facial expression and demeanor. In some fundamental way, he seemed to have given up on his life.

As his session begins, Jeremy reveals that being here on Earth in a physical body has always been accompanied by a deep sense of loneliness and alienation. As Jeremy opens to embrace these feelings, his experience moves into new territory. He is taken out into galactic space, to a place that feels like his true home. For a long time Jeremy simply floats in the vastness, absorbing its blessings.

Jeremy's face softens and opens, releasing the tension of lifetimes of pain. When he is able to talk again, he reveals that he feels immeasurably comforted, reassured that there is a place for him in the universe. Tears of joy stream down his cheeks. He can handle being on Earth, he says, now that he has tasted the joy of his home-region and the comforting stillness of his true being.

As the session comes to a close, Jeremy expresses gratefulness for his wise little son, who knew there was something Jeremy would receive in his session that would bring him soul-support for being here on Earth.

As his consciousness expanded beyond the confines of earthly life, Jeremy transcended his limited, physical self sense. He awakened from his amnesia and re-experienced his true nature as a vast, multidimensional presence. Experiencing the peace of his celestial home provided healing sustenance that would help him endure third-dimensional existence on a strange world. What a relief to remember who he really was, and to know that this Earth life is but a temporary chapter in an endless unfoldment.

16

The Oversoul and Beyond

    As the story of Jeremy's session in the previous chapter reveals, when we travel inward toward the soul, we may be lifted far above the level of the human self to domains in which we re-connect with our inherent vastness. We may float in limitlessness, meet our higher Self (also called the oversoul), or be absorbed into the Source of All That Is. As we awaken to the soul as our true na-ture, the soul simultaneously reconnects with its origins in the Eternal Infinite.

    This chapter presents a process for consciously connect-ing with the higher-dimensional levels of the Self. If you do not yet feel strongly established in being able to connect with your inner divinity, we suggest working with the soul-induction process in Chapter 14 for a while longer. Setting aside time each morning or evening to go within and commune with your sacred core invites awareness to rest more deeply there over time. When you can easily access that sense of inner stillness and oneness whenever you like, you are most likely ready to explore the vaster realms of the Self. As in all things, let your inner knowing be your guide. If now is not the time, simply skip the guided induction that follows and go on to the next chapter, which contains many experiences of the higher-dimensional realms. It often helps to first read about a new area of experience before tasting it for ourselves. When the mind opens to a new possibility, it paves the way for the rest of our energy to follow.

    The soul-connecting induction in Chapter 14 and the guided inner journey below provide practical technologies of grace to facilitate awakening. The process below picks up where the soul-connecting induction ends, and assumes that you have made

...scious connection with the soul. Just as consciously connecting with the soul forms the basis for awakening and can become the cornerstone of our spiritual practice, extending our awareness up into the transcendental realms of the oversoul and Source reveals the fullness of who we are as emanations of the One. The following experience is intended to support this expansion of consciousness, as all levels of being reunify.

Experience/Activation: Connecting with the Oversoul and Source

Feel how much you want to consciously connect with the higher levels of being and the Source from which you emerged. Feel your desire to commune with your vastness and transcend all human suffering and limitation. This is the path to birthing your true, Luminous Self.

Remember that this is not something you can do. It happens as you totally surrender to the vaster levels of being. They know exactly how to guide your journey into full reunion.

Ask now to be taken through this journey, guided by the oversoul and Source levels of your being. The process we share here is but a possible template for this voyage. Any time you feel guided to go in another direction, simply surrender and follow where the path leads.

Let your eyes close as your body finds a comfortable position it can maintain for a while. Invite the breath to carry your awareness into the inner sanctum of the soul in the center of the chest. Breathe and feel the unique frequencies that tell you that you are Home. ...

As you rest in the center of your soul, become aware of a vertical flow of energy through the core of your body, both upward beyond the body and downward into the core of the Earth. From the center of the soul, allow your consciousness to descend through the lower chakras until you reach the edge of the auric field just beneath the feet. Continue down into the dark, magnetic realms of Mother Earth until you come to rest in her core. Rest here for as long as you like, feeling the strong anchoring her womb provides. ...

When this feels complete, invite your awareness to travel back up, carrying the magnetic energies of the deep, dark feminine with you. Continue to ascend through the Earth, reentering the auric field below the feet. As your awareness rises to the base chakra, pause to feel your strong grounding into the core of the Earth. You may want to visualize a magnetic cord between the Earth's core and the base chakra that is firmly, continuously attached. Once you have reached the heart soul center, rest there and allow your being to settle into and integrate the grounding connection. ...

When you feel ready to continue, become aware of the upward vector of the central column. Invite your awareness to travel from your soul center up through your neck and head, exiting through the crown chakra at the top of your head. Continue up the central channel into the higher-dimensional realms of the higher Self or oversoul. Ask these vaster levels of being to reveal themselves through inner feelings or images. Commune with these realms, experiencing whatever arises in consciousness, for as long as you like. ...

Now, turn your awareness upward yet again to a point somewhere between fifteen and fifty feet above your head. Ask the I AM Presence and Source levels of being to come into your conscious awareness, sending your heartfelt desire up the central channel with this request. Continue to project your awareness upward until you sense a presence above you. ...

Feel the power and magnificence of the Presence. Allow your subtle senses to open to whatever comes into your experience. As you commune with this vast level of Self, you may sense infinite love, intelligence, and luminosity. ...

When your experience feels complete, allow your awareness to gently travel back down the central channel, through the top of the head and into the body, coming to rest in the soul center just above the heart. As this occurs, continue to feel the connection through the vertical channel into the vast realms of being above. ...

You may still feel or sense the oversoul and Source aspects of your being. Rest in the heart of your soul and commune with them as long as you like. Allow all the energy that has descended into your body to gently radiate through your form and out into your energy fields. ...

Finally, allow whatever time is necessary for these energies to ground and balance within your being. It may be helpful to feel your connection down the vertical axis into the center of the Earth. Invite any excess energies to flow down and ground in the planet's core. When you feel balanced and grounded, let your awareness come back out into normal waking consciousness.

Communion with the vast levels of Self may happen quickly or unfold over time through many inner adventures. Trust that it will happen in its own time, and continue to periodically work with this unification process as guided. Once the connection with the higher realms happens, the circuits are open. We can strengthen the connection to our vastness and further open the central channel by regularly devoting time to communing with the oversoul and Source.

Experiences of the Oversoul

A distinctly different quality of energy and consciousness manifests when the vaster realms of the oversoul are contacted. The scope of being of the higher Self is far beyond even the soul's luminosity, loving compassion, and wisdom. These rapturous experiences cannot be fully expressed through words.

When Ann invited her awareness into the soul center, she was blessed with a direct experience of her oversoul as an all-intelligent, loving, and beneficent presence. At first this presence seemed to be a separate being, but later he is revealed to be a part of her own vast beingness. Here is how she described this encounter:

There's a person in a robe, and I see a halo around him. I'm thinking, "The halo's not supposed to be there!" But it is still there, so it's supposed to be.

His hands are held out...He wants me to hold his hand and go on a journey. We're floating over the mountains...it's very peaceful. It feels really good in my heart.

He's telling me how easy it is to be peaceful and happy in everyday life. He's showing me the beauty of the Earth, looking at the world from afar. There's so much more.

I want to live my life knowing that...to keep the peace of the mountains within me. He's a very good man, very wise...

It's so easy...He says I tend to try to complicate things too much. I need to have periods when I just let go. I need to take time to feel the peace and understand how much more there is and let go...

He helped me understand...We went way out....

Next, Ann is taken to a place that figured prominently in another lifetime. After she has seen what she needs to know about that life, they continue on.

I'm taking the guide's hand -- [his name is] Peter. It's nice and floaty feeling, light as a feather...He's bringing me back...Now he's just watching, way up there...The halo is still around his head...He kind of looks like Jesus...

I'm asking him more about himself...He's a guide, a part of me...I'm connected to him...He's always there...we're tied...he's part of me...He's on a high, high plane...He's come to me before, only he's saying more things this time...I'm seeing the halo around his head...

I'm not a bad person...it's time for me to peel off the layers, get rid of the guilt...I am very innocent...I don't have to feel guilty. I am good...The golden halo is part of me...

He's a wise man...He cares for me...He's a part of me...

Now he's just floating and watching...I got what he wanted me to get...If I think about him, he'll come.

It isn't just a visual journey; I can feel it. When I first saw him I got an explosion in my chest. I have it again now. It's a wonderful feeling.

He's very, very powerful...We all are...We get too much into the complications instead of just getting above it and letting go.

There's that feeling in my chest again. I know a place now I can go whenever I need to get really in tune with myself, whenever I want to get back. How lucky I am to have this place to go, and to have found my spirit, my guide, my Self.

Ann experienced the oversoul as an overlighting presence that was a part of her, yet operating in an octave beyond that of the embodied soul. The "explosion" in her chest let her know beyond all doubt that she was contacting the most sacred, sublime levels of herself.

Glimpsing the Multidimensional Universe

Richard's experience of the oversoul realms beautifully conveys what can unfold when consciousness merges with the vaster dimensions. From this perspective, we glimpse the spacious expansiveness that characterizes the oversoul.

I see a whole reality, an entire universe. It's all gridded out. The lines and gridworks extend out into all directions. I see myself as a blip, a bell-shaped curve that is formed as a curvature in these gridworks. Below, I see a torus (a geometric shape that resembles a doughnut) and a five-pointed star. The star is a sort of direct echo of the human body.

Richard witnessed exactly what quantum physicists assert, that everything, including ourselves, is a ripple or wave emanating from the universal matrix. Interestingly, the torus is thought by some physicists to be the basis of both wormholes and black holes, which are postulated to be doorways between dimensions.

In his second session, Richard once again found his consciousness merging with the oversoul levels:

I'm floating in grace...There are galaxies everywhere...I am one of them. I am a galaxy...From this place I can see there are many parts of me...I exist in many places all at one time...

As Richard's awareness expanded into the galactic level, he transcended the limited identity associated with inhabiting a physical body. He clearly apprehended that he is far more than the human being called Richard; at a larger level, he exists as a vast, galactic presence.

Richard's journey continued through a series of lucid dreams. During one, he simultaneously witnessed someone dying, experienced himself as the person dying, and woke up, reborn in another life. Experiences like Richard's dissolve our exclusive identification with the small, third-dimensional, human self, and remind us that, as Walt Whitman so eloquently expressed, "I am vast -- I contain multitudes."

Reflection

During countless inner voyages in the Chrysalis, the true Self came forth and provided solutions to even the most challenging earthly dilemmas. The superconscious love and wisdom that issued forth from those with no special spiritual pedigree were reminiscent of the sublime declarations of saints and sages. As the soul and oversoul realms revealed themselves to one client after another, we were filled with ever-increasing awe at the glory of each human being's vast, divine nature. No matter how thoroughly the personality self belied it, what lay dormant and unseen beneath and beyond the surface of every one of us was magnificent.

Not even the most stupendously beautiful outer structure can even remotely compare to the grandeur of the inner divinity of the soul. When we experience the truth of our divine essence, everything changes at the most fundamental level, as the idea that we are a limited, imperfect, temporal being is thoroughly dispelled. Though full awareness of this may require deepening in the numinous presence over time, absorption into the soul's luminosity steeps us in the magnificence that lies within us as our true nature.

The inner realms of the soul are revealed through grace alone. The journey inward happens without one iota of human effort or intelligence being expended. In fact, the less we do and the greater the surrender, the more easily and rapidly we are led to our sacred core.

17

Discovering Our Soul Purpose

Karen: The Evolution of my Soul Symbol

Just as the soul realm offered new discoveries to everyone who experienced it in sessions, it presented unexplored territory for me, too. During morning meditations, I brought my awareness into the soul center above the heart, asking the soul to come into my conscious awareness. Day after day, I saw and sensed nothing but a big, dark cave in the center of my chest. This didn't seem very promising. Did other people experience a dark cave when they went within?

Once again I seemed deficient, devoid of all spiritual sparkle. My inner world reminded me of a poem I had taped to the wall of my college dorm room. It had only two lines, but they said it all: *My soul is gray. Please pass the paisley crayon.*

My inner world did not in the least resemble a paisley crayon, and although I faithfully brought my awareness into it each day, nothing even remotely spiritually spectacular came forth. As much as I wished for something different, I had no choice but to go with what presented itself. Inwardly, I'd walk into the enormous, dark cave and sit on the hard stone floor, waiting for something to happen. Nothing did.

I continued to invite my soul to unveil itself to me, and day after day, nothing happened. Familiar feelings of disappointment and hopelessness threatened to overtake me. *You're a spiritual failure*, the ego-mind insisted. *This is a waste of time.*

And then, one day, when my awareness traveled into the cave, a tiny flame glowed in the middle of the vast, dark expanse. Faint shadows flickered on the curved walls of the cavern. I could barely see the little flame, but it was there. Everything had changed!

Now, whenever I ventured into the cave, the small but steadily burning flame magnetically drew me to it. I'd sit near it on the ground, comforted by its presence. As I spent more time communing with the little light, it grew. Each day when I'd enter the cave it appeared a little bigger and brighter.

I continued to go into the cavern each morning, and the flame kept growing. It occurred to me that the growth of the flame offered a metaphor for my growing soul-awareness -- not just during meditation time, but throughout daily life. This did not strike me as particularly impressive or flashy, but it did seem encouraging.

Now the light had stabilized in size and brilliance. It resembled a small campfire, blazing steadily with a reassuring feeling of constancy that began to pervade my outer life, as the emotional turmoil that had forever plagued me slowly transformed into an ever-increasing calmness. Trusting my soul to lead the way, I felt more and more confident during sessions. No longer fearing that my facilitation might not be effective -- or, worse, that what I said or did would somehow damage people -- a new level of soul-presence imbued whatever it came to me to do or say.

One morning, my awareness traveled into my inner world yet again, only to discover the flame no longer burned within the cave -- it now blazed atop a sturdy staff suspended at the entrance to the cavern. I could pick up the torch and carry it wherever the light of the soul was needed!

As I stood at the entrance to the cave absorbing this big, new change in my inner landscape, I turned to look around. For the first time, I realized that adjacent to the cave grew a garden, a place of exquisite beauty and peace, lush with greenery and flowering plants. I looked back at the cave and inwardly heard the words, *the Cave of the Resurrection*. While my inner being wandered about the garden, absorbing the intensely present stillness and grace, I heard, *This is the Garden of the Resurrection.*

I continued to bask in the refined vibration of this extraordinary place, when words suddenly blossomed within my consciousness -- a series of simple words that forever altered my sense of who and what I am: *You are the Garden of the Resurrection.*

For years, I had wanted nothing more than to play a transformative role in people's lives. Because I had suffered such intense emotional storms, I yearned to assist others in going beyond their trauma and unresolved pain. In sessions, I had often vicariously glimpsed what lay on the other side of all human travails: the direct experience of our true magnificence. During the long years of turmoil, I had often wondered if I would ever become stable or transparent enough for the Divine to work through me. No matter how far I came, I still seemed to have such a long way to go.

Suddenly, in one moment, years of self-doubt were obliterated by the realization that *I already was* everything I had sought without. There was nothing I needed to do, or learn, or become! In that moment of crystal clarity, I knew beyond all doubt that *I AM the space in energy and consciousness that facilitates Resurrection in those who are ready for that to happen.*

Karen: I AM the Garden of the Resurrection

After this profound inner experience, during morning meditation I often repeated aloud, "I AM the Garden of the Resurrection." Hearing the words and contemplating them day after day planted their life-changing truth deep within my being. Almost immediately, the highly charged phrase began to manifest in my outer life. I found myself facilitating sessions with a succession of women who dove into the intense emotional trauma stemming from childhood sexual abuse. I marveled at their absolute willingness to go wherever the journey took them. Each of these courageous souls seemed as if she had been waiting all her life for this opportunity.

At first I felt puzzled: Why were they drawn to work with me, when I'd had no history of abuse? My mind apparently held the belief that only those who had suffered through a particular kind of challenge were equipped to support others in their healing process. But these potent sessions proved that this belief, like all others, simply wasn't so. Now that I was realizing my fundamental nature as the Garden of the Resurrection, my presence was exactly what these women needed.

They seemed determined to get to the very bottom of the pain they had carried for decades. After feeling layer after layer of emotion, a process that often went on for an hour or more, these indomitable women were carried into a state of soul-communion, in which a vaster perspective about what they had experienced came forth. For the first time, many felt the ever-present shame lift, replaced by exquisite empathy for themselves and what they had endured. When they had basked in the limitless compassion of the soul for as long as they needed to, their awareness spontaneously turned to inwardly face the person whose actions had led to so much suffering.

Now, the wisdom of each woman's soul emerged. One after another saw that the perpetrator of the abuse had also been wounded, and could do no differently than perpetuate the pain. Some immediately shifted from hatred into forgiveness, as they saw the tragedy of all lives involved. As the soul revealed the totality of the situation from an expanded perspective, others were amazed to discover that nothing remained to forgive. They found themselves at peace with what had occurred, ready to go forward free of the burdens of rage, hatred, resentment, and self-pity.

Through these sessions I came to understand that being present to any kind of pain makes us able to be there with all other forms of suffering. I had deeply felt the sorrow of my mother's suicide, and had survived other harrowing life challenges. I had suffered, and others must have sensed their suffering was safe with me. As woman after woman unburdened herself, I felt blessed by their implicit trust, and deeply moved by their courage in facing and ultimately prevailing over the biggest traumas of their lives.

Over and over I was awed by the wise, compassionate way each woman's true Self guided the process. There were no hints from me about how the session should unfold, for I had no idea what would be in the highest for each woman. I offered no contrived exhortations to forgive, for I knew that would only happen when all had been fully felt and faced and released. Layer after layer of pain and trauma and rage and deep grief arose, were felt, and dissolved away, creating space for the next, deeper layer to emerge.

These sessions instilled some profound truths in my awareness. When all feelings are allowed to be what they are, forgiveness occurs as a spontaneously arising act of grace, far beyond a mentalized "should." As the Self removes veil after veil of all that had prevented seeing the other with compassion, the anger and resentment of the ego-mind give way to the peace of the soul, whose eyes can only bless ourselves and one another with love. The soul's eyes see all others as Self, and that clear seeing lets us join, blend and merge, even with those who have harmed us. Souls know that every human being has suffered, and find commonality in that shared experience.

The revelation of my role as the Garden of the Resurrection had led to this profoundly moving series of sessions, and I felt deeply grateful to take part in them. These experiences of death, rebirth, and resurrection blessed me at least as much as those who came for the sessions. At first it was a challenge to remain fully present through the emotional intensity, but over time I became more comfortable, knowing that the deeper a person went into the pain, the greater the potential for healing and wholeness to be restored. Through this series of potent sessions, I learned there was no need for me to "do" anything -- no need for me to be clever, or "therapeutic," or any other quality the ego-mind was sure was necessary. All I needed to do was be myself. The rest would unfold from there.

Reflection

"Each of us is born in answer to a need," wrote the esoteric astrologer Dane Rudhyar. We may have wandered through countless experiences and situations, attempting to determine the nature of the need that only we can fulfill. The ego-mind believes our purpose will be found in outer doing. *If I only learn enough, or become enough* of whatever it thinks is important, the train of thought goes, *I will find success and fulfillment.*

But our true purpose and destiny can only emerge from within the inner realms of the soul, where we directly experience our unique celestial blueprint. This divine pattern of energy~consciousness contains two primary facets. The first is the singular expression of the Divine that originally emanated from the Godhead -- that which makes us who we are, unique in all the worlds. The second encompasses all the ways that primal beingness has been "formatted" during our many incarnations, as the soul was sculpted through its experiences in matter. The divine capacities and qualities that are central to our nature have been honed and refined from one lifetime to the next, building an irreplaceable treasury within each one of us.

As we commune with the divine pattern inscribed within the soul space, its essence unfurls like a bud opening into a resplendent flower. As the soul lotus opens, the outer world comes into sympathetic resonance with its energetic signature, and sculpts itself into a manifest expression of what is unfolding from within. A new, divinely aligned "program" can now run through the operating system of our subtle bodies and chakras.

Expressing our divine nature ever more fully is a natural byproduct of awakening to the soul. This is not something we have to figure out how to do; in fact, it is just the opposite. The egoic "doer" dissolves back into its essential nothingness as the soul comes forth. The mind's ideas about how we might best express our purpose are likewise eclipsed by the radiant brilliance of true soul-knowing.

A specific form of outer activity may or may not occur as our destiny unfolds. It may be that simply living in an embodied, awakened state is the perfect fulfillment of this life's purpose.

Whether or not we also carry out a divine "assignment" that has a specific form, to walk through life in an open, loving, and luminous state may be the greatest gift and service we can offer to Earth and humanity. Whatever our purpose is will be imbued with the grace of our true, divine nature, and expressing it will be the most uplifting gift we can give to this planet.

18

The I AM Presence
and the Ascended Masters

Barry: Pearl and the Ascended Masters

Upon reading about her in a book by Barry and Joyce Vissell, Karen immediately knew we needed to meet Pearl Dorris. In the 1930s, Pearl had been part of the I AM movement, which brought the teachings of the Ascended Masters to the world at large. She now lived in a small town near the pilgrimage point of Mt. Shasta in northern California. Bill, her younger assistant, invited us to attend the gatherings he and Pearl held early each evening.

Pulling up to the appointed address, we instantly noticed the luminous energy field that emanated from the otherwise nondescript little house. Tall, dark-haired Bill welcomed us in with a friendly smile and introduced us to a petite, elderly woman. With her short, bowl-cut strawberry-blond hair, pink sweatshirt and pants and bright white sneakers, Pearl exuded a childlike sweetness.

We joined the handful of people sitting on folding chairs, and soon the meeting began. Bill offered a short invocation, calling to the I AM Presence and various Ascended Masters, beginning with St. Germain and including El Morya, Quan Yin, Lady Nada, Jesus, Hilarion, and Paul the Venetian, asking them to pour their blessings into our little circle. The room was immediately inundated with refined yet extremely powerful energies. We sat absorbing them in silence for a while, and then Bill opened *Ascended Master Discourses*, one of the "Green Books" authored by Godfre Ray King. As the volume made its way around the circle, we took turns reading a paragraph or two aloud. The divine presence in the room intensified, and we found ourselves transported into mystical, transcendent states. For some time afterward, we sat transfixed in silence while the inpouring energies suffused our beings. As the gathering came to a close, we realized that Pearl had said little throughout the meeting, but her light and love had flooded the room.

We later learned that the I AM movement originated with a most unusual encounter on the slopes of Mt. Shasta. Thirsty from his hike, Godfre Ray King was about to drink from a mountain spring when a being appeared before him, saying, "My brother, if you will hand me your cup, I will give you a much more refreshing drink than spring water." When the being returned the cup, it was filled with a magical elixir.

"While the taste was delicious," he related, "the electrical vivifying effect in my mind and body made me gasp with surprise."

Thus began a series of fascinating adventures in which the being, who later revealed himself to be Ascended Master St. Germain, imparted age-old teachings through impromptu discourses and experiences designed to expand Godfre's consciousness. During these astonishing journeys, described in *Original Unveiled Mysteries,* quoted above, and *The Magic Presence*, the existence and work of the Ascended Masters were revealed for all of humanity. The stories in these books are not only highly engaging, they also carry profound transmissions of the sublimity and limitlessness of the ascended state.

Over the following months, we attended many gatherings in Pearl's little home. Bill often gave spontaneous discourses that conveyed the simple, practical essence of the I AM teachings. His message always focused on getting in touch with the I AM Presence, which, he said, most people experience as residing fifteen to fifty feet above their heads. This Presence, Bill explained, is the individuated aspect of God that anchors in our heart and uniquely expresses itself through and as our soul.

The goal of human existence, Bill emphasized, is to surrender our outer, human personality sense and "call" the I AM Presence or Divine Source to take dominion over our body, mind, emotions and world. The primary practice to accomplish this involves raising awareness from the heart center through the top of the head, ultimately ascending to contact the I AM Presence. Then, we are to commune with the I AM Presence, call it down into our heart and soul, and allow its light to fill the physical body and radiate out to permeate the aura. Whenever we did this during the little gatherings in Pearl's living room, we felt ourselves dissolving into a luminous, blissful field of pure being.

While connecting with and bringing down the energy and consciousness of the I AM Presence forms an essential aspect of the Ascended Master teachings, Bill stressed that this is far more than just a meditation practice. Whenever a human need, problem or conflict arose, we were to go immediately to the I AM Presence, "make the call," as Bill and Pearl put it, surrender all personal will as to the outcome, and let the Presence do the rest.

Once the request was made of the I AM Presence, we could also ask the Ascended Masters for their help. The teachings repeatedly insisted that immense assistance is always available from these great beings if we but make the call. They have completely mastered all human challenges and achieved liberation and ascension, perfecting themselves to be full manifestations of their God nature. The Ascended Masters want nothing more than to be of service to humanity, especially during this highly transformative time on planet Earth. Who better to guide us than those who have already transcended all human limitation?

The Masters serve as ideal way-showers, not only dispensing guidance and inner instruction, but also bestowing powerful emanations of grace that accelerate our spiritual evolution. While they are always available to assist us, the Ascended Masters cannot do so unless we ask. The universal law of noninterference requires that we consciously request their assistance as specifically as we can.

We felt overjoyed that the Masters' assistance was available any time we asked, and knew their presence would assist us in carrying out our soul purpose. Each time we remembered to call for their help in the midst of discord or difficulty, the process of doing so became more natural and automatic. Whenever an issue arose, we first brought our awareness into the heart soul center. Once in communion with it, our consciousness traveled up to the I AM Presence. Then, with heartfelt sincerity and passion, we asked for assistance from the I AM Presence and the Ascended Masters. Finally, we fully released the issue, surrendering all ideas about when and how its resolution would occur.

As energy poured down from the Presence into our heart soul centers and filled our auric fields, shifts occurred in our energy and consciousness, and the discord related to the issue often lessened right away. Typically, within a few minutes we received the higher wisdom that would lead to the resolution of the "problem." Some matters resolved right away, while the way through others was revealed over time. Calling to the Masters always imparted a deep comfort, along with a knowing that we could relax and let go, for They would handle the request. We knew all was held within the perfection and infinite grace of the ever-unfolding Whole.

The Ascended Master teachings stressed not giving power to the "world of appearances." We were not to react to inharmonious inner or outer events, for they were but relative appearances obscuring the deeper reality of wholeness and perfection. Instead of engaging the ego-mind and its coping strategies, or getting lost in runaway thoughts and feelings, we were to take the concern into the soul and offer it up to the I AM Presence. According to the teachings, spiritual law dictated that once the call was made, the highest and best resolution for all beings would unfold.

During this time, fear and worry often arose about how our earthly needs would be met, so we had ample opportunities to call to the Presence for help. Turning everything over to the Divine helped the ego-mind to disengage and let go of control. Again and again we were tested; the world of appearances seemed so believable, so rock-solid, so *real*. But the teachings stressed that it wasn't, ultimately, and we encountered countless situations that seemed custom-designed by Those on High to bring the message home. The outcome always confirmed the living reality of the "law," often in an amazingly short time and in ways that bordered on the miraculous. Our minds could never have orchestrated the ingenious delivery systems that provided what we needed. Over time, calling to the I AM Presence became a spiritual habit, and to this day we continue to "make the call" when pressing personal or planetary issues arise.

The Ascended Master teachings proved to be endlessly useful in our daily lives. Over many months, the 5:00 meetings with Pearl and Bill gradually deepened us in the teachings and strengthened our communion with the I AM Presence and Ascended Masters. We studied the Green Books and Pearl's *Step by Step We Climb* series, often reading passages aloud and then contemplating them. Dozens of informal conversations with Bill, who had lovingly devoted many years to absorbing and integrating the teachings, further immersed us in their timeless wisdom.

A stroke some years earlier had left lasting impacts on Pearl's overall functioning. Then in her early eighties, Pearl usually said very little during the daily gatherings, but when she did speak, the message was always simple and profound. Pearl stressed getting in touch with the "inner flame," and with a blissful, reverent countenance she'd place her hand on the area just above the physical heart, the place we had come to know as the center of our being. Pearl's peaceful, radiant presence demonstrated the effect of merging with the inner flame. She frequently exhorted us all to "be simple, be humble, be natural," and she and Bill epitomized this teaching. Their gentle, humble presences emanated divine love, which Bill counseled we were to pour out to all of life continuously.

The teachings spoke of an incoming Golden Age during which the Earth and humanity would be lifted into a higher-dimensional, heavenly realm. Pearl often saw visions of the new Earth, which was very real and already present for her, just above the third-dimensional planet. According to the Ascended Masters, Earth changes would occur at the end of the age as part of the necessary cleansing of the discord that had accumulated from humanity's disconnection from the God within.

The transition into the New Age would unfold as humanity reconnected with its inner divinity -- the inner flame, as Pearl called it. More advanced souls would expand up into their I AM Presence and fully bring it down into human embodiment. Thus would be born the radiant Christ Self. When a sufficient number of human beings had fully realized their luminous, divine nature, the Earth and humanity would ascend into a higher dimension of reality. There, they would be forever free from the illusion of limitation and the resultant suffering that has long plagued the human race.

According to the Ascended Masters, the Christ is not just associated with the man known as Jesus or Yeshua, but represents a universal principle: God fully incarnate in and as the divine human being. Christ Jesus, the avatar of the current age, demonstrated the fullness of embodied divinity as an icon of possibility for us all. The next step is for humanity to follow in his footsteps as the Christ within ourselves comes forth.

Hearing these teachings detached the unconscious association of the Christ with Christianity that had colored the term since our childhood church experiences. We now recognized the word *Christ* as defining a particular state of spiritual attainment, just as the terms *buddha*, *avatar* and *shaman* connote various levels and types of mastery. We also became aware that the word *Christ* carries a particular vibration that links us to a field of spiritual presence. While associated with Christ Jesus, its scope is universal.

Pearl demonstrated the living reality of the Christ-conscious state, for she seemed to exist in it fairly continuously. The indwelling flame that Bill and Pearl repeatedly directed us toward was none other than the golden star that Anna had seen and felt within her heart of hearts. We now understood that establishing a continuous connection with the I AM Presence above the head and inviting it to pour its blessings into the heart soul center would fan this flame until it infused our entire being.

This was clearly humanity's next evolutionary step. *What would it be like*, we mused, *to walk this Earth surrounded by be-*

ings who have ascended into the Christed state -- and to be among them ourselves?

For decades, Pearl had quietly, humbly assisted countless human beings to journey toward that state. During the flowering of consciousness that took place in the 1960s, many souls made the long trek from the San Francisco Bay Area to her simple abode in Mt. Shasta. Over the years, Bill shared many examples of Pearl's wise, spontaneous counsel to those who visited her. One of our favorites was her advice to a young man whose busy mind frequently controlled his consciousness.

"Come out of the office," Pearl began, gesturing to his head, "and into the cathedral," she finished, pointing to his chest.

We often repeated this to clients and friends plagued by the mind. Many later told us they said this to themselves whenever the thinking mind started to take over. In the gentlest of ways, it never failed to redirect their consciousness.

Reflection

The I AM teachings expanded our understanding of what had occurred during Anna's session and the many other direct experiences of the soul we had witnessed. The Chrysalis had been designed to accomplish what was necessary to connect with and embody the I AM Presence, which the teachings described as the final chapter and ultimate goal of human existence. In the teachings, we found an experiential working model of how to further our mission and purpose of catalyzing awakenings to the God within. Since connecting with the soul and I AM Presence could be accomplished at any time to accelerate awakening and resolve issues as they arose, the Chrysalis was suddenly no longer essential; consciousness was the key.

The process of connecting with the I AM Presence and the Divine within is simple, and takes place within our subtle "soul anatomy and physiology." The soul center above the heart provides a doorway to a vertical column or channel that links the chakras. It begins at the base of the spine and proceeds out the top of the head, extending up through the higher, oversoul levels all the way to our individualized aspect of Source, the I AM Presence. We are built to experience a continuous, ongoing flow of energy~consciousness through this channel, which connects our multidimensional vastness to our embodied humanness.

Going to sleep to our true nature takes place when the lotus of the soul closes and we are no longer able to access this vertical channel to the higher levels of our being. As these channels open once more, we awaken and realize our essential divinity. First, the outer-acting personality turns inward to reconnect with the soul, which also reawakens as it opens upward through the central channel to the oversoul and ultimately the Godhead.

When we bring awareness to the vertical axis and the I AM Presence above our heads, we can commune with it and ask its frequencies to pour down into our humanness. This invites its energy and consciousness to descend through our chakras and anchor in the soul center above the heart. The soul lotus then opens like a flower, and the luminous divinity at our core comes forth. The I AM Presence progressively descends and unfolds through the soul, alchemically transforming our human nature into a radiant expression of the Divine. A being in this state walks the Earth as a Luminous One -- an awakened Self in whom the Presence of God has completely embodied. Esoterically, such a being is often referred to as a Christ or a fully Self-realized being.

The process of birthing the Luminous Christ Self, then, contains a number of distinct steps. The first occurs as the outer-acting personality awakens to the soul as its true nature. This is the initial stage in the spiritual journey, when we begin to realize we are more than the human being we see in the mirror. As we awaken to the soul, we naturally find ourselves desiring an ever-deeper communion with our essence. We also recognize the importance of supporting its unfoldment in and through all aspects of our earthly life, even when this means making substantial changes in our life pattern.

While our awareness of the soul is increasing, it, too, progressively awakens as it begins to "remember" and reconnect with the vaster levels of being that contain it in an inextricable unity. We refer to these levels as the higher Self or oversoul. As this reawakening to our vastness occurs, we may directly connect with a presence or expression of beingness that resides in the higher dimensions -- a wise, loving, and more complete or perfected aspect of who we are. Gradually we merge with this level of ourselves until its energy~consciousness descends and anchors in the lotus of the soul. This process can result in transfiguring experiences like the one Anna was blessed with when she discovered the golden star shining within her heart of hearts.

The last phase of birthing the Luminous Self occurs as we rise beyond even the oversoul domains and connect with the Source or Godhead levels, where we reestablish conscious communion with the I AM, the individualized God-being synonymous with our absolute nature. As this divine presence fully descends, the small flame within the lotus of the soul becomes a conflagration that alchemically transfigures us into a fully realized, luminous, divine human. Now, we walk the Earth as a blessing-being, an agent of grace bestowing the gifts of the spirit that have been entrusted to us. Our illuminated presence ignites the spark of the Divine in the soul centers of all who are ready for that to occur.

This simple description of the metaphysics of awakening may seem to belie the enormous complexity, and, at times, the utter difficulty, of the inner journey. Soaring up into the bliss-filled transcendent realms is highly attractive for nearly everyone, while the complementary submersion into the dark, subconscious realms may seem to be a daunting facet of the awakening process. Nonetheless, a working knowledge of the various aspects and stages of awakening can provide a reassuring reality check when we are faced with challenging moments along the way. It also helps to remember where we are going, and that arriving at our destination is assured. From the moment we left the Godhead to embark upon our adventure in embodiment, our essential Self knew that one day we would return, all the richer for our myriad experiences within the world of matter.

19

The Figure 8 of Soul Evolution

As we digested the I AM teachings and applied them to our lives, we longed to be forever established in the perfect peace, love and joy of the oversoul -- the eternal, transcendent expression of the I AM Presence. Lifting our awareness along the vertical axis to the I AM Presence and Source, we wanted to believe that eventually we would reach escape velocity and leave all shadows behind. But this was not borne out by our experience. In fact, we noticed that with each new opening to the transcendent dimensions, another layer of unresolved mental-emotional material arose. The higher we soared into the bliss-filled realms of light, the deeper the subsequent nose dive into the darkness of the subconscious.

The law of duality seemed to dictate that the more light we seek, the more fully we will need to embrace its opposite. It only made sense that the converse would also be true, and this was borne out by our experience. Sessions that began by diving all the way to the bottom of the suffering nearly always transitioned into an infusion of light and expanded consciousness, accompanied by significant shifts in perspective. The most powerful awakenings, including Anna's, had occurred in this way.

Yet Anna's session and those that followed had demonstrated that the journey of awakening consists of not only ascents and descents; it also carries awareness to a center-point within us, the place where divine presence focalizes in the upper part of the chest. The I AM teachings had confirmed the existence of such a central focus of consciousness, describing it as the inner flame and the home of the God Presence or Christ Self. Through many more sessions and life experiences, we came to understand that the soul, as a nonphysical presence within a physical body, weaves all levels of consciousness into its experience of being. In the soul space, light and dark, heights and depths merge and blend into the all-enfolding wholeness of the true Self.

This unification takes place through a continuously moving flow of awareness that travels the path of a figure 8, extending up into the superconscious, higher-dimensional realms and down into the deep, dark shadows of the subconscious. As we awaken, higher-dimensional light cascades down and is progressively absorbed into the deepest realms of our humanness, while the darkest aspects of earthly life are raised up into the illumination that continuously pours in from Beyond. The soul's "conveyor belt of consciousness" unendingly carries our awareness wherever it needs to go next. All we are asked to do is follow the flow of energy and consciousness wherever it takes us and say "Yes" to whatever we find there. To the degree that we can be present to what we encounter, all aspects of our experience and beingness -- light and dark, superconscious and subconscious, inner and outer, past, present, and future -- are eventually woven together in the grand tapestry of the Self.

And the central processing unit for this ever-unfolding journey is the embodied soul. This is the focus of Self that is not only capable of reaching up into its vaster nature to access more of the limitless love, intelligence, and power of Creation, but also knows exactly which parts of the shadow are ready to be faced and reunited within our totality. How do we know which parts those are? They are what is staring us in the face!

Our ever-unfolding understanding of the figure 8 process informed and matured our session facilitation. We were able to reassure clients who thought something was wrong when they encountered big, deep pockets of pain after a session that had taken them up and out into All That Is. We now expected some version of this to occur, and informed people that a plunge into the depths might well take place after a profound spiritual opening. For most, this entailed facing yet another aspect of unresolved mental or emotional material, a relatively short-term process. Relationships and other outer life circumstances often called out for renovation or elimination, as well. Occasionally, someone was thrust into a Dark Night or other alteration of consciousness that lasted for months or even years. If the opening into the higher realms had been especially profound, a correspondingly enormous amount of mental-emotional excavation typically occurred, so the illuminated, expanded consciousness had a place to land and take root within the embodied self.

"When the light pours in, it cleans house," we told clients. We explained that it goes into the deepest, darkest areas of the subconscious and literally brings to light whatever is now ready to be seen, accepted, and ultimately transcended. "The key is to be with whatever is present," we'd add, "not just partway, but 100%." As Barry's friend Charles had counseled years before, we now knew that this was the key to moving through suffering to a place beyond it.

No longer did we prize higher openings as the ultimate goal in the spiritual journey. We now knew descents into unresolved mental-emotional material are exactly the way the light is invited into every nook and cranny of our being. How else, we realized, could it be deeply and permanently embodied?

Reflection

Elegantly and impeccably, each soul orchestrates the weaving together of its spirit and matter aspects. Throughout our lives, consciousness flows up and down the figure 8 continuum of being. The unique way this process unfolds is custom-designed by the powerful, loving intelligence of the soul to be absolutely appropriate for each of us, every step of the way.

When wholeness, not some imagined standard of spiritual perfection, is the ultimate goal, the unification and integration of opposites becomes a central feature of the spiritual journey. Not one iota of Creation can be held outside the all-encompassing embrace of the One. Just as Absolute Oneness encompasses all polarities and aspects of being within its infinite expanse, our awareness becomes capable of the same spacious inclusivity as we awaken. Our orientation shifts from the either/or polarization of the ego-mind into the both/and perspective of the soul. No longer do we "make decisions," weighing this against that. Instead, we simply listen within and pay attention to the subtle feelings that prompt us to act or wait. If an inner "Yes" is present, we move ahead; if not, we pause until a clear signal presents itself.

As we evolve into a level of awareness that transcends duality and polarization, we find ourselves exploring all kinds of places within ourselves, from the exalted heights to the deepest depths of the human condition. Journeying into whatever is calling out for our attention can be challenging in a culture that does not support dropping into the depths. We are taught to buck up and bear our suffering, to take a pill to rid ourselves of our physical, mental and emotional pain, rather than educated in how to find our way through our malaise by being present to the inner world of sensations and feelings and turning them over to the Divine.

Many of us are afraid to make the descent because of fearful misconceptions about darkness. We might believe: *If I acknowledge what is there, it will be overwhelming.* Or: *There's so much emotion inside of me I'll never get done feeling it.* A core fear may arise: *If I face the darkness within myself, it will mean that is who I am.*

To override what is present within us, we attempt to preoccupy our awareness in countless ways. We smoke, drink, use mind-altering substances, overeat, watch TV, and shop, among a host of other pursuits, hoping to fill the chasm of emptiness within. We may even divert awareness from the inner world in seemingly "spiritual" ways. If we have adopted the view that all on this level is maya, or illusion, we might believe we have no need to deal with mental-emotional material. Concluding that we can transcend it all through raising consciousness to the higher realms or by exclusively identifying with and residing in the emptiness effectively stops us from diving into the uncomfortable domains of unfinished business, which, although we may be doing our best to ignore it, nonetheless plays out in disturbances and inharmony in our relationships and life situations.

For thousands of years, the dark feminine has been repressed and demonized during a planetary cycle dominated by the cosmic masculine principle. Our god became the Father in Heaven, the sky god or solar deity. The prevailing spiritual traditions turned away from the dark mother goddess and her life-giving nurturance, which had formed the spiritual core of the previous age, and looked only upward to the masculine god residing somewhere above. While opening to the transcendent, absolute vector was a necessary evolutionary step, the simultaneous judging and suppressing of the cosmic feminine has split us off from an essential part of our being. One has only to look at the state of life or planet Earth to see the results.

Taoist philosophy reminds us that everything eventually reverts to its opposite. Yin flows into yang, which in turn empties into yin, and so it goes forever within endless eternity. Darkness is eradicated by light, while light is inevitably absorbed back into the primeval darkness of the Fertile Void. The more light we embody the more darkness it will want to illuminate. The more darkness we bring into conscious awareness, the greater the infusion of light that rushes in and fills the inner space shadow material once occupied.

If we have believed that by going up into the light we will transcend our suffering, we can be sure that at some point we will find ourselves descending into the deep, dark realms of the divine feminine. There, we will meet aspects of our beingness we may have cut off from and rejected in our skyward ascent toward the Ultimate. We may not consciously choose this descent; we may rebel against it and resist its downward pull. We may even believe that if we just try harder to go up, we can avoid it altogether. But when Divine Mother calls us down and in, it is futile to resist!

Conversely, if our spiritual path has focused on the earthy, embodied aspects of the journey -- purifying our diet, practicing yoga, tai chi or other body-disciplines, connecting with the nature kingdoms, and so on -- awakening will not be complete until consciousness extends up into the realms of the immaterial. Body-identification will be broken down through experiences that demonstrate our vast, ethereal beingness, extending far beyond the physical form.

The Divine does not exclusively reside "up there" somewhere in a disembodied realm of perfection. Any truly comprehensive definition of the One includes both its transcendent and immanent aspects. If God is all that is, then everything must be contained within Its infinite beingness. All aspects, all parts must be included and realized if we are to experience divine union.

As the light of spirit descends, it naturally seeks to be absorbed into the rich darkness of our deep feminine nature so that it can take root and grow. Each infusion of higher light carries a holographic packet of energy~consciousness from Source and our higher Self, which, when clothed in the dark, feminine matrix, becomes our manifest expression of being. When we have incorporated vast amounts of our ultimate Source, embodying the higher frequencies of spirit here in these earthly forms, we walk this Earth as divine humans, following in the footsteps of the sages, saints and masters that have shown us the Way.

As our ethereal, spiritual bodies expand in scope and radiance, we naturally manifest divine qualities and capacities. Translation, liberation, and ascension occur when our embodied presence expands beyond the vibratory rate of this dimension. As the experience of Self becomes too vast and luminous to be expressed through a physical body, we literally "outshine" this density as we are raised into a new level of vibration in the Father's and Mother's "house of many mansions."

Through the never-ending movement of the figure 8 of soul evolution, the sacred marriage of spirit and matter takes place. The white light, or Father aspect, and the dark light, or Mother aspect, continually merge and birth ever-expanding dimensions of our being. As all levels and facets blend and synergize within us, we step into our true estate as a Holy Daughter~Son of the One.

PART THREE

✧ ✧ ✧

The Living Laboratory of Soul Awakening

✧ ✧ ✧

20

A Crash Course in Faith and Trust

As our education continued through facilitating sessions, the University of the Soul's curriculum diversified and extended beyond the confines of the Chrysalis. Just as clients had reported, the realizations gained within the microcosm of the session environment began to spontaneously outpicture in our lives. It was time to live into the understandings, and Life provided plenty of situations to help us assimilate and embody what we had learned. Daily life turned into a living laboratory in which all that we had studied, intuited, and witnessed in sessions was now put to the test.

In short, our lives became one big soul-awakening session. We followed the "trail of crumbs" through the ever-changing landscape of the world, doing our best to fully meet whatever Life placed before us. When things got challenging, we breathed, felt, and turned everything over to God, just as we had with clients during sessions. It was time to integrate the vertical axis that extended up into infinity and down into the depths of density with the horizontal axis of being in the world and relating to our fellow beings. As our lives became an ongoing, ever-unfolding "field trip," the soul repeatedly demonstrated its profoundly transformative grace.

All along the way, Life presented endless opportunities to let down our masks, face our shadows, and deepen in the soul. Each new chapter in our ever-unfolding journey of soul awakening helped us to release our identification with the ego~personality and become ever more firmly established in the true Self.

Karen: Hitting Bottom

After traveling around the western U.S. facilitating sessions, we felt homesick for our beloved Kaua'i. Many months without a home base and facilitating hundreds of sessions in the Chrysalis had left us feeling a bit wispy, ethereal, and ungrounded. We needed a place to slow down and drop back into our human selves, where we could enjoy the simplest aspects of everyday life. What better spot than the Garden Island? This time, we hoped to establish a permanent home on the island that was our favorite place in all the world.

We arrived in early 1992 with just enough money to secure a camping spot and purchase an older car from a friend. At Salt Pond Beach Park, we met our new neighbors, a loose-knit "family" of people living beyond the edge. Many had pitched their tents on a sandy spit near the official campground, where no fees were collected. Most of our new neighbors seemed happy with their circumstances, and some had actually chosen to live this way.

But this wasn't always true for us. We could have been in Paradise, within as well as without. Here we were, on a tropical island, camped in an idyllic spot right on the ocean, with little to do but walk along the beach, swim, and enjoy life. Yet, as minds are wont to do, ours found plenty to be concerned about.

During my two decades of adult life, I had never found myself without enough money to rent a home. I grew up in a solidly middle-class environment, and although we were by no means wealthy, our family's existence was well-padded with the comforts of the American way of life. There was never a threat of our being thrust into homelessness, or even of having to do without the little luxuries we took for granted.

Barry's family life, like my own, had its emotional challenges, but he, too, had always lived in a home filled with food, furniture, and whatever else the family needed and wanted. Having a home -- a nice, comfortable home, with many rooms and running water and indoor plumbing -- had never been in question for either of us, until now.

I had been raised to assume that my adulthood would be at least as prosperous as my parents' had been. But my life just wasn't working out that way. And now, renting even a modest abode appeared impossible with the resources on hand, and it would take time to establish ourselves here professionally. Although we had received plenty of income from facilitating sessions, expenses had somehow eclipsed what came in, which led to accumulating credit card debt. Now, with no money for a home, we wondered, *What has happened to our lives? Are we falling out the bottom of our culture? Will we be able to find our way back in?*

The fears and self-judgments that had often tormented me in the past returned at full volume. At times I felt so overwhelmed all I could do was lie on the floor of the tent, crying. My belly churned with fear that this was the way my life would be from now on. With alarm verging on panic, my mind wondered, *What if I never have a home again?*

My worst fears -- fears I didn't even know I had -- were coming true, and I had no idea what to do about it. I felt deeply ashamed that my only home on the planet was a 5 x 7 foot nylon enclosure that barely provided enough room for us to sleep. I was an intelligent person with a college degree and abilities I'd spent years cultivating. What was I doing living in a tent?

The mind insisted that the fact that my home was now a tent left no doubt that I was a failure. I was still so identified with this voice I could not find my way beyond it into a place of acceptance and peace with the situation. The tirade of shame was so loud it all but obliterated the "still, small voice" of the soul, which would have provided reassuring comfort and given meaning to this latest challenge.

A little money came in from sessions with clients on the Mainland, but in the days before cell phones, we had to use a public telephone at the beach park for our sessions. It stood out in the open without even the smallest canopy or enclosure. Downpours sometimes drenched us as we struggled to remain present with a client's process. In the absence of any type of chair or ledge, we had no choice but to stand for an hour or more as we facilitated each inner journey. During a particularly crucial moment in a session, a queue might form, and we'd have to reschedule. With any luck, the neighbors' boom box wouldn't be blaring their one reggae tape, every note of which we had come to know during the nonstop barrage of sound that filled most days and nights.

Having traveled for many months, we both felt a deep need for an ongoing home, a place where we could do sessions, offer groups, and live our lives. Right now, though, all of that seemed far off and unobtainable until our financial situation changed. I was willing to get a job, if that would create some grounding. It would have been a relief to receive a regular paycheck and slowly dig ourselves out of this hole that seemed to be engulfing us. *Even the most menial job,* I often thought, *would be better than this insecurity.*

In meditation, we repeatedly asked what we could do to create some financial stability in our lives. When we wondered whether we should get jobs, the inner answer was always the same: *There's no need to go to work -- just enjoy life.* Rather than advising us to get busy providing for our earthly needs, our souls clearly had another agenda. But hearing this didn't make it all instantly easy for me.

"What if this is the way our life is from now on?" I went on wailing to Barry. "What if we never manage to have a home again?"

"Then that would be what God wanted us to experience," he'd calmly reply.

All of this was far easier for him. Barry was delighted to be back on his beloved island, even if it meant we had to live in a tent. And that was not a hardship for him, either -- he loved being able to walk down to the water for a swim whenever the mood struck, and the sunset views from the beach were spectacular. From time to time he wondered why we had to go through all of this, though, and he, too, occasionally succumbed to fear. At times Barry felt sad and hopeless; he had been given the wonderful gift of the Chrysalis, yet so few people seem interested in availing themselves of its evolutionary opportunities. Still, as he often reminded me, "If we have to be homeless, being on the beach in Hawai'i is as good as it gets."

Gradually, after more than a few meltdowns, it became clear that this was simply the latest in the ongoing series of challenges designed to break down every last vestige of the ego-mind's control over our consciousness. We began to reframe it as an opportunity to go beyond "giving power to the world of appearances," as the Ascended Masters taught. When fear and panic threatened to overtake one or both of us, we went into our tent to lie down. After breathing and feeling whatever was arising, we'd take all the discordant thoughts and feelings and surrender them Upward, offering them to the luminous Presence of the I AM for resolution. While in communion with the God Presence, we'd often pray, *Show us the way.*

When we felt particularly lost about what to do next, we prayed as we had learned from Bill and Pearl: *Open the doors that need to be opened, and close the doors that need to be closed.* Sending requests to the omnipotent One helped us to surrender our personal wills to the divine plan.

The outer appearances of our lives gave us plenty of opportunities to face and see through the mind's fearful illusions and future-based projections about what might befall us. In truth, we always had enough to eat, the ocean unfailingly refreshed us, and the skies overhead remained blue and clear, even when our internal weather turned cloudy and gray. Living at the campground also brought gifts of grace we would not have received in any other way. The aloha spirit of Uncle Louis, the unofficial campground host, overflowed to bless us all during his daily round through the little tent community. One day, he took the two of us home to meet his wife, Alice, who gave me a bag of rare and precious Ni'ihau shells. I was deeply touched by her gift, and took it as a sign that all would be well.

When we weren't feeling overwhelmed by the challenge of being with what was going on, within and without, we recognized that this latest test was taking us ever deeper into the ability to accept What Is and live from our souls. We had learned a lot about faith and trust during soul-awakening sessions. Now it was time to live into these divine qualities, and that can only occur through direct experience. All the while, we were growing stronger, clearer and more grounded in our essential selves. Each time we hit another edge and surrendered into the death and rebirth it asked of us, our beings expanded yet again to embrace still more that we had rejected and judged as unworthy of love.

It seemed that a second figure 8, rotating on a horizontal axis, was weaving together the inner realms of the soul and the outer realms of the personality. The crises stimulated by outer circumstances took us deeper into our souls, bringing our awareness to all that did not resonate with our essential divinity so it could be transformed. As our inner worlds changed, our outer worlds soon morphed to reflect the evolutionary shifts.

During this time, we learned a lot about the ways money and the power it affords buffer us from many of the unpleasantries of life. The fear and vulnerability that those at the bottom of our society experience were suddenly part of our lives, too. Yet we also noticed how kind and generous so many of the materially poorest people were; what little they did have, they willingly shared. Having arrived at the nadir of worldly wealth, they had found that life did, indeed, support them, even in the absence of houses, credit cards, and cars. We aspired to the freedom and equanimity that simply, quietly colored their presence. They may have inhabited the bottom of the socioeconomic scale, but the divine qualities they embodied certainly put them right at the top of any spiritual hierarchy.

Karen: An Unlikely Teacher of Faith and Freedom

As we drove back and forth from the beach park, we often saw a very pregnant young woman and her daughter standing at the roadside in the hot sun, hitchhiking. We soon learned that they, too, lived in a tent near Salt Pond. Jody and her six-year-old daughter, Sarah, had come to the islands with practically nothing, seeking a new life. Jody never seemed to fret about her earthly needs, nor was she preoccupied with meeting them. Radiating like the sun, Jody simply loved life and approached each new day as an adventure in which anything could happen.

One day Jody told us that she felt it was time to have a car. This seemed sensible to us, given her circumstances, even as we wondered how it would ever happen. Jody said she had let God know that she was ready to have a vehicle, if it was in the highest for her to have one. *God,* she prayed, *if you would like Sarah and me to have a car, we would gratefully receive one!*

Within a few days, Jody drove into the beach park in a Cadillac convertible that had seen a lot of life but still appeared to be in good, roadworthy condition. For the little family, this big boat of a car was the ultimate in practicality. It was capable of carrying all their possessions, and wide enough that Jody and her daughter could even sleep on the seats if they liked. Astounded, we wondered how it had come into her life.

That evening she related the story. Walking home from the store, carrying bags of groceries in one arm and holding Sarah's hand with the other, she was offered a ride by a man driving the Cadillac.

"I've seen you hitchhiking along the road before," the man revealed. They got to talking, and before long, the man was offering to give Jody the car if she wanted it.

"My wife and I have another car," he went on, "and you look like you need this one more than we do." Within a few hours the title and registration were in Jody's name.

One day, we asked Jody about her plans to birth her baby. Smiling, she said she thought that she would go down to a still pool at the end of the beach when she knew it was time to deliver. What better than to lie down in the ocean and allow the baby to swim out into the world, embraced by the great Mother of all? Once again, Jody demonstrated her absolute trust that whatever she needed was right in front of her.

In every interaction with Jody, we received a living transmission of the underlying reality that engenders faith and trust: She knew in her bones that Life provides. Every breath came and went in the deeply calm knowing that she was carried by the infinitely loving, all-powerful Divine.

Barry: From a Tent to a Mansion and Back

When a dear friend invited us to join her for a few days in an oceanfront home on the Big Island, it sounded like a welcome respite from our intense immersion in the tent-living hologram. The inter-island flight would mean another charge on the credit card, but it felt like the right thing to do.

Joan was staying with wealthy friends right on Kealakekua Bay, a spectacular expanse of calm water in which spinner dolphins frequently came to swim with locals and tourists. With its five thousand square feet of luxuriously appointed opulence, the Point House inhabited the opposite end of the socioeconomic continuum from our tent on the beach. Here, guests whiled away their days lounging on the lanais that hovered just above the coral-filled waters. We happily swam with the dolphins, ate sumptuous meals, and enjoyed the sensual pleasures of this way of life.

But there was a dark side to all of this privilege. One evening we all returned from a restaurant to find a group of native Hawaiians gathered just outside the house. This was one of their sacred places; a Hawaiian temple, or heiau, sat just above the beach. The Point House literally overshadowed the beach and restricted visual and physical access to parts of the bay. As we waited for the automatic garage door to go up, we saw and felt angry, resentful Hawaiian eyes upon us. The tension in the air was palpable, and we didn't feel like invited guests in the hearts and souls of these Hawaiian people.

But overall, the interlude at the Point House was a gentle one, and we felt grateful for it. Although we were welcome to stay longer, we felt called to return to the Garden Island. As we arrived back at Salt Pond Beach Park, we realized we were not sad to be back in our "homeless" home. The simplicity of living on the beach seemed more deeply nourishing, in a way, than life at the Point House. There was something comfortingly forgiving and allowing about it all. With nothing to take care of, nothing to worry about keeping clean, polished, and in perfect condition, we felt free. Being outside all the time seemed to be more of a gift than ever. It didn't matter what you looked like, what you wore or drove; everyone at the park lived in the same type of humble abode. The easy camaraderie with our itinerant neighbors reminded us that we were part of a family here. In this multicultural "neighborhood," racial and economic divisions didn't exist. There was little to separate us from anyone, and many things that united us with everybody who passed through the park.

Through the juxtapose of the two realities, we realized that our happiness wasn't dependent on whether we were in a tent or a multimillion dollar house. In many ways we preferred the simple groundedness and communion with life that living in the tent offered. When we considered the state of the Earth and humanity, this way of life felt far more real and sustainable than that of the opposite end of the spectrum. We had discovered the value of simplicity, and were now choosing it as an important component of our life together.

Karen: A Miracle Reprieve and an Unexpected Realization

We rarely attended spiritual gatherings, but seeing a flyer for a meditation group centered around *A Course In Miracles,* I had a strong feeling we were to go. During the meditation, I felt an unusually beautiful, peaceful emanation coming from behind me. When the meditation ended, I turned to see who was there, and the eyes of a willowy woman with long brown hair met my own. Thus began our friendship with Katharine, who had been taking care of a series of properties and was now ready to have her own home once more. Would we like to take over for her and finish out her obligations?

Would we ever! Our immersion in tent living had put me up against more evolutionary edges than I'd known existed. Thanks to Katharine, for the next couple of months "home" alternated between million-dollar abodes and the tent on the beach. Back and forth we went, from teak floors and marble bathrooms to sleeping bags and communal outdoor showers. It became a dance, even a joke, as we segued from one reality to another every few days.

At some point it occurred to me that this back-and-forth movement was dissolving all the ways my sense of self had been dependent on outer conditions. So much suffering had stemmed from believing that if I lived in a nice, stable home, I was a good, worthwhile person, whereas if I was "homeless," living on the beach, there was something wrong with me. Now, it suddenly dawned on me that *who I was had nothing to do with where I found myself living.* Whether I was in the tent on the beach or a luxurious mansion, I was the same!

Reflection

~∾ ~∾ ~∾

Our outer lives had become the macrocosm in which all that had awakened within us during the sessions in the Chrysalis would now be tested, annealed, and embodied. In Its infinite wisdom, the Divine choreographed the exact outer circumstances needed to free us of our inner entanglements. Wave after wave of fear, doubt, and ego-resistance surfaced as we were taken through experiences that would, if we fully met them, deepen the realization and embodiment of our true nature.

Many hours were spent facing and feeling all that was arising. The simple formula we had often repeated to clients, *Breathe, feel, and give it up to God*, became our primary practice. The ongoing challenge was to stay present to our experience, especially the fearful, troubling thoughts the mind endlessly generated. Again and again we were asked to turn our lives over to the Divine.

Inevitably, awakening brings us face to face with whatever prevents us from living continuously in the freedom and peace of our souls. One way or another, we find out what we are attached to and identified with. If our self sense is defined by where we live or what we drive, we may be asked to give up these things, at least for a while, until we realize that nothing *out there* ultimately defines or validates who we are *in here*. We may not all need to forego a stable home and live in a tent, but who among us hasn't had to let go of a job, a relationship, a home, or another facet of our lifestyle when it became an evolutionary limit?

Letting go of whatever we believe has the power to validate our existence and prove our worth carries us into the place beyond attachment. As we release the beliefs themselves -- the ideas, concepts and self-images that give rise to our suffering -- we become unfettered. When we no longer need the home, car, bank account, or other circumstances to be the way we thought they had to be in order to feel good about ourselves, we discover the freedom that is an inherent part of our true, divine nature.

This is how we come to understand that the Divine, which lives in us just as much as we live in it, is complete and sufficient unto itself. Everything we truly need is always provided, and when we are in a unified state of consciousness we know it. We rest in the awareness that having our real and true needs met is the nature of things; it is how Life works. Our gratitude for the abundance that comes our way opens the channels for even more of Life's infinite goodness to not only flow into our lives, but also pour through us to bless others.

We were discovering these spiritual principles in the ways our souls had lovingly set up for us, circumstances impeccably designed to obliterate the falsehoods that had cluttered our minds so the eternal truths could shine through. Even the best therapist could not have known or set up the conditions that would most effectively propel us into greater freedom and peace. While our human selves were melting down into puddles of nothingness, our divine Selves were flourishing in their ever-present fullness.

21

Transcending Dis-Ease

Karen: A Close Encounter with a Jellyfish

A few months before we met, Barry stubbed his toe on a vacuum cleaner. The toe swelled up, turned color, and appeared to be broken. This "accident" turned into a transformational experience during which the multileveled nature of dis-ease, and the means to transcend it, were revealed. Barry was taken through a series of steps in consciousness that eventuated in the complete healing of the toe in a very short time.

Now it was my turn to experience what he had been shown. We were on O'ahu, taking care of a friend's beautiful, oceanside home, and although the outer conditions were idyllic, my inner world continued to be fraught with turmoil. As was often the case, our financial situation looked precarious. Although breakthroughs in faith and trust had occurred while we lived in the tent on the beach, I still worried at times about how it would all work out. Intermittent thoughts continued to insist that my impecunious outer situation reflected some fatal flaw in my inner being.

Today was one of those days when guilt and shame alternated with feelings of helplessness and overwhelm. Tired of the whole thing, I decided to go out for an afternoon swim. As always, the weather was sublimely undisturbed, even while my internal outlook had become clotted with clouds of worry. As my body glided through the azure waters in as perfect a setting as can be found on this Earth, my mind was consumed with fear.

Suddenly, my upper body felt as though it was on fire. *What is happening?* Long, thin tentacles were tangled in my hair and wrapped around my arms and chest. Desperately, I yanked at the stinging streamers, attempting to free myself from their grasp. My hands stung; the task seemed impossible. Large, red welts already ran down my arms. They hurt like hell.

This is no simple jellyfish, I realized. *It's a Portuguese man-of-war.*

As I ran screaming through the shallows toward shore, Barry came out of the house to meet me. Through the sobbing, I conveyed what had happened.

"Would you like to work on this?" he asked. This was clearly the only thing to do, so we went inside and I lay down while Barry sat beside me. He prayed for divine help, and we turned the entire situation over to the limitless One: *Show us the way through this, God, as only you can.* Barry then connected with the I AM Presence and held a sacred space for all that I was about to experience.

We began with the most obvious symptom of dis-ease, the physical pain, which was overwhelming. *This must be what Agent Orange feels like,* I thought, recalling those infamous images of naked Vietnamese children running down dirt roads, their skin hideously burned, helpless to do anything to lessen their suffering.

"Breathe into the pain," Barry counseled. "Stay with it -- feel it all the way."

I did my best, occasionally opening my eyes to check on the raised, red welts stretching down my arms and running across my shoulders and upper chest. They looked terrible. It was better not to look.

After many minutes of breathing into layer after layer of sensation and releasing it on the outbreath, the physical pain began to subside. Then the emotions arose, one after the other, as tangled together as the tentacles of the jellyfish had been with my hair. Intense and overwhelming, the feelings vied for attention and spilled over into waves of tears. Grief and deep sadness alternated with anger and frustration: *What kind of planet is this, anyway? You go out for a swim and the next thing you know you're covered in weeping, blazing, excruciating sores.*

As the deep dive went on and on, I eventually arrived at the existential fear that life would always be hard on this strange, cruel world. At the bottom of it all lay heartsick hopelessness and utter despair.

Barry encouraged me to breathe into each layer of emotion and feel it to the bottom. One opened into the next, which in turn led to a still deeper level of pain. As the feelings unwound, the thoughts driving them surfaced: *It's no use. It will always be painful here on Earth. I might as well give up. No matter how hard I try, something awful always happens here.*

With as much detachment as I could muster, I witnessed each of these thoughts that led to nothing but suffering. I did my best to not buy into it, but rather to simply see it for what it was -- a thought that *because I believed it* had created mental and emotional torment. Through giving voice to the ideas, and observing them without believing them, they eventually passed through.

Then judgments arose: *I'm a victim of a cruel world. There's nothing I can do to change it -- bad things will always happen to me here.* Again, all that was needed was to witness these potentially damaging concepts without accepting them as true. They certainly *seemed* true, but in reality they were just the products of a mind that had based these assessments on its experience, generalizing from a few difficult moments to conclude that Life is horribly unfair.

Beneath the judgments were identity patterns: *This is the kind of person I am -- someone who tries so hard to live right and do good, and yet these kinds of things happen anyway.* Within the reality bubble I occupied, it didn't matter how hard I tried, I couldn't prevent painful things from happening. *Other people have homes and newer cars and enough money and a life that works, while in my reality those things seem elusive. They are for others, not for me. Life is hard.* At the bottom of the pile lurked the familiar refrain: *What's the use?*

It took all the free awareness I could access to see through this reality bubble and realize there is a world outside of it, unaffected by the identities I had adopted as "Who I Am." First, I had to experience the suffering of living within this matrix -- the limitation and constriction this identity pattern had placed around my free, limitless divine energy and consciousness. Life within this reality bubble was definitely not fun!

While the contents of the mind spilled out, Barry patiently listened, not engaging with any of it in any way. As layer after layer arose, he reminded me to be fully present to each one, and let it all pass through on the outbreath as I released everything back into Life.

After experiencing and releasing each level of dis-ease in turn, beginning with the physical sensations and continuing with the emotions, thoughts, judgments, and identities, I finally hit the subtlest yet most causal level of all. This was the wall of separation that divided me from myself, from Life, and from the very circumstances that now consumed my awareness. Viewing myself as a helpless victim of the man-of-war led to nothing but suffering. Within this world view, events occurred in random, happenstance ways, with no meaning or reason. Blind to the larger purpose for this situation, I seemed to be alone and isolated in a world that did nothing but perpetuate pain.

The feelings of existential desperation continued to pour out in torrents of tears until there were no more. I grew quiet, as all the tentacles of emotions, ideas, beliefs, judgments, identities, overarching perspectives on life, and separation that had wrapped around me fell away. And then, from within that silent void, the breakthrough emerged and the "miracle" began to unfold.

In the spaciousness that was now present, the truth about the experience stood clearly revealed. I was shown that the water, as a powerfully conductive medium for consciousness, had carried my feelings of fearful despair out to all who inhabited this stretch of ocean. In response to this call, the man-of-war had come to literally zap me out of the trance that had overtaken my awareness. *This was not a punishment,* I realized. *It was an act of love!*

Gratitude washed over me as I saw the gift in the experience. *The jellyfish had come as my savior!* Its venom had delivered an impeccably exact mirror of what I had been doing to myself through focusing on thoughts of impending doom, when, in fact, it was a beautiful day in Hawai'i and I was out for a swim at one of the most sublimely gorgeous beaches in the world.

Waves of gratefulness continued to wash through me healing all levels of my being in a refreshing, life-giving deluge of insights and thankfulness. What had begun as the most physically painful experience of my life had transformed into one of the greatest healing blessings I could imagine. *The man-of-war was not my enemy! It had come not to needlessly torment me, but to bless me into remembrance!*

Opening my eyes, I immediately noticed that the angry red welts on my arms and chest had subsided considerably. The agonizing pain was now merely a dull ache. While I continued to absorb the great gift of this experience that had so recently seemed like a cruel tragedy, the stings diminished even more.

Barry looked at a clock and we realized that in just half an hour, through being with all that had arisen, we had participated in what seemed to us to be a miracle of healing. By now, the stings were barely noticeable. Where vivid crimson welts had once covered my upper body, now rows of faint pink spots ran down my arms and over my chest. Best of all, the excruciating pain was gone!

Reflection

≈ ≈ ≈

This incident reminded me in an absolutely unforgettable way that it is foolish, if not dangerous, to give power to the world of appearances. While my future looked uncertain and scary, at the moment everything was fine. We had a beautiful place to stay, plenty to eat, and many other blessings, but these considerable gifts had been veiled from my awareness by the fear and doubt that darkened my mind. Giving power to these unconscious elements had led to their outpicturing in the form of the jellyfish.

Through fully meeting all that was present and feeling everything to the bottom, and with the help of Barry and the Great Ones assisting me from above, I had been freed from a serious physical-level challenge to my health and well-being. Stories of healing "miracles" had always thrilled me, and I had long believed in the possibility of sudden, amazing breakthroughs. Now, I had experienced one. The possibility had become a living reality, encoded within my being forevermore.

While it usually doesn't appear so at the time, whatever befalls us is based in love. I now knew that the man-of-war had appeared as a "jelly angel," as a friend would later put it, to wake me up. When dis-ease on any level is fully faced and embraced, it no longer has a purpose in our life. God doesn't want us to suffer, and when it is clear that we have received the gifts such experiences come to deliver, healing can occur in an instant.

But this doesn't mean that all dis-ease is something we should be able to transform immediately. Typically, a number of factors are involved when physical conditions manifest. Chronic maladies, in particular, may carry considerable past life history, and are usually core to the mental, emotional, and spiritual issues we are to resolve in this lifetime. Some people have taken on physical conditions that will not be healed in this life, for reasons only their souls can understand. And for those of us who are meant to transcend our maladies, the healing process and the resulting awakenings and realizations may need to occur over time, rather than all at once. In this way, the journey takes us down through all the layers to the very bottom, and over time we receive all the insights we need to transcend the issue permanently.

Ultimately, it is grace that brings about healing, and there had been plenty of grace in this situation. What if Barry had not been there to facilitate my process of untangling from all the layers of suffering? That earth-plane grace was accompanied by the divine grace that pours in when we open to receive it. We both were more than willing to be blessed by the grace of the One as it guided us step by step through the inner labyrinth of painful sensations, thoughts, feelings, judgments, and all the rest.

In addition to opening to receive the grace that is always waiting to pour down upon us, there are two things we can do to expedite the process of getting free when we face a daunting challenge. We can sincerely and humbly turn the whole matter and process over to the Divine and ask for help. And we can surrender into the experience and be willing to be fully with it, holding the sincere desire to become conscious of the gifts it has come to deliver.

22

Safe at Last

Barry: Waves of Grace

One day Karen and I had a really painful conflict. With those old, familiar feelings of hopelessness and desperation, I put on a swimsuit, grabbed a towel and walked down the road to Anahola Beach. On this stormy midwinter day, the waves were high and choppy. I headed to the end of the beach and dove into the water without any consideration.

I had learned over the years to deeply respect the Ocean Mother. She had moods, and at times she made it clear it was best not to come in. But today, I wasn't listening to anything but the pain within.

Paddling out beyond the shore break, I noticed I was moving out to sea very quickly. I turned to paddle back toward shore, but to no avail. As a strong swimmer, I could almost always buck the currents, but today, despite giving it my best, I continued to drift out. I was in trouble, and the beach was completely devoid of people.

I swam to the right a bit and tried again to move toward the beach. *Nope...still going out.* I maneuvered back and forth, attempting to find a place without the strong undertow, but I continued to float out to sea. My body was rapidly becoming exhausted from battling the high surf and strong currents. I had to face the real possibility that this was it...the day I would die.

Then a ray of hope surfaced -- I saw a man walking on the beach with his dog. I started to yell and wave my hands in the air. The man stopped and seemed to look directly at me, causing me to wave and yell even louder. I felt certain he saw me. Yet with no acknowledgment of my distress, he continued walking and exited the beach through the bushes.

Maybe he didn't see me, after all, and the crashing of the waves might have obscured my calls for help. But the impact of his leaving the scene was deadening to my heart and soul, maybe even more devastating than the specter of death. My mind insisted I had been abandoned. *How could a human being witness me fighting for my life and simply not seem to care?*

The overwhelming grief and sadness wore away at my tenacious hold on life more than the raging waters. One of my chief wounds throughout all my lifetimes on Earth surfaced: *No one really sees me, gets who I am, or cares about how much I am suffering.* Maybe this was a good day to die, after all. Why not?

I continued to swim parallel to the shore, first toward one end of the beach and then to the other. Every so often I'd stop and tread water for a while to regain my strength, which was rapidly waning. I wouldn't last much longer. In the distance, palm trees waved to and fro in the strong wind, silhouetted against the grey, mottled sky.

Love for the precious gift of life, this blessed island that had always felt like my home on this planet, and my beloved Karen arose in my breast. The faces of others I loved crossed the screen of the mind. It felt as though these were my final moments; this might be the last time I would look from these eyes. Gratitude for having been alive filled me, along with an overwhelming love of this life. Bittersweet tears rolled down my cheeks, mixing with the salty ocean. Such beauty...had I ever really seen it before?

I envisioned simply letting go, sinking down into the dark waters, taking that first deep, liquidy inhale and then the blackness and void. Yes, this I could accept. It would be OK.

But then I felt a final surge of gratitude for being in a body, and a desire to once again experience the joy of doing one of the things I enjoyed most in this form, swimming. I turned toward shore and began to stroke against the current, hoping somehow, magically, I might make it in, but not really believing it possible. More than anything I just wanted to feel the joy of being in a body in the water, arms and legs in synchronous motion, one more time. *Yes, this is why I came to this Earth: to experience the gifts of physicality.*

Then something happened -- a parenthesis in time and space, a moment of nothingness that I was unaware of until later.

Suddenly I found myself standing in knee-deep water near the shore. At first I wasn't aware of what was going on until I looked out and saw where I had last experienced myself as being

Obviously I was no longer out there, but no memory existed of what had happened between here and there.

Stumbling home in an altered state of amazement, grateful to be alive, I noticed a sense of being far less glued into being here, far less impacted by the seemingly difficult circumstances of my life. Things just didn't seem to matter as much, in light of what I had just been through. Forgiving Karen was no problem -- in fact, I was overjoyed to see her again with these eyes.

After sleeping for hours, I awoke with the lingering question of how I had gotten to shore, and what had happened to time and space during that lost period of my existence. Into the mind came the words "tractor beam," and with them the sense that I had literally been beamed from out in the bay back to the shore by beings who were lovingly and mercifully watching over me. I briefly mentioned this to Karen and never said much more about it to anyone.

With this came a quiet reassurance I had not known before. It wasn't my time to go on that day. I now knew that there are indeed beings "up there" watching over and taking care of us, making sure we do what we came here to do, despite ourselves.

Reflection

A decade and a half later, we were sitting around a kitchen table in Eugene, Oregon with some friends after a group we had facilitated. The energy was very expanded, and we began to drift into the higher realms. We were talking about a man named Mike who had been part of a similar group in Ashland, Oregon for a short while before he left his body to take another assignment. Intuitives had reported that he now happily piloted a space craft in service to the spiritual brotherhoods, working to assist the Earth in making her evolutionary leap.

Suddenly Mike's presence was in the room with us, and he began a mind-to-mind communication with me. Reminding me of the time I was rescued from drowning on Anahola Beach, he confirmed that a space ship had literally used a beam to "move" me directly to shore. His message conveyed that no matter what happens in the days ahead, we are being closely watched over by beings like him, and that nothing will happen to us that is not in our highest good.

A relaxation settled into my being after that conversation. It eased much of the remaining fear of Earth changes I still held, and confirmed with absolute surety what I had known at the time. Here was yet another repetition of the theme that had become the central "law" of our life: When we sincerely turn our life and our very being over to God, enormous grace is always right there for us. When this inner attitude and consecration are present, there really is nothing to worry about. No earthly power or force, including the strongest forces of nature, can ever be more powerful than the Divine Presence that directs our lives.

When we trust the grace of God alone, we see and know that life is safe. We experience its blessing-grace, no matter what is going on. Nothing can happen to us that is not in our best interest. Even an "accident" has no power over us -- for in truth, "mistakes" and "accidents" do not exist. It wasn't my time to leave this earthly experience. And even when the day arrives that it is time to go on, we are safe, held in the loving embrace of the One throughout eternity.

All along the spiritual journey, we hit this edge and, through grace, find our way through and beyond it. We encounter small moments of letting go, and big tests and initiations, like my experience in Anahola Bay. During these watershed moments, our comfort zone is blown to bits, shattering the dominion of ego. We are brought up against our biggest questions: *Is there really a God that cares for me? Am I truly safe here? Or do I need to constantly be on the lookout for danger?*

The experiences that take us beyond the edge of what we thought was possible demonstrate that Life is wholly devoted to furthering our existence. If we really knew that to the bottom of our feet, we would be masters. As Jesus said, "If ye but had faith the size of a mustard seed, you would move mountains." The most shattering, fear-inducing experiences can catapult us into the realization that Life is Safe. Through them, our faith becomes increasingly unshakable, no matter what the challenge.

Moments like those in Anahola Bay destroy the illusion that we are in control. They make it clear that even the forces of nature are rendered impotent when the Divine moves. The further we walk on the path, the more we come to embrace those moments when we stand at the edge of the cliff facing the abyss of the unknown, for we know that it's safe to let go and jump into the Mystery. The invisible hand is always there, and will lift us up even in the darkest, most overwhelming situations. Even when the death of the body becomes the outcome of the situation, who we really are remains as it always has been and forever shall be -- eternal and undying, unlimited by any outer condition.

23

The Grace of Earth Changes

Barry: The Miracle of Hurricane Iniki

September of 1992, with its balmy, late-summer weather, was a magical time on the north shore of Kaua'i. At Hanalei Bay, the water looked as smooth as glass, and our long, early evening swims were blissfully idyllic. Life resembled a 3-D Maxfield Parrish painting with a Polynesian theme. We often commented on how perfect it all seemed, in a way that bordered on surreal. These soft, gentle days were as close to heaven on Earth as we'd ever known.

But at times, just behind this Edenic experience, lurked a feeling of something ominous, a nameless, faceless danger we couldn't identify. The sense that this level of earthly perfection could not last instilled a bittersweet feeling of just how ephemeral it all was.

Soon after we began a new caretaking situation, the impulse arose to go out for a special dinner. We put on our finest clothes and drove south to a restaurant overlooking a glistening bay. On this perfect evening, warm trade winds caressed our skin, while the Hawaiian music in the background enhanced the carefree ambience. We lingered over our delectable meal, enjoying the fragrances of the flowers, the island music, and the gentle breeze. After dinner, a quiet walk on the beach with the Pleiades twinkling above carried us into a space between the worlds. In every way, the unforgettable evening epitomized the beautiful existence that was possible in the Islands of Aloha.

As we drove back to the house, a weather bulletin on the radio warned of a tropical storm heading west across the Pacific, a few hundred miles south of the islands. It wasn't expected to intensify. Still, I sensed there was something to pay attention to here.

The next day I arose with the feeling to take a trip to town to buy groceries. Driving down the coast, I noticed how large the waves were, along with the unusual humidity in the air. The surfers were having a great time, but that ominous feeling returned, despite the beautiful, sunny day. With a car full of gas and bags of groceries, I headed back to Kilauea for a quiet evening with Karen in our new home.

The grey light of early morning was punctuated by the loud ringing of the telephone. Hearing the German-accented English on the other end, I wondered why one of the owners of the house, who was staying in a cabin in the mountains, was calling at 6 a.m.

She went straight to the point: "A Category Five Hurricane is headed directly toward Kauai, and landfall is expected around 1 p.m." A Category Five hurricane, she explained, had sustained winds of 160 mph with gusts in excess of 200 mph. We were on our own, she said; she was going to weather the storm in the mountains. "Good luck and God bless" were her final words.

The mind processed the meaning of that information like a supercomputer, and the data output was simple and conclusive. A real and present danger to our lives required immediate action to do everything possible to insure our physical survival. It doesn't get any more basic and compelling than that!

In direct response, the body leaped out of bed as if self-propelled. Karen got the whole picture from my end of the phone conversation and almost simultaneously jettisoned from her side of the bed. We had entered into a new reality bubble. The normal sense of time was suspended, and despite the immensity and intensity of what lay before us, we felt surprisingly calm, with virtually no inner mental chatter or outer conversation. Our souls had taken over, and each inner knowing instantly led to its outer manifestation.

Moments later we were in the car, headed for the nearest hardware store. The shopping center was crowded, as we'd expected, but with great relief we saw that everyone had lined up at the grocery store, waiting for it to open. Waves of gratitude rippled through me for being guided to get groceries and gasoline the day before. We were being taken care of, and the strength of that guiding presence was intensifying.

I felt for the masses of people worried about food as we drove past them to the hardware store. A full belly is always a priority, but having your house turned to rubble with you in it wasn't a good option either. Running into the hardware store, we each grabbed a shopping cart. Clutching our halves of the shopping list,

Karen started on one side of the store, I on the other. It all felt like a play that had been pre-rehearsed. Up and down the aisles we raced, gathering hammers, nails, ropes, tarps, rain gear, flashlights, batteries, and everything else we'd been prompted to add to the list. We were checking out as the first of the throngs who had just finished buying groceries arrived.

Back at our temporary home, we began the construction project at hand -- securing a bunker within the house that would sustain 160+ mph winds. The master bedroom in the corner of the house beamed out as the obvious place. I would need wood to cover all the windows. The hardware store did not have any, but, as fortune would have it, under the house we found sheets of plywood for just that purpose. A few hours later, all of the master bedroom windows had been boarded shut.

The single-story house had been built into a hillside. While the living areas opened onto the front yard and driveway, the basement and outdoor shower were adjacent to the lower-level back yard and garden, which could be seen through the living room's huge, single-pane windows. We were unable to reach those sheets of plate glass from outside the house, much less cover them. What would happen to those big windows during the storm?

Well, the answer to that question was out of our hands, so we got busy storing water in every available receptacle, including the bathtub. The radio continuously announced the progress of the storm, whose initial trajectory had aimed straight toward O'ahu, the next island over from Kaua'i. During the night, it had made a 90 degree turn and now appeared headed for an exact bulls-eye hit on the Garden Isle.

All our survival and emergency supplies were safely in our "bunker bedroom" by the time the first gusts arrived. As the wind began to buffet the trees, we walked outside one last time. We turned to look at the house; would it survive the storm?

If there was ever a time to connect with the higher beings, it was now. We asked everyone who was part of the Office of the Christ to join with us to build an etheric pyramid over the entire house, just as we had always erected a Christ Pyramid over the places in which we set up the Chrysalis. The Universal Christ Presence descended and we felt the presence of many divine beings energizing the pyramid. As we finished our prayer, the winds propelled us back inside, and after taking a last look around, we entered our "bunker" in the corner bedroom.

We had done everything we could to protect the house, and, by extension, ourselves. Now the storm would have its way with the island and all of us who lived there. As the winds rapidly built, a combination of anxiety and spiritual excitation escalated within us. We hunkered down in our stronghold with Lady, the resident dog, and prayed.

The noise of the wind became deafening, as though a jet hovered over the house under full throttle during takeoff. As the roar intensified, so did the inner fervor with which we asked God for help. I kept praying that the walls would hold; if the structure were breached, we would be in deep trouble.

As the winds accelerated, a shift happened in each of us simultaneously. Lying on the bed with the dog at our feet, we found ourselves face to face with the fact that our lives were in imminent danger. It was obvious we were absolutely powerless and unable to do one more thing to protect ourselves. There was no place to run or hide, no way to avoid the specter of what might unfold next. This was it. Just us and God; life or death.

In that moment of absolute intensity, our egos surrendered and we were bathed in a peace that was beyond sublime. We had come to the edge of clinging to our humanness. Now, the storm's grace had pushed us right over the precipice. As we floated in the freedom that comes from true surrender, it was obvious that the One was omnipresent in and as everything we were experiencing. No matter what happened, we knew beyond all doubt that we would be fine. Death didn't have a place in that state of consciousness, even if this was the time we would leave our bodies.

As the freedom of this epiphany suffused us, the storm continued to rage. I found myself getting up and going out into the living room. A sense of invulnerability welled up within me. It was euphoric, almost giddy, and very luminous. Somehow I knew that nothing could harm me.

The big, unprotected picture windows revealed the storm's full splendor. Shredded masses of foliage careened, crashed, and tumbled across the landscape. A grove of large acacias at the end of the lane caught my attention. These mature trees, with trunks two to three feet in diameter, were bent further toward the ground than seemed possible. I watched the first towering grandfather tree being snapped off halfway up as though it were a matchstick in God's fingers.

Many of the ironwood trees that lined the long driveway had already suffered the fate of the acacias and lay across the gravel drive. It suddenly hit me that a half dozen of them stood right outside our bunker bedroom, in easy position to crash down on our abode of safety. A brief wave of fear and powerlessness rippled through my being. Looking again, I observed that while more than half of the ironwood trees were already lying on the ground, not one next to the house had fallen. I was struck by the absolute improbability of this. As I stood there in awe, a loud crack just a dozen yards beyond the house announced that another massive ironwood had come crashing down. Although some were listing twenty or thirty degrees, no small feat for the stolid ironwoods, all the trees next to the house continued to stand.

Suddenly the front door began to creak and the door frame cracked. I called to Karen for help and looked for something to bar the door shut. With a piece of a two-by-four, a hammer and some nails, we approached the door, now slightly ajar. As I attempted to close it by pressing all my weight against it, the stronger force of the hurricane pushed back and the door opened a foot or so. Adrenaline coursed through us as we shoved back with all our might and managed to close it. More nails and wood across the door frame insured the door would ride out the remainder of the storm.

Back in the bedroom, we heard the winds begin to subside. Everything became still, as though the storm were over. The eerie calm, though, did not communicate that it was time to relax and begin cleaning up. No, we were in the eye of the hurricane.

In the preternatural stillness, we gathered our energies for the second half of the tempest and surrendered more deeply into the Mystery. Soon the winds again began to blow, from the exact opposite direction. This was good news -- if more of the menacing ironwood trees fell, they would probably not land on the house. But now the big, unframed pieces of glass we hadn't been able to cover began to rattle. How would these flimsy, unsupported windows ever survive 160 mph winds, let alone a flying piece of wood or another projectile? Even while this thought crossed the mind, no fear arose, just the knowing that things were as they were and there was nothing to worry about. At some level it didn't matter; it was all OK.

Within fifteen minutes, the wind built back to hurricane force. The jet plane again hovered over the house in perpetual takeoff, but inside, the peace and calm were as hushed as a cathedral. From the doorway of our bunker bedroom, we watched in awe as the outer destruction escalated. What was once a lush garden lay in waste. Torrents of wind crashed like a runaway bulldozer against the trees, uprooting some and shearing others as though they had been hit by an enormous axe. Foliage swirled, flying toward the wall of unprotected windows. The avocado tree had been stripped nearly bare. Would one of the hard, unripe fruits crash like a grenade through a window and into the living room?

Observing the mayhem, I noticed that the flying debris somehow never made it to the house. Even stranger, the huge, plate-glass windows barely vibrated in their loose framings; some were not moving at all. *How could this be?* One hundred and sixty mile an hour winds with even higher gusts would surely make quick work of such brittle vulnerability. Yet there they stood, untouched.

I walked across the living room and stood within a few feet of the windows, watching. Was there no wind striking them, or did it simply have no effect? Again, the deep peace prevailed in a surreal juxtapose to the crescendo of violence going on a few yards away. I shook my head and laughed. There was no answer other than grace. We were obviously being protected.

Then, a review of recent events flashed across the mind. The ominous forebodings during swims in Hanalei Bay on those almost too idyllic late-August days. That perfect evening out for dinner, like a scene in a movie set in a Tahitian paradise. Being guided to go to town the day before the storm to secure the groceries and gasoline that allowed us to be one step ahead, giving us easy access to everything we needed at the hardware store. The plywood under the house, awaiting our need. The ironwood trees nearest the house refusing to follow suit with their brothers and sisters along the driveway. The door just managing to stay intact, and our "luck" in closing it in the face of the roaring winds.

Yes...Grace, Omnipotent Grace...And the flimsy panes of glass continued their muted rattle, as if it were a normal Kaua'i day with gentle trade winds caressing all they touched.

Within another hour or so, the howling winds subsided and the rains stopped. Darkness descended, obscuring the ravages of the storm. Exhausted, grateful to be alive, and delighted that the house had survived relatively intact, we sent our thanks to Those on High who had shepherded us through the raging tempest, protecting not only our lives and that of our canine friend, but also the house that was in our care. With that, we fell asleep in our bunker room, wondering what would be revealed by morning's light.

Barry: Awakening into a Different World

We woke at dawn to a deafening stillness. Gone were the soft swishes of the palm trees and the calls of birds happily greeting a new day. Looking out the window, I found myself wondering whether I was in the Mojave desert. Where verdant mountains once rose into a bank of clouds at the center of the island, barren rocky crags now jutted up against a clear blue sky with the full moon suspended over the peaks. Not one shred of foliage could be seen.

A bit shell-shocked from the previous evening's intensity, we walked around the house, taking inventory. With the exception of a few broken jalousie windows above the living room and some missing roof tiles, the house had survived virtually unscathed. We could still hardly believe the huge plate-glass windows were intact, but there they remained, as though nothing out of the ordinary had transpired.

There was no way to traverse the debris-strewn driveway with the car, which had survived the storm intact after being parked in the center of the front yard, far from any trees. We knew power lines would be down, blocking the roads, wherever we went. So we got on our bikes and headed to Kilauea, the nearest town. We needed to see what had happened in the larger world, and hoped maybe we could be of help in some way.

Coming into town, the level of devastation nearly over-whelmed our ability to process the immensity of the destruction. Outer reality had morphed into a surrealistic movie. We felt as though we had been projected into a news story about a bombed-out area in the Middle East. But no, this was present-tense reality on Kaua'i, the Garden Isle, and by the looks on everyone else's faces, they were having as difficult a time fully processing this as we were.

At least half the homes in town were heavily damaged or destroyed. Many had lost two or more walls, peeled back as though by a huge can-opener. We peered into the houses, now open to view like life-sized dollhouses. The contents of entire rooms had been tossed about and now rested where they had landed. Formerly hidden elements -- pipes, plumbing fixtures, structural framing -- could be seen amidst appliances and heavier pieces of furniture.

Each front yard had become a multicolored patchwork, resembling a bizarre, random statement by a deranged artist. It looked as if it had rained clothes and assorted personal belongings during the night, and they now lay where they had fallen. Residents dazedly milled around, picking up an item or two and placing them somewhere else, rarely speaking. Most were obviously in shock, overwhelmed by the radically transformed world they now inhabited.

Bicycling to town, we'd wondered whether bodies would be lying amidst the rubble. We fully expected to encounter stretchers bearing the wounded, but to our amazement, we didn't see anyone with more than a small bandage over a minor scrape or cut. Not one seriously injured person was anywhere to be seen. It looked as if a reverse neutron bomb had hit the island. While neutron bombs destroy all the people and leave the buildings standing, here, the buildings were in shambles but the people seemed un-touched.

In front of a convenience store, a man sat at a picnic table with a couple of lemons before him. We went over to find out how he was doing.

"These two lemons are all I have left," he revealed by way of introduction.

He related his story, a pastime that would occupy islanders for months to come. He was in his house, he told us, as the storm built towards its peak. As the windows began to break, he found himself flying around his living room, commingling with the furniture in violent, painful ways. After a few somersaulting revolutions, he heard an explosive noise as one wall blew outward, expelling him onto his driveway. As "luck" would have it, he landed right next to his pickup truck and was able to roll over a few times and find safe haven underneath it. During the remainder of the storm, he watched the rest of his home be leveled.

The next morning, neighbors came by to see how he had fared. When they saw the state of his house, they surmised that he might be inside, and wondered aloud whether he had survived.

"I'm over here!" he shouted. They looked around, but couldn't see him beneath his truck. Again he yelled, and finally someone discovered his whereabouts.

Now, he sat at the picnic table with his lemons, his rueful smile punctuated by an occasional grimace as he told his tale. Even if he had nothing left, he was happy to have come through his ordeal with only some aches and pains and a few cracked ribs.

During the following days, we all shared our stories. The devastation all across the island seemed to be as severe as what we had witnessed in Kilauea. Yet the same joyous refrain was heard everywhere -- serious injuries and deaths were so few as to seem miraculous. While half the homes on the island had been heavily damaged or destroyed, only a handful of fatalities had occurred, and not one of these was directly related to the violence of the storm.

Within a few days the initial shock had passed. The Red Cross and U.S. Army arrived with food, water and supplies, the most precious of which may have been the huge, bright blue tarps that now covered more rooftops than not. Cleanup began in earnest, and within a week it was possible to drive around the island. While the losses had been major in all areas, during our first drive to the other side of the island we saw nothing but smiling, happy and upbeat faces. The aloha spirit remained in full bloom.

One day, we stood in a very long line in the midday sun to apply for food stamps. Even though we all had to stand unsheltered for hours, everyone seemed congenial and cooperative. Not once did we hear someone complain or grumble. Wherever we went throughout the coming days and weeks, the resilient spirit of the people of Kaua'i prevailed.

Since no traffic lights worked, everyone had to stop at each intersection and connect with the other drivers. Cooperation became essential in almost every activity of daily life, and virtually everyone rose to the occasion. After the first few days of backyard barbecues, refrigerators had been emptied. Many people found themselves eating in Army mess tents, where the wealthy sat next to the homeless. A few days before, they might never have given one another the time of day.

Princeville, an upscale enclave of homes clustered around a championship golf course, now resembled a scene from a third world country. Its perfectly manicured landscaping had become a distant memory. Under normal circumstances, the rules forbade even draping a wet towel or bathing suit over a balcony railing. Now, clothes and linens hung everywhere, and furniture and possessions of all kinds littered the grass. The elite edifice of a previous identity had been shredded by the fierce, loving winds of Iniki.

Iniki's Intense Grace

As the weeks passed, it became clear that Hurricane Iniki was less a disaster and more a movement of grace bringing everyone back home to their souls. All across the island, neighbors joined together to secure and repair their homes. Without power, TVs didn't work, so after long days of clearing debris and patching up their homes, people relaxed and "talked story" with friends and family.

With no running water, getting cleaned up became an issue. One day, we stopped at a roadside waterfall to join dozens of others enjoying their first real cleanup since the storm. There we all were in our swimsuits, lathering up in a beautiful, communal shower. People of all sizes, shapes, colors, and religions happily showered and played together. Another day, we went down to a river, where people large and small, light and dark soaped up and rinsed off in the cool, refreshing water. We all joked and laughed together, enjoying the newfound intimacy. The aloha spirit was growing faster than the green blush already returning to the bushes and trees.

Military vehicles and people in uniform showed up everywhere, and locals welcomed them. This was quite a shift from the long-standing resentment of a missile testing base that had been inappropriately sited right next to long-term enclaves of native Hawaiians. For years there had been an ongoing rumble about a movement to get the base removed. But now people greeted the military with open arms as they worked tirelessly helping to clean up. As we drove around the island to see what had happened, we saw a white bed sheet draped across one battered home, spray-painted with MAHALO (deep thanks) U.S. ARMY. On the front door of another house had been painted GOD BLESS THE MILITARY. The door and its wooden frame were all that remained of that abode.

What she destroyed materially, Hurricane Iniki gave back many times over in soulfulness. Adversity and having less seemed to bring everyone into who they really were. Hearts flowered, and with them, the soul of the island. And through Iniki's potent grace, all of us seemed to receive exactly the experiences we needed. One woman we heard about traveled regularly to the Mainland to offer spiritual workshops. She had called her friend during the height of the storm in a state of grief-stricken panic. Crouched down in the laundry room, the only place in her condo that had not been invaded by the tempest, the teacher exclaimed, "Everything I've worked for has been lost!"

Karen's immediate response upon hearing the story was, "If that's what she was working for, it had to go." We empathized, realizing how often our own clinging had resulted in loss. Yet we also knew the freedom that lay on the other side of seeming tragedy, and hoped this woman would discover it for herself.

The results of fear and attachment colored many Iniki stories. On many streets, some homes had been destroyed while the houses next door remained intact. Before the storm, many who loved the island felt that Kaua'i was becoming energetically imbalanced due to overdevelopment and the influx of people from the Mainland. Rush-hour gridlock choked the main road that circled the island. Businesses for locals were being replaced by tourist-serving enterprises. Housing costs skyrocketed, causing some longtime islanders to leave or move in with friends, and many locals had already emigrated in search of work.

And now the idyllic tropical paradise of Kaua'i had been devastated. Beaches were eroded or gone altogether. Hotels and restaurants, including the site of our fateful dinner on that perfect evening that now seemed long, long ago, would remain closed for renovation for months or even years. The foliage had been so severely pruned that the island looked as though it had endured chemotherapy. The number of tourists dropped off dramatically and the tourist-fed economy took a nosedive. Insurance claims often took months to be paid, and the remaining businesses suffered.

The destruction and loss had been considerable, and normal life would not resume for a long time. Yet the impeccable grace that pervaded the storm and its aftermath instilled greater faith and trust in the infinitely loving intelligence of life in more than a few hearts and souls. The many stories of Iniki's fierce grace were later collected in a book called *The Miracle of Iniki*.

Reflection

When that early morning phone call came, there was no time to think about what to do next. In that moment, our minds gave way to our souls. Suddenly, we were "channeling" Infinite Intelligence, which guided us to do and obtain exactly what we needed to weather the tempest in the best possible way. Just as we found during Hurricane Iniki, in the uncertain times to come, being in touch with the soul may turn out to be one of the most important survival skills we can possess.

Hurricane Iniki showed us that Earth changes are informed by an infinitely intelligent and loving power that cares for each one of us beyond anything we can imagine. Far from being a punishment from God, as some believe, these "catastrophes" are actually profound movements of grace in disguise, acts of love that help us come home to what is real and eternal. Iniki took away much that was unnecessary, and gave back far more of the essence of life. Happy to be alive for another day, we delighted in the slightest treasures -- a leaf still on a tree; the sun overhead, warming our hearts as well as our bodies; our animal friends, who seemed unperturbed by it all. We bathed with strangers, shared stories, food, and water, and knew that we were all in this together.

Our experiences during Hurricane Iniki instilled great comfort in facing what might lie ahead on planet Earth. Even in the apparent chaotic destruction of a hurricane, divine grace is controlling, with absolute perfection, all that occurs. The reality that prayers are answered was brought home graphically by the many miracles that took place. Hearing, day after day, one amazing story after another about the miraculous way the hand of Grace had moved in the midst of the disaster, changed our lives. A deep imprint, a sacred remembrance of what is real, had been engraved on our hearts and minds.

Within minutes or hours, Earth changes and natural disasters wipe the slate clean. We are suddenly, starkly aware of What Is, without all the props that support our conditioned, consensus reality. One day on Kaua'i it was business as usual. The next day it was all gone.

The large-scale evolutionary catalysts called Earth changes provide "processing tanks" for thousands, even millions, of beings to go through exactly what is needed to propel them forward in their soul-unfoldment. Natural disasters instantly remove immense amounts of egoic debris, and plunge us into our true, divine nature if we are able to surrender into what is happening and open to receive its spiritual gifts.

A catastrophe can dismantle so many mental and emotional layers so quickly that, if we are able to open to the evolutionary catalyst it provides, we emerge from the challenge far more awake than before it arrived. Ideas and concepts about "how I have to have things" and "what I require to be happy" are rendered obsolete when it is no longer possible to maintain life as we have known it. Sooner or later, we must surrender into What Is, and the sooner we do, the less suffering we experience. In terms of our soul evolution, one Hurricane Iniki can propel us forward faster and further than many years of sitting on a meditation cushion.

Living in separation from its true nature, the human family has created a lot of distortion over many millennia. The material manifestation of all this misqualified energy is a largely toxic, life inhibiting culture that threatens the Earth and humanity. The planet will inevitably be cleansed of these impurities, and the consciousness that spawned them, as it is raised into its higher-dimensional state. A primary way this occurs is through Earth changes and natural disasters.

And we human beings cannot make the transition without purification and cleansing, either. While many of us are already focused on releasing emotional baggage and earthly attachments, sometimes a powerful catalyst is needed to take us further. From our human perspective, the results of Earth changes may seem cruelly unfair and unbearably tragic. Those of us who were spared view others who have gone through such catastrophes as victims and wonder why the innocent must suffer. With our human eyes most of us cannot see or know how our experience is serving us or why millions of others must go through harrowing cataclysms. We have no idea what is being balanced out over many lifetimes through the suffering we or others endure during a massive crisis. Few of us grasp the larger forces at work, or how our own experience is part of a far more comprehensive purgation and cleansing.

But through the eyes of the soul, we know that nothing is out of place, and not one thing can happen unless it is part of the larger Plan and Pattern that hold all of our lives within their all encompassing, all-loving embrace. We see life beyond the tempo rary appearance of duality, and know that in truth there are no victims. Each soul is going through exactly the life experiences needed to deepen it in the divine qualities it has taken embodiment to cultivate. Many souls are now here to play their parts in the collective evolutionary leap, even if that means their earthly lives appear to be "cut short" from our limited human perspective. The soul knows that each life lasts exactly the right amount of time for its purposes, whether that turns out to be two or eighty-two years of earthly existence. A massive loss of life in a collective catastrophe may be what is needed to awaken other sleeping souls to the necessity of a radical reorientation so life can endure. Sometimes many seemingly innocent beings suffer great physical loss, not only to expedite their own soul evolution, but also to serve the rest of humanity as it digs deep within and finds a soulful response to what is unfolding. As souls are aware, even in physical injury and death, nothing is truly lost.

Rather than seeing life through the mind's either/or orientation, the soul holds all in its both/and perspective. Yes, we human beings suffer deeply when we see other souls in pain and trauma. And yes, it is all part of a larger unfoldment that, in the end, honors and exalts every bit of our experience as essential to awaken us all from our soul-forgotten amnesia. Seen from this level, there are no disasters, tragedies, or "accidents." All that unfolds in every moment of earthly life serves the evolution of each soul.

The swift sword of natural disasters and collective crises cuts away our coping mechanisms, leaving us naked and vulnerable in the face of the awesome power of Life itself. Catapulted far beyond our comfort zone, we may suddenly realize the only sane option is to surrender to a higher power. This opens the door to finding the pearl hidden within the rough exterior of seeming catastrophes -- the opportunity to experience the miraculous. We may find ourselves showered with the spiritual blessings we have always dreamed of through the catalyst of these sudden, shocking outer events. When we experience sublime, transcendent bliss in the midst of life-threatening conditions, we deepen in the realization that we are eternal and free.

Experiencing the hurricane provided another chapter in the ongoing saga of strengthening our faith and trust through the living experience that nothing can happen to us if it is not in our highest good. Even the seeming "laws" of physics are powerless in the face of the omnipotent grace of the Divine. And if Earth changes coincide with the moment it is time for us to return Home to the One, we can trust that even that is held within the ever-unfolding perfection of Life, which goes on forever.

24

The Gift of Less

Karen: Used Food and Other Travails

We had returned to Kaua'i with the idea of staying on our beloved island for the rest of this earthly embodiment. We felt happy each day as we awoke to the sounds of geckos chattering and roosters crowing. As clients found their way to us, we grew confident that this time, we would be able to create a sustainable life on beautiful Kaua'i.

But when Hurricane Iniki struck, our plans were changed overnight. Suddenly, we had no clients at all; everyone was busy repairing their homes, not to mention their lives. With electricity and phone service wiped out, phone sessions with Mainland clients became impossible. Still, because we thought of Kaua'i as our home on the planet, we hoped to somehow play a part in the island's reconstruction process, which we knew would take years.

Instead, one morning we received the guidance to return to the Mt. Shasta area and write a book. We grieved as we said yet another goodbye to the island we loved, but we trusted our inner guidance above all else. We settled in the little town where Bill, Pearl's assistant during her last years, still lived.

Life was lean in Yreka. Having sold our car in Hawai'i to finance the move, we biked to the laundromat through rain and snow, our bags of laundry balanced on the handlebars. With little furniture, Thanksgiving potluck was shared on a tablecloth laid over the dining room carpet. Before Christmas, we splurged on a taxi to bring home a tree, which we decorated with thrift store finds. Many evenings were spent gazing at the twinkling tree in humble gratitude that we had a home to put it in. As we sat in quiet reverie, reliving the memories of previous yuletides, gratefulness for all those precious moments with loved ones filled our hearts to over-flowing. This simplest and humblest of all holy seasons was filled with the Christ presence, the true spirit of Christmas.

Buying discounted produce at the grocery store, we grimly joked that our next step might be eating used food. With no money for entertainment, I'd sometimes bicycle to the supermarket and read the greeting cards, just for something to do. Yet through it all we felt we were in the right place, doing what the Divine wanted us to be doing. As difficult as it felt at times, we knew our souls were taking us through these experiences for reasons our minds couldn't always understand.

Barry: Getting the Gift

This was the first time in my adult life that I couldn't get in the car and go where I wanted, when I wanted. A huge hole had been created by the absence of something I had taken for granted as an essential part of my life. Feelings of fear and unworthiness surfaced when the urge to turn the key and drive away overcame me. Biking to the store, I suffered, not so much from the cold, but from the feelings of vulnerability and low self-esteem.

Karen and I spent many hours sitting quietly, being with all the thoughts and feelings our situation triggered. With each experience of facing another seeming crisis and coming out the other side unscathed, we reacted and suffered a little less, and over time we became more deeply anchored in the peace of the soul. We felt less and less victimized by what seemed to be our difficult circumstances. It was becoming clear that our path consisted of being continuously taken beyond our comfort zone to face the subconscious fear and doubt our psyches still harbored.

Some days, biking through the snow or buying the dinged, discounted food others had passed over evoked nothing but calm acceptance, and happiness formed the background of our experience. At these times we believed we had mastered these "lessons" and assured ourselves we wouldn't have to experience any more hardships. But we couldn't deny that fear and doubt still arose, although the ever-lessening severity and frequency provided some consolation that we were, indeed, getting free, and that a purpose and gift lay in the midst of our apparent deprivation and lack.

Barry: Peek-A-Boo God

More than anything, each of us longed for a deeper communion with our true Self. This made it all the more painful when we got caught up in fear and lost our sense of connection with the Divine and each other. The juxtapose of ego and soul was becoming stronger and starker with each passing day. This only deepened our consecration to developing an unshakable communion with our divine core, for we knew that was the only way we would experience continuous freedom and peace.

All our egoic coping mechanisms and personally willed efforts came up short. No matter what we tried to stabilize our finances, from applying for jobs to attempting to increase our client base, nothing seemed to work. Over and over, we were brought back to the obvious solution: Give the whole matter to God.

Our constant prayer became *Thy will be done.* The focus of our lives continued to shift from activity dictated by outer considerations to following the movement of the presence of God within. All we could do was travel on, as the pathless path of the Mystery unfolded before us in each moment, surrendering all fear and resistance to whatever we met along the way.

Despite our trepidations, things had a way of working out. Even during the most challenging passages, we never really needed anything we didn't have. And if a true, soulful desire arose, it was nearly always satisfied in ways we could not have planned or predicted. The Divine seemed to be playing a giant game with us, showing us its magic and grace in the most imaginative ways, making it abundantly clear we were always watched over and taken care of.

At times the tests intensified and we fell into doubt, believing we had been abandoned by God. Our minds cited our precarious outer circumstances to validate these feelings. But just when the sense of being forgotten grew most painful, the Divine would poke its head into our bubble of forgetting and wake us back up.

The Source of All That Is seemed to be toying with us through a series of lilas, or divine plays. For instance, now that we were back on the Mainland, I longed for the beauty and aloha spirit of Hawai'i. I really wanted a papasan, a big, round rattan chair with a plump cushion that would remind me of the islands. Remembering Jody's way of praying, we voiced our own request: "God, if you'd like us to have a papasan, we'd gratefully receive one!"

One Saturday morning Karen got on her bike to go to yard sales. She soon returned with the news that she had bought a papasan chair -- a block away! Before long, we were happily carrying the papasan home, laughing together at the pure magic of it all.

Thanking our Friends Upstairs, we sensed we weren't the only ones chuckling.

Over and over, God manifested as a loving trickster, the ultimate coyote teacher, masterfully choreographing an ever-unfolding divine play designed to anneal our faith and trust so it would withstand all threats. Dangling us further and further over the cliff only to have grace appear out of nowhere seemed to be the focus of the game. Just when we thought, *This is it, we're headed for a crash*, a celestial hand would appear from the least expected vector and with a magic wand, wave the whole illusion of our imminent demise away.

One particular month looked really bleak financially, and we had no idea where the rent would come from. Would we have to call the landlord and tell him we didn't have the money? How would he react?

A man we'd never met called to schedule a session in the Chrysalis, referred by his friend in Colorado who had worked with us there. We enjoyed our phone conversation with him, and he soon arrived for his session.

Afterward, Roger sat quietly. It was clear that he'd been deeply moved by all that had taken place during his session. Finally he said, "You've given me back my soul." As he looked into our eyes, the deepest gratitude was shining from his own.

Roger then handed each of us a check, saying, "I was told to give you one of these on the way here, and during the session was told to double it."

We looked at the checks. Each was for $500.

Before he met us that day, Roger didn't know that our bank account was empty, or that the rent was due. Now, the rent was covered, with money left over! During the next few years, Roger became our fairy godfather, offering us friendship, wise advice, places to stay, and even his old computers when he bought new ones.

But during the rest of this long, cold winter, no more Rogers arrived to deliver a financial boost. As the cold lingered into March, we often thought about how nice it would be to swim in warm, tropical ocean. One day, we borrowed a car and drove to the next town. We'd filled out a contest entry form, and needed to deposit it at the mall. The first prize was an all-expenses-paid trip to Cancun, Mexico.

We hadn't been anywhere on vacation in a long time. And our last experience in the tropics had been less than relaxing since it involved a Category Five hurricane. Throughout this cold, wet winter, we'd been confined to our little town, riding our bicycles over the potholed streets and walking long distances when it was too stormy to bike. *Wouldn't it be great,* we fantasized, *to lie on a beach and do nothing for a week or two?*

We held the little piece of paper between us and prayed as Jody had taught us, "God, if you'd like us to win this trip, we'd gratefully receive it!" We imagined what it might be like to stay at a resort, soaking up the luxurious ambience that would be such a contrast to our frugal little life. We dropped our entry into the box and drove back home.

A week later, the phone call came. We'd won!

"You can't imagine how much this means to us," I heard Karen respond. "We don't even own a car!"

The trip to Mexico was a delight. We swam in the bathtub-warm waters, snorkeled, and enjoyed siestas in a hammock each afternoon when it got too hot to do anything else. The Mayans who staffed the huge resort were the only people we connected with. As we passed them sweeping the grounds or pruning the foliage, we'd smile and say, "Hola!" -- happy to use one of the few Spanish words we knew. The small, brown-skinned Mayans invariably smiled back and returned our greeting, looking astonished that anyone was talking to them.

Winning the trip told us Life hadn't forgotten about us after all. Returning home, we felt buoyed up. We were clearly being seen by the far bigger eyes of the Whole, which knew how much this trip meant to us. This experience reinforced the budding awareness that God has an infinity of delivery systems to supply our true, soulful desires. These mini-miracles were really nothing unusual, we realized; they are the way life works when we put our faith and trust in the Divine instead of the ego-self.

Karen: A Delightful New Home

The Yreka experience was growing dry. We knew no one but Bill, and there wasn't much that nurtured us in the little town. When friends in Ashland, Oregon relocated in August of 1993, we decided to move into the house they had been renting. The little postwar bungalow looked homey and inviting, nestled beneath mature trees on a rare unpaved street in this rapidly developing town.

Lenny and Alana had painted the interior in festive colors. The rose pink living room, with its burgundy and deep blue trim, felt Tibetan, while the sunny yellow hallway positively glowed. My office enfolded me in deep indigo, and the kitchen radiated a happy green. The bathroom needed painting, and Barry chose a hue that turned out to be named Ascension Blue. We loved the heartfelt essence that permeated our little home, thanks to the life energy

Lenny and Alana had poured into embellishing it. The colorful walls and vibrant energy expressed their soul-presence, which lingered long after their departure, enveloping the house, and us, in its nourishing warmth.

We had not only inherited a home full of life, but also two cats, a big yard, Lenny's organic garden, and a five-acre pasture we rented to a neighbor for his sheep and horses. The open land next to our home created a much-appreciated psychic buffer, while a spring and an irrigation ditch kept everything lush and green. As we settled in, the furniture we envisioned magically appeared at nearby yard sales, and the little house began to feel like the first real home we had had in years.

We enjoyed growing some of our own food and gathering blackberries from the thick tangle of bushes that bordered the back yard. One late-summer day I was perched high on a ladder, filling a bucket with juicy dark morsels, when snuffling sounds interrupted my reverie. Turning my head, I found myself looking straight into the eyes of a gentle horse, who seemed just as interested in the berries as I was! We soon established a picking and eating rhythm: *one for me, one for you, and one for the bucket.*

Barry and I still didn't have a car, so we walked and biked everywhere. My part-time job at a clothing consignment shop brought me into contact with lots of people and provided an ever-changing wardrobe. I became well-known among yard-sale shoppers for carrying home all sorts of things on my bike. A vintage croquet set provided an interesting balancing challenge, while a voluminous, cloud-like featherbed prompted one man to comment that I looked exactly like the people in China, who transported everything imaginable on their bicycles. *I'm living a third world existence,* I thought. A life-brightening assortment of inexpensive treats and treasures came our way through the castoffs of the affluent first world dwellers who surrounded us in this upwardly mobile little town. We felt happy to reuse and recycle their no-longer-wanted items; our low-impact way of life resonated with our souls and honored our Earth Mother.

As much as I enjoyed this simple existence, at times I wondered why more clients didn't come for sessions, when they were so transformative for those who did find us. Occasionally I felt sorry for myself, remembering when I'd had a car, a stable home, and a steady income. I'd taken all of this for granted, never dreaming that life would not always be so easy. One evening, walking home in the dark after a long day at work, I was soon drenched, even under my big umbrella. Self-pity reached a crescendo as car after car zoomed by, splashing me with muddy water. Not one person stopped to ask if I'd like a ride. I felt invisible, and thought, *They have no idea what this is like.*

Barry: Discovering Real Abundance

Each time we left our little haven on the quiet, unpaved street, we entered another world. When we had last lived in Ashland a few years before, rents were affordable, older cars were common, and the quiet streets were lined with shops for the local people. The inhabitants struck us as classic Oregonians, who valued a simple, healthy lifestyle that included hiking and other outdoor activities, organic food, and sustainable living. Now, the streets were crowded with shiny new cars and well-dressed tourists who frequented the trendy new shops and restaurants in which down-to-earth locals were rarely seen. An ever-escalating urban influx caused real estate prices to soar. We were fortunate to have inherited a humble little home with low rent, but many of the people we had known before had already migrated to nearby towns seeking more affordable places to live.

Friends and clients sometimes commented about our seeming impoverished lifestyle. Some wondered, "If I live from my soul, will I have to live like you do?" We told them we didn't know, but in our experience, whatever we were attached to had to be let go of so we could be freer and less encumbered. Far from reassuring them, this only seemed to heighten their anxiety.

Others voiced New Age philosophies that supported their perceptions.

"You're just caught in poverty consciousness," they insisted. "It doesn't have to be that difficult. Life is supposed to be abundant and joyful."

This caused us to question ourselves: Did we think that it was better, or more spiritual, to be "poor," or were we simply unable to get our lives together? There were certainly times when we felt like victims as we looked at the world just beyond our quiet street. Most of the time we loved our colorful little bungalow, but sometimes we wondered what had happened to the days when we'd lived in large, well-furnished homes.

At these times we had to face that there was still a part of us that didn't feel good about ourselves. Our emotional reactions to the judgments of others alerted us that they were mirroring our own subconscious self-criticisms. When we believed those evaluations, the greater wealth of those around us engendered a sense of unworthiness, inadequacy and incompleteness. Despite all that we had been through during the last few years, we had to admit that our egos were still clearly identified with certain material objects and conditions, and our very value as beings was attached to having these.

Our minds often insisted, *Without a car, a good income, and a nice place to live, I am not OK.* Deeper levels of judgment sometimes surfaced: *Something's wrong with me. I don't seem to have what it takes to live in this world. Others manage, but I'm not doing too well at it.*

Observing our culture, we realized how deep this attachment and identification runs. The sleek new car, the perfect house, the successful career and burgeoning investment portfolio are widely shared cultural identifications by which we collectively define our personal value. Having them bolsters our sense of self, while their absence means we are "un-together" and unworthy, based upon societal group agreements. Although we had left our professional careers long before, our sense of self was still, to a degree, influenced by these ideas. We, like most of those we saw around us, had mistakenly thought that our worth and value were related to the things we possessed.

As always, the longing for the things of the world dropped away as we came home to the true Self. Resting in this place in consciousness, it didn't matter if our clothes and furniture were secondhand; in fact, we preferred this way of life, for it felt sustainable and real. From time to time, the not-OK feelings returned, alerting us that we were succumbing to forgetting, comparing, and judging ourselves. But as we settled into our new way of life, we discovered a deeper sense of rightness about it.

As our sense of interconnectedness with the Earth grew, we became ever more aware of the imbalances and destruction the Western way of life causes. We knew the environmental footprint of the United States was the world's largest by far. Part of our dharma seemed to be about providing a juxtapose and a balance to the over-consumption that surrounded us. Yet while our standard of living was downwardly mobile and rapidly approaching poverty level, we knew we still consumed more resources than most people in the world.

As our awareness of these issues deepened, we felt more in harmony with life, and experienced a deeper sense of oneness with those the world over living at the lower end of the economic spectrum. Gradually, we felt ourselves opening to receive the blessings of our simpler way of life. Walking slowed us down and made us aware of the subtle sensations of nature. As we biked through town, we admired the artistic ways people embellished their homes and yards, and stopped often to smell the flowers, watch the birds and clouds, and commune with the cats and dogs

The banquet of Life spread out before us, and as we complained less and less, we enjoyed the rich feast more and more.

We were discovering an abundance that had been hidden from us during our seemingly more prosperous days. The more we slowed and deepened, the more it appeared all around us. In the spring, a couple who saw us walking by each evening gave us artichokes that grew in their front yard, scrumptious delicacies they had no interest in eating. When autumn came we harvested the windfall apples and walnuts that littered yards and streets until removed as trash. It was thrilling to find nourishment in the living things that surrounded us, especially since they seemed like afterthoughts to almost everyone else. We were far more excited to come home with pockets stuffed with nature's simple gifts than to unpack bags of food from the store.

We slept in the backyard until the heavy frosts came, falling asleep under the starry sky and enjoying the subtle shifts in the weather. At times we'd be tickled awake by a moist sensation on our outstretched fingertips. It was the resident skunk, coming over to sniff us as it made its nightly round. At dawn, we'd poke our heads out from beneath the covers to greet a neighbor friend on his morning walk.

The crispness of fall tinged the air as darkness enveloped our neighborhood one evening. As we got ready for bed, we suddenly heard excited voices out in the street. Running outside, we saw clusters of faces tense with anxious awe as they looked to the east. Turning to see what they were gazing at, we spotted a rapidly growing wildfire descending the mountainside across the highway. Faster than a human could ever run, it traversed a mile or more as we watched, mesmerized. Would it cross the freeway and tear through the subdivision just below us? What would we do if it did?

As quickly as it had sprung up, the fire vanished. People wondered aloud how that had happened, and various theories were put forth and debated. Small groups huddled together in the dark, sharing their frightened awe at the raging power and stunning, scary beauty of the fire before they wandered off that night. We enjoyed the brief, rare sense of community this potential threat had spawned, recalling the far more pervasive coming together Hurricane Iniki had engendered.

One early morning not long after the fire, we were once again ensconced in our makeshift outdoor bed when the earth undulated beneath us from feet to head, waking us out of a sound sleep. A graceful, perfect wave had just rippled through the ground. Realizing we had just experienced a mild earthquake, we looked at each other in awe at the power and magnificence of the natural forces that had set it in motion. Our smallness, vulnerability and dependency on our Mother were never so evident. The recognition of the Earth as a vast, living being, the true source of all nurturance for our lives, had been engraved on our hearts and souls as never before.

Barry: Finding and Losing a Sanctuary

I had turned our large, finished garage into a private retreat where I spent most of the day writing, communing with higher beings, and dropping down into the never-ending fountain of issues bubbling up from the subconscious. One day a man came to the door to tell us he had just bought the property and that we would have to move. He also mentioned he would be removing the garage as part of his planned construction project, which would place a housing development on the five adjacent acres.

A few weeks later, with no notice, a large bulldozer was unloaded in the field behind the garage. In one day, it ripped up every bit of living matter on the land, even burying the spring from view. By nightfall, all that remained was an unsightly swatch of brown, with all the previous vegetation clumped into piles strewn around the property.

Before my eyes, my garage sanctuary was turned into sticks within minutes. The bulldozer even backed into our vegetable garden in the midst of its late-summer glory. Down went the glorious, six-foot-tall sunflowers as Karen watched, crying, from her office window.

Rape was the word that summed up our experience of this traumatic change. We had loved that piece of land. Now, we felt the pain of the earth as its lush, green covering was stripped away. The energetic balance that this largely undisturbed haven of life had held was gone, replaced by a strong sense of tension and dis-ease.

The true stewards of the life of the land were the owner of the sheep and horses that grazed there, who leased the land, and ourselves. That one man with no soul connection to the land could denude it of life in one day came as a massive psychic shock. It was also a reality check: This was how things were on this planet and we had to face what seemed impossible to ever accept.

Now we knew something of what people in the third world experience when multinationals desolate the land that is their home to extract resources, factory farm, or produce cheap goods for export. Here was the poignant gift hidden in the destruction. Our deep sense of displacement and loss served to open our hearts to those all around the globe who suffer the same fate, day after day. We now knew what it was like when the rich, beautiful fabric that weaves us together with the soul of the Earth is shredded.

Reflection

This cycle began as we relinquished our souls' home on the planet, the island of Kaua'i. As if returning to the Mainland after our dreams were stripped away by Hurricane Iniki wasn't enough, in Ashland even more of the cultural conditioning that sculpted our idealized sense of self was burned away. The metaphysically aware in Ashland often joke, "They don't call it 'Ash-land' for nothing." Like so many others, we were brought to this little Oregon town so that more of our egos could be purified away in the hot fires of transformation, leaving nothing but the proverbial ashes.

The unconscious self-image we both still held was the possibility of being spiritually enlightened, materially abundant, successful "light workers." Even before *The Secret* became a huge phenomenon, this New Age identity had become a goal for many spiritual seekers, who believed that God wants us to be abundant, and that our level of material accomplishment attests to our spiritual attainment.

The idea that human beings were never meant to live in deprivation made sense to us. At the same time, we had noticed that what our culture defines as "enough" would be considered egregious excess in many other parts of the world. Observing the growing material affluence all around us, the quest for more of what the culture tells us we should want seemed soulless and self-centered. So many people seemed caught up in worshipping their material trappings and deifying the pursuit of more of them. In response, we coined a new mantra: *Mmmooorrrre....*

The spiritual climate of the time was epitomized by a popular book entitled *You Can Have it All.* As much as parts of us wanted to experience this widely shared dream, we found ourselves taken in the opposite direction. The soul qualities we were to develop were not, it seemed, furthered by "having it all." They apparently could be best evoked by putting us into situations in which we had less. And sometimes even the less was lessened, so deeper fears and attachments could be faced and released. The priceless gift from watching things be taken away and seeing our dreams go unfulfilled was that it all served to take us deeper into our true nature.

In the process, we saw that the world of culture tends to operate in ways that are diametric to the ways of the soul. Cultures tend to enshrine certain idealized images of the way to live. These shared beliefs form powerful energetic fields that, in effect, hypnotize people to seek externally for what is of value instead of looking inward to the wisdom and truth of their souls.

As our values shifted to reflect soul-essence rather than culture, new ways of being emerged. With the ability to buy our way through life all but gone, our perception opened to the web of life all around us. We realized that it, not the world of endless consumption, held us in its embrace, showering us with an abundance few others seemed to even notice. Picking blackberries and gathering windfall apples brought a richness to our lives beyond anything found in stores. Watching the living world around us respond as the seasons came and went connected us to something far more fundamental -- the gentle, loving embrace of our Earth Mother.

As our communion with the natural world deepened, it occurred to us that the purging and dissolution we had endured might serve a larger purpose. Our newly simple way of life provided a balance, a counterpoint, to a world headed in the opposite direction. But even this needed to go to yet another level of relinquishment for our hearts and souls to be opened wider.

Watching our beloved pasture and garden be decimated, we went through a minor version of the displacement that many who live close to the land all across the planet have experienced. While our level of communion with the Earth was nowhere near that of indigenous peoples, we glimpsed the pain and suffering that they and the planet endure when the web of life is desecrated. Our hearts registered the wound to the soul of Gaia that takes place whenever any aspect of our living, sentient planet is violated for human gain.

As we dropped into the deeper, earthier parts of our soul, we connected with the intelligence of the divine feminine that knows what nurtures and fosters life. From that perspective, when such a large percentage of human souls becomes disconnected from the soul of Gaia, life starts to spin toward chaos and disintegration. Any planetary awakening, we realized, would have to include the healing and wholing of this split and fragmentation within our individual and collective psyches. It was clear the path lay in reunion with the deep, feminine soul of the Mother.

Outer possessions are not inevitably stripped away as we awaken. What must be given up are the attachment and identification that eventually become an evolutionary limit. Sometimes that occurs without having to physically relinquish the object of the attachment. But the two of us must have needed to go without in order to free ourselves, for that is the way things often unfolded. Once the attachment was severed, the very things and conditions we had been forced to let go of usually came back later in grace-filled ways, as gifts from life. And how much deeper our appreciation of them was!

Time after time, we had to face that our sense of self was wrapped up in outer achievements, where we lived, and what we owned. Through having things taken away -- things we didn't see how we could live without -- we learned we weren't diminished in any way by having less. In fact, we tapped into the richness and fullness of life as never before. As things we believed essential to happiness were taken away, our sense of victimization slowly transformed into gratitude. Our deepest consecration had always been to become free and awake. This was the way our prayer was being answered.

When our egos were no longer able to take control and manifest our desires through personal effort, the door opened to show us that Life always provided everything we truly needed. As each outer layer of security was dismantled, we were brought ever more deeply into the capacity to rest in God. While cars, homes, and bank accounts vanished, the corresponding veils in consciousness also dissolved. We became more transparent and naked as we found that our possessions and accomplishments didn't provide safety, security or self-worth. With less on the outside to support our illusory sense of self, we had to dig ever deeper within to find who we really were.

In the lives of many of the world's greatest spiritual icons, including the Buddha and St. Francis, a similar journey took place. Both of these great beings were born into wealthy families, but walked away from all the power and privilege when they awakened. Their living example resonated with what our souls knew to be true and gave us courage to continue on.

Many offerings in today's spiritual marketplace pander to the greed, materialism and egoism that are exactly what stand between ourselves and Self-realization. Popular teachings advocate going after the things of the world in a "spiritual" way, using our meditation time to envision what we would like to have more of in our lives. While it is possible to create what we want with the power of the mind, this is not always in our best interest. If our goals arise from personal desires and attachments rather than the truth of the soul, we might end up with a nice, big spiritual ego -- a new and improved version of the personality self with shiny new "spiritual" attachments and identifications. It's still the same old ego, masquerading as the soul.

The ideas that we are the "doer," that we make our lives happen, that our sense of self equates with what we outwardly achieve and possess, will inevitably be deeply examined on the way to realizing the true nature of the Self. The false self, or ego, which perceives itself as the CEO of our being, must be faced and seen through all along the path Home. Its incessant doing and accomplishing, its planning and time-management and goal-setting, give it the sense of control and importance it craves, while preventing it from surrendering into the movement of the Divine from within.

The true Self is not identified with anything. It has no need to prove, demonstrate or control anything, and nothing is necessary to validate its worth. It knows Creation is manifesting continuously through it, since it is an integral part of a unified Whole. In truth, there is no separate "I" doing anything on its own. To realize this, our true nature, all unconscious identification -- everything that keeps us believing we are a separate self steering the boat of our being -- will inevitably be dissolved.

Many years after this time, we heard Ammachi, the Hugging Saint of India, sum up this process simply and beautifully: "When you are a zero, you'll be a hero." In that moment, we knew beyond all doubt that this was the path we were on. All along the way, we have been brought up against the parts of us that wanted to be somebody, to experience worldly success, to have what our egos craved -- in short, to be anything but a zero.

25

The Burning Ground
of Relationship

Karen: The Agony and the Agony

Although we seemed to be making spiritual progress in other areas, our connection continued to be fraught with conflict. Barry and I were intense mirrors for one another; being in each other's presence often brought up so many feelings that we sometimes seemed to be drowning in the intensity. Although we had each experienced easy closeness and harmony in other connections, these qualities were elusive in ours.

Our approaches to daily life seemed to be totally opposite in just about every way. My mind insisted, *If he really loved you, he wouldn't be so careless with your things. He'd clean up after himself.* Digging deeper, it continued to recite the litany of woes: *If he really cared, he'd welcome what you have to say, instead of belittling and criticizing it. He'd be interested in the things that light up your life.* Finally, it summed things up in a way that seemed too obvious to miss: *If this connection were really working, you'd be close, enjoy each other, and have fun together!*

This thick, dark, mental stew of judgments fed the hurt, vengeful outrage that lived just beneath the surface, ready to vent at the slightest provocation. I found myself getting angry, impatient, and irritated with Barry over trifles that suddenly seemed all-important. When my ego wasn't raging out of control, I felt shocked and ashamed of my behavior. I'd never been so short-tempered and mean with anyone else. What was going on?

Friends wondered why we remained together when it was so hard, and some counseled us to go apart. "You deserve to be happy," they said. "Why stay together when you aren't having fun?"

Their well-meaning questions echoed our own inner voices. Our egos were sure we were heading down the wrong path, and did their best to make the other into a villain that was ruining our life. Projection and blame often tainted even the simplest of conversations. We knew we had been brought together for a spiritual purpose, but our personalities were so different that we wondered at times if it made sense to stay together. Were we addicted to suffering? Or just fooling ourselves?

Not only was daily life a constant challenge, we were also attempting to write a book together. That did not go smoothly, either. Our wills clashed in just about every discussion and planning meeting. Barry said he wanted my input, but whenever I made a suggestion he'd point out why it wouldn't work. He felt I was not fully "showing up" and wanted me to be stronger and more definite, a tall order for someone whose consciousness was as diffuse and unstructured as mine was in those days.

It was during this time that our dear friend Roger commented, "You two seem to be coming from opposite ends of the universe -- no wonder it isn't easy to be together." We found it nearly impossible to appreciate our differences. Instead of seeing that our energies actually complemented each other's quite well, we found fault with one another and wished we were more alike. We rarely experienced unity, while separation was a frequent occurrence. Sometimes, the gap between us seemed incapable of being bridged.

During one of these times, I came close to moving out. But when it came time to sign the lease on the apartment, my soul wouldn't let me do it.

"Stay with it," the inner voice urged. "All of this is going somewhere."

It repeated this often, whenever things seemed too difficult to bear. In response, I'd hear my mind whine, *But **when?** And how much more of this will we have to go through until it gets easier?*

Barry: Eating Shadow Pie

After my awakening experiences, I thought I was pretty much free and clear of emotional baggage. When I got together with Karen, the illusion of this perception was starkly and painfully revealed. Now, in the appropriately named town of Ashland, what remained of my ego was being turned to ashes at an ever accelerating rate. I'd emerge from one hot fire only to enter another; the larger divine forces that had taken dominion over my existence seemed intent on wiping out any vestiges of self.

My financial situation had never been more perilous, or so my mind insisted. Despite the fact that all our needs were being met, I worried about money continuously, and often felt Karen didn't understand. She seemed unable to really see me and my situation. It was bad enough that our day-to-day expenses were not matched by our income. Even bigger, a huge IRS issue from years ago loomed overhead, threatening to crash down at any moment.

One day Karen announced she was taking a two-week trip to Sweden with her family. Her father had given her $1000 that she felt was to be used for this journey. Anger and hurt welled up in me, and all the pent-up feelings began to spill out toward her.

I exploded, "You're going to use your money to go to Sweden with your family and leave me here in this mess? We could use that money to pay down my credit card!"

When Karen replied that she felt guided by her soul to go on the trip, my anger, based on the beliefs that I was being betrayed and abandoned, escalated. I couldn't bear to be near Karen, so I accepted a housesitting opportunity nearby. Whenever I spent any time around her the anger ignited and deeper hurt welled up. My mind continually reiterated its summary stance on the whole matter: *This is it! This relationship is toxic and a demonstration of my lack of self-love. The healthy thing to do is leave.*

While I attempted to witness these thoughts without giving them any power, they were anchored deep within the subconscious and strongly affecting my inner world. I even began to lose track of the underlying oneness I had always felt with Karen during even the direst of times. Despite my ego's resolve to leave, the pull of my soul always brought me back into contact with her. Every so often I'd run into her unexpectedly and we'd experience a moment of joy at seeing each other. At a deeper level we both knew this was yet another hot fire of ego-death that we would have to endure, just as we had all the others.

The intensity passed and I moved back into the house, though I often continued to sleep on my own. Attempting to write a book together only escalated our ego-clashes. After a few weeks of work, I had finally completed a few chapters I felt really good about. As I handed them to Karen for proofreading, I felt relieved and happy that we now had at least one section of the manuscript ready to go to a publisher.

The next day, Karen began to reveal some new ideas for this section that had come in during her morning meditation. I blew up.

"We're never going to get this book done!" I ranted. "Where were you back when we were having our initial discussions about the vision and outline for these chapters? Now I've wasted all this time and effort. I don't know if I can work with you any more!"

I stormed out of the room to stew in my garage hermitage.

That night, after a cold, silent dinner, I had curled up alone in my makeshift bed when the Christ presence came to me. In an instant I was shown a rerun of my behavioral antics earlier that day. It was torturous to see the anger and hatred I had leveled at my beloved. My heart was splitting open with pain, grief and shame. Torrents of sobbing convulsed me into a fetal position as I faced the part of me that was full of judgment, anger and separation. I prayed fervently for help. I didn't want to go on living if I couldn't love.

As the inner storm passed, Christ answered my prayer with three simple words: *Love and Forgiveness*. Like a sharp sword of light cutting through my trance of separation, the words instantly telegraphed the way through all our relationship dynamics. But first, I needed to apply this wisdom to myself, and stop beating myself up over how I had treated Karen. Loving and forgiving her for what I thought she had done was easy in comparison.

During this period I ate "shadow pie" almost continuously. The intense mirroring going on with Karen seemed to be a gigantic spotlight God was shining on my ego's tendency to judge and separate. As yet another previously hidden, gnarly personality aspect was bared, my previous self-image as a kind, loving person was immolated before my very eyes.

Facing the part of me that hated and fostered conflict to enforce its sense of separateness was one of the most difficult aspects of the journey I have ever encountered. This angry, venting ogre so deeply contradicted the kind and loving person I had envisioned myself to be! To this day, Christ's guidance of "love and forgiveness" as the way through and beyond the separate self remains a precious touchstone held within my heart and mind.

Reflection

≈≈≈

Karen:

We had already been put through countless experiences designed to annihilate what remained of the separate self, but nothing compared to our relationship as a burning ground for the ego. Conversely, we had to admit that there didn't seem to be any more powerful way to learn about love than in connection with our fellow beings -- and specifically, each other. Again and again, in the depths of conflict and despair, something would inevitably happen that brought our awareness back to the only truth, that love is more powerful than even the most gripping illusion of separation. Over and over our egos were humbled as the flimsiness of their *me, me, me* "reality" was revealed. Time after time, the calm, steady presence of our souls prevailed over all our egos were doing to drive us apart.

We have often joked that we must have the two most stubborn egos on the planet. Yet here we are, more than two decades later and still together. Occasionally even now this seems to be a miracle of unparalleled proportions. It has taken us many years to deeply value the perspectives we each bring to life, and to consistently see our differences as a precious gift. Through innumerable hours of listening to one another as we struggled to understand, hearts that had slammed shut opened back up to truly take in what the other was saying, rather than impatiently waiting to make our own point.

As we deepened in the soul, we stopped trying to remake each other to be more like our pictures of the perfect partner, and began enjoying each other just as we were. The complementary nature of our energies became ever more apparent, and years later, in the groups we offered, people often commented on it. Their appreciation of our dovetailing energies helped us to see the synergistic perfection in our vastly different ways of being. The larger whole that is created in our being together enables us to more powerfully and effectively facilitate awakening.

Living with someone who is very different stretches us past the limited identities that naturally form as we go through life in our own particular way. Little by little, the sharp edges of the small self are smoothed away, as the alchemy of relationship unifies personalities within the bigger container of the souls involved. In proximity to another soul in the human experience, we realize that all our ideas about how it is best to live are optional, and that another, very different set of suppositions seems just as real and true to the other person. We are able to open to and embrace radically different ways of being when we see they are just as valid as our habitual modes of responding to life.

During the years of our partnership, we have come to see that each of us has developed soul qualities that are exactly the ones the other needs to be complete. I now willingly open to Barry's structured, focused orientation, which has helped me to write this book and accomplish many other tasks. In turn, he has welcomed in more of my diffuse, feminine perspective than he would ever access on his own. In the process, we both feel more whole and complete.

Far from feeling less ourselves through being in relationship, we have been enlarged, expanded, and immeasurably enriched. Our fears of losing ourselves in the relationship have transformed into appreciation for what we each bring to one another's lives. A deep gratitude for the gifts we receive in each other's presence now permeates the love we share, a love that transcends the personal levels of being that worked so hard to take us apart.

More than anything else could, our own direct, ongoing experience has demonstrated that there is, beyond all doubt, something stronger and more enduring than the ego. If we had not accessed that, we never would have been able to remain together through all that we faced, within and without, during these years. If anyone needs a testament to the power of the soul, all they have to do is look at our relationship.

26

Grace in Unexpected Places

Karen: Falling in Love with … L.A.?

The destruction of the pasture behind our home so that 26 houses could be built was the beginning of the end of our "turning to ashes in Ashland" experience. Now, the dwelling we called home had been sold. When our landlord announced we had two months to move out, we were surprised at how little anxiety arose. Years of living with little visible means of support had shaken most of the fear and doubt out of us. Having lived through innumerable experiences of feeling as if we were about to fall into the abyss, only to find God's loving hand there to support us, we were coming to know that the Divine is the source of all that sustains us.

This time the divine hand came in the form of a phone call from a friend in Los Angeles. Her new partner owned a property that had been damaged in the '94 earthquake; would we like to be its live-in caretakers until it sold? In the absence of any other offers or ideas, this looked like our next step. Again we packed up our belongings. We said goodbye to our beloved, colorful cottage, soon to be surrounded by a subdivision, and headed south.

I'd never thought of myself as an L.A. sort of person. *I like nature and quiet and solitude,* the inner monologue went. *Why in the world would I ever want to go to Los Angeles?* My mind overflowed with judgments: *It's all about materialism, greed, and glamour there; like Hollywood, it's the height of artifice. There's nothing real about the place!*

Yet Life seemed to want me to spend some time in this metropolis. I had learned to trust the Mystery, so off we went to the

City of Angels -- or Lost Angels, depending on who you believed. We would have to live into discovering why we were being sent there. Our walking and biking way of life would never work in the San Fernando Valley. So, with a loan from our fairy godfather, Roger, we bought a sleek, secondhand Celica that would be fun to drive on the freeways.

The house we were to look after turned out to be part of an upscale development overlooking the Valley's vast expanse, just below the bare, wild hills where cougars and coyotes roamed. Instead of the cramped, crowded urban environment I'd expected, spaciousness and clean air surrounded us. Mornings, we walked to the park at the end of the street for yoga and meditation. At day's end we hiked up the hill to watch the sun set, sending our love and blessings to the valley full of people below.

No one ever seemed to be home in this high-end development, even on the weekends. We wondered where all of our neighbors were. When we drove through the Valley, we soon figured it out: The enormous shopping mall parking lots were perpetually packed. Judgment after judgment poured out of us: *How shallow! How materialistic! How lost!*

But then we began to see the bigger perspective. In the grand scheme of things, those parking lots could not remain full forever. At some point, even the most matter-enthralled souls will wake up and realize the fulfillment they seek can never be found in acquiring ever more things. Eventually, even the most dedicated shoppers will come up empty.

And that is when they will turn -- or return -- to the soul.

Realizing this, we began to bless those vast parking lots full of cars. "Have fun shopping!" we'd call out as we drove by. was a benediction, a coming to peace with What Is. In my heart and soul I knew that all that material seeking could only carry them back Home. *Everything* can only carry us back Home, eventually. When I saw that, I was free.

From then on, I felt at peace as I walked down our empty street. I knew that the souls who lived there were doing exactly what they must to fulfill this phase of their evolution. At dusk, I happily sent out wishes for happiness to the millions of people in the valley below, shopping their hearts out. Marveling at the perfection of it all, I felt nothing but love for every bit of it.

Karen: Feed my Sheep

I felt inspired to write a letter to the ministers of all the metaphysical churches in the L.A. phone book, letting them know that our life's work was helping people to get in touch with the soul. "We're available to give talks during Sunday service, lead workshops, and facilitate soul-connecting sessions," the letter went on.

The only response came from a minister in Pasadena, who wrote, "You're the answer to my prayer." Kathy invited us to speak during Sunday service at the Church of Truth, and we offered several evening classes and day-long workshops there. Many members of the congregation experienced the peaceful, loving wisdom of their souls during private sessions. We loved interacting with this group of sincere souls and felt blessed to have been invited into their lives.

Kathy had weathered many challenges as a minister. One day she confided that she had long been worried about the church's financial footing. Expenses continued to increase, while it seemed that no matter what she did, the congregation remained rather small. Finally she prayed to Jesus Christ about it.

His response? *Feed my sheep -- don't count them!*

Whenever our own faith and trust wavered during the years to come, this wonderfully pithy counsel has come to mind. Remembering Kathy's willingness to continue on into the Mystery of how things would work out, we've done the same. What would any of us do without the countless teachers Life sends our way to help us reawaken and remember the truth?

Karen: Cells in the Body of God

Driving on the L.A. freeways looked more than a little daunting to me, so whenever we went someplace, Barry, who had lived in Los Angeles before we met, happily drove. On balmy evenings as we traveled the freeways, I'd find myself transported into states of bliss, dreamily watching the streams of headlights and taillights advancing and receding endlessly, like the rivers of red and white corpuscles flowing through the bloodstream in science class movies.

Occasionally I managed to rise up out of my reverie to speak. "We're all cells in the body of God!" I'd exclaim, the revelation scintillating in every cell of my being.

Who could have guessed that the freeways would become a sacred ground of awakening? Every outing was an opportunity to rejoin the One in all its multifaceted splendor. I'd marvel at the way it all seemed to effortlessly flow along. I knew that everything did not always work out, but there seemed to be so few accidents compared to the number of beings rapidly pulsing through the space. Somehow, all the individual units of consciousness in their big and little metal boxes seemed to find their place in the larger Whole. For the most part, everyone cooperated with one another in a stunning display of group mind, heart, and soul. Yet most of the beings involved probably had no conscious awareness that they were part of this phenomenal, synchronized dance.

By the time we left L.A. four months later, I'd developed a deep, unexpected fondness for the place. We had supported at least a few souls in awakening to their true nature. We'd enjoyed walks on the beach, hikes in the hills, and drives on those amazing freeways -- hotbeds of enlightenment in disguise. In Los Angeles, we'd gone beyond more judgments and separative places in our consciousness than we'd known were there. We never dreamed so much awakening would happen during our time in the metropolis!

Reflection

During these years, the Divine continued to shave off the bristly stubble of the identities that had bound us. The humble, simple existence that barely resembled our previous lives served as God's barbershop chair. Like kids getting their first haircuts, we squirmed and fidgeted as the Divine restyled us into more appropriate vessels for It to pour through.

Although egoic resistance and struggle arose every step of the way, the life that our souls gradually sculpted turned out to resonate more than anything we had previously known. For us, less truly was more, and the newfound simplicity became a cardinal element in our ever-unfolding life pattern.

Yet even as we were brought into a more soulful life through letting go of old identities and attachments, a new identity came into being. Now we had become outsiders, "eco-renunciates" who eschewed the excesses of Western culture in favor of living in greater oneness with life. Newly imbued with a subtle form of separation and egoism, we didn't feel comfortable amidst the upscale, "yuppified" culture that surrounded us. Our minds judged that world as a place where the Divine was absent, in which people could lose touch with their souls.

This set the stage for the next level of ego-shredding, which unfolded when we were thrown into the "heart of the beast" in Los Angeles. As our beliefs and judgments surfaced, veils were quickly stripped away, revealing the eternal, divine substratum beneath the surface appearance. On freeways streaming with gas-guzzling, polluting machines, filled with people preoccupied with acquiring more material objects, the mind's projections were unexpectedly eclipsed by the ever-present reality of oneness. In yet another divine lila, the place we once deemed most unspiritual proved to provide fertile ground for awakening.

Watching people flock to the shopping meccas, the new cathedrals of American culture, we realized that even there, all the souls busily gathering in more earthly goods were on the path to God, just as all souls are everywhere within Creation. Not one being could ever, in any way, be separate from the only One that is. To be sure, the glitz and glare of L.A. can numb the finer senses; while a teeming metropolis might not be the first choice for a monastery or ashram, this city still catalyzed awakening, even as it had for Barry years before. We were blessed to meet many heart-opened, soul-awake beings there, which reminded us that there is no place where soul is truly absent. We left the city with a greatly deepened love for the collective human soul in all its pursuits and pastimes. We felt nothing but gratitude to have witnessed the Infinite Ineffable moving through the earthly maelstrom that is Los Angeles.

If the One is omnipresent as All That Is, how can any person, place or activity be separate from the Divine? Conversely, when we are lost in the separate self, even the most sanctified temple can seem devoid of spirit. In L.A., soulful connections occurred everywhere we went. Yes, greed, glamour and materialism abounded. Yet beneath all outer appearances, the Divine serenely held it all in Its infinite embrace.

27

Descending into Endarkenment

Barry: Down, Down, Down...

While Karen was being blessed with epiphanies, for me, the pervasive sense of dissolving away that had begun in Ashland continued to deepen. As much of what had occupied my world disappeared, so, too, did parts of who and what I had thought myself to be. Feeling vulnerable and raw, I was no longer sure I knew how to navigate the outer world. This new uncertainty was the exact opposite of my former confident, powerful persona. The downward spiral keep pulling me deeper, bringing me face to face with personality aspects it was time to see more clearly.

A more fundamental issue than the loss of cars, possessions, and resources was the yawning chasm of despair I felt about our work. In public talks, we shared the profound magnificence people experienced in sessions as they communed with their souls, but few people responded by setting up appointments. At times the pain was almost unbearable. We had been given the most wonderful, meaningful gift to share, one that could make a significant impact on planetary awakening. We couldn't imagine what we could offer that would be more important. Why hadn't our work taken off as I had always thought it would? Was there something we weren't getting, something missing within us?

An inner cauldron of feelings and judgments bubbled over with unworthiness, inadequacy, self-doubt and overwhelm. The sense of an existential lack of safety plagued me. Some days so much shame bubbled within, it was difficult to leave the house to buy groceries. Gone was the Barry of the banking days. I'd lived in a world of three-piece suits; now, my clothes came from the free box or yard sales. All personal will to make things different, to "get a life," seemed to have vanished. I was too dissolved to muster any major egoic effort to make anything happen anymore.

We felt sure our work would take off once the book was published. When, after many rejections, a publisher looked at it but declined at the last moment, I lost hope. My true purpose was clear: I had come to this planet to facilitate awakening. Why would I want to stay here if I couldn't do that? During so many lifetimes I had come to Earth to be of assistance, and they all seemed to have failed in one way or another. Was I doomed to experience that again?

Our home had provided a sheltering refuge during this time of continuous death and dissolution. No matter what else was going on, we had our humble little haven on the planet, the one place we always felt safe and comfortable. We cherished this, for we had not had a home for any length of time since we had met.

Yet as my meltdown continued, this, too, was taken away. When the landlord told us he'd sold the property and we would have to move, we were again reminded that nothing on this planet is permanent. How quickly we'd grown accustomed to having a refuge of our own! Now it, like just about everything else in our lives, would have to be relinquished.

For the first time since the awakenings Don and Linda had catalyzed years ago, I began to feel divorced from the presence of the Divine. Even God didn't seem to matter. Everything felt extremely empty and dark, within and without, as all the spiritual moorings I trusted dissolved. I seemed to be accomplishing nothing even close to my purpose. Worst of all, I felt like a failure in serving God. That thought was unbearable.

As if all of this weren't enough, money also remained an issue. I had made hundreds of thousands of dollars while working at the bank, yet I left L.A. with only $15,000. Then my grandfather died, leaving me a quarter of a million dollars. After the awakenings, I was on a wild ride, living completely in the moment and doing exactly what I wanted to do. I moved back and forth from Kaua'i to New Mexico and traveled where and when I pleased. I also channeled considerable time and money into developing the Chrysalis.

By the time Karen and I got together in 1989, money was running low. I had great plans for the Chrysalis, and envisioned light rooms all over the planet. I had always found that when I set my mind to something, I never failed to make it happen. Until now I had believed I was powerful, a manifester of what I wanted. "Successful Barry" was who I thought I was.

Well, things just didn't happen as I projected they would. I had slowly but inexorably run up my credit card towards its limit. Then there was the matter of the $85,000 tax bill from a tax shelter the IRS had ruled against. There was no choice -- I had to face the financial mess I was in.

The hardest part was taking responsibility for creating it. I blamed the IRS, former coworkers at the bank, Karen, and even God. Finally I had to look in the mirror and see that I was the one whose name was on the credit cards, and every charge was one I had made. Falling through the veil of denial, I encountered the hidden guilt and shame I had been unable to face.

The only hope seemed to be declaring bankruptcy, but all the financial advisors I talked to said it was absolutely impossible to discharge tax debt through bankruptcy. My research appeared to corroborate this. Checkmate, as it seemed.

Barry: The Bankrupting of my Ego

I could think of no way out of this one. There was nothing left to do but surrender and give the whole thing to God. Still, visions of payments to the IRS for the rest of my life haunted me. How would that work out? I was barely surviving as it was.

Taking responsibility looked like the first step. It became easier as I remembered that Life wasn't punishing me, but was actually putting me in a position where I would be forced to face and resolve karmic patterns. Reframing the situation as a gift and an opportunity immediately caused the energy to shift. I prayed fervently to be shown how I had created this mess, and how I might get through it.

Magically, as always, I came upon an obscure book discussing clauses in the tax laws that allowed for the discharge of tax debt through a Chapter 7 bankruptcy. After I read the book a few times, I felt sure that despite what every tax lawyer, CPA, and financial advisor had told me, a way existed to discharge taxes through bankruptcy.

Once again, the light shone down from above, revealing the way through. With no money for lawyers, I ordered a bankruptcy kit by mail and began the process. While a number of "credible" people told me the whole project was an unrealistic fantasy, the inner knowing kept telling me it would work.

The ordeal of filing the papers led to many realizations, one of which unveiled the insidious nature of debt. In the Beatitudes, Christ Jesus taught to "make no oaths to any man." To incur debt is to "make an oath" that requires living in an imagined future over which none of us has any control. In doing so, I had created a mound of debt that felt like a heavy weight on my soul. It hung over me like a thick, gray cloud that darkened my future, stifling my spirit and life energy. Worst of all, I couldn't do anything about it -- or so I thought.

During the days I was filing the bankruptcy petition I came across the statement, "Man plans and God laughs." Those five words presented a billboard-like tribute to the impotence of my ego. Until the last few years, I had never envisioned myself not being able to manifest money. I'd always felt in control, and trusted that what I willed would happen. But Life had other plans. Living in the present instead of in a fantasy future was more in alignment with the central, most cherished goal of my life -- to be awakened and in full union with God.

A strong dose of humility looked like the prescription for this ego. Through grace I once again saw that I had no personal power to do anything that wasn't supported by the Divine. During all the years when money flowed to me in a continuous river, I thought I was the one making it happen. The arrogance of this came home as never before. Clearly, all the success and wealth had been a gift from God. Who was I to take credit for it?

Not long after I filed the papers, an official-looking letter arrived, announcing that both the credit card and tax debts would be discharged. Once again the Omnipotent One had come to my rescue. My debt was soon behind me. Financially, at least, I was free. I felt some relief as the burden of the debt lifted, but I didn't sense I had reached the bottom of my descent. This intuition proved correct; the next chapter in the downward plunge would soon begin.

Reflection

Barry:

My life had become a living manifestation of the figure 8 of soul evolution; I was learning through experience that the higher we go, the deeper we must also descend. The higher-dimensional light from all the awakenings and sessions in the Chrysalis shone like a bright laser into the murky clouds of lifetimes of darkness. My ego was rapidly dissolving, and with it the coping mechanisms and armoring also disappeared, exposing the gaping psychic wounds that remained. Painful emotions that I hadn't been able to fully feel at the time now rose to the surface, and I felt like the small, vulnerable child I had been when the wounds originally occurred.

As intense as all of this felt, the descent delivered a gift of grace, for now I could finally face what had always been there, hidden beneath my "successful" mask. I had constructed that persona early in life to hide the underlying fear, insecurity and self-doubt I harbored within. As the shadows cleared away to reveal the true, eternal Self, I could finally access enough consciousness, integrity and love to redeem the wounded aspects and bring them all home to the soul.

A chapter in *The Dawn Horse Testament* by Master Adi Da Samraj helped me to frame what I was experiencing. Through profound awakenings such as kundalini experiences, Adi Da wrote, the integrity of the false ego~personality structure is shattered. It may fall apart quickly or over time, but fall apart it will. As this occurs, the familiar egoic defense mechanisms fail. These are designed to keep the personality intact by walling off the subconscious shadow material the ego believes would destroy it if allowed to fully surface. The ego forms in response to the core woundings; its job is to keep the psyche intact and ongoing.

During awakening, Adi Da went on, the energetic shell of the ego is breached as the crown chakra opens. The individual may feel out of control, overwhelmed by subconscious forces. Extreme vulnerability and an inability to cope are common passages as the separate ego self dissolves. The good news, as I was discovering, is that the will, power and intelligence of the true Self are always guiding the process. This inner integrity can be totally trusted, even if it is not always consciously felt. As I learned to trust more, I also loved and nurtured myself as never before. My vulnerability and psychic healing process required lots of "womb time" to rebirth myself as my psyche was dismantled.

At times I was torn by the seeming dualities of my experience. I would soar into the vast, supernal, transcendent realms in which I knew my wholly pure, loving, and luminous higher nature. It always existed there, just above the clouds, and often I would be catapulted back up into it to help me remember. But then, before long, I again plunged into the darkest depths of fear and shame and vulnerability.

Reconciling the two states of being presented a quandary. *How do I remember my luminous, higher nature when I descend into the shadow worlds? How can I accept the dark, shadowy aspects of self and not attempt to spiritually rise above and escape them? How do I hold them both as parts of who I am, equally important dimensions of being essential to Self-realization?*

As we had invariably found, no matter the question, th soul is always the answer. Its essence contains the all-inclusiv love that bridges and unifies both our transcendent, spiritual natu and the depths of our earthy humanness. Resting in our heart hearts, we find the place within that can hold both of these aspec of our being.

The larger oneness of the soul synthesizes and unifies a seeming opposites in our experience. We are that holy, pure, ar perfect luminosity that is forever descending into the imperfectio chaos and limitation of the human psyche. This alchemical, tran mutational process takes place as our capacity to face and er brace all parts and pieces continuously expands and deepens. Th never-ending weaving together of spirit and matter carries the so into ever-vaster realms of being, until it includes all dimensions the One and becomes its perfect manifestation.

28

A Dark Night of the Soul

Barry: The Meltdown Continues

In the spring of 1997 we moved to the small town of Arcata on the northern California coast. We had always loved to visit Humboldt County to commune with the Pacific Ocean and towering redwoods. This part of the world felt like an enfolding, countercultural womb, in which eccentricity, simplicity, and living without masks were commonly shared values.

It also proved to be an appropriate place for the next step in my journey of descent. With the filing of the bankruptcy papers, gone were the credit cards. As I cut them into pieces and threw them away, I felt like I was losing my membership cards to a world I once belonged in but now could barely relate to. There was a finality to it all that brought a sense of great relief and completion, right alongside the fear of what might lie ahead.

Roger had counseled us to no longer rely on spiritual work as our primary means of support. I knew he was right, and saw that this had kept me bound to needing clients, creating a subtle but pervasive distortion that tainted the purity of what we offered. I stopped seeking clients, and few made their way to our door. As a result, very little money flowed in, and the options looked bleak. Getting a job seemed like an overwhelming prospect as I cascaded further into the dark night of the soul that had been deepening for a few years.

While I looked for work, I attempted to patch things together by getting food stamps. This was a new low for me. There I stood in the long lines with the people I had silently judged as failures, those who couldn't make it in the world. Now I was on the verge of becoming one of them.

I continued to go for job interviews, but nothing felt right. As much as I wanted to get a "real job" and crawl out of the seemingly bottomless pit I felt myself falling into, I just couldn't imagine myself working at any of the places I visited. Nothing had any energy at all. I was so depressed, vulnerable and hypersensitive that I had no psychological stamina for anything as stressful as the work world. What was left of my ego was collapsing. My entire sense of self continued to dissolve at an ever-accelerating rate.

I felt so desperate I decided to apply for a job at Walmart. Maybe I could function as a greeter or a stock person. But sitting in the car outside the store, I burst into tears, realizing I wouldn't be able to exist inside that building for more than a few hours at most. I couldn't continue trying to make it in this world anymore. I just couldn't do it.

A few days later in the food stamp line, a scruffy-looking but kind-faced man wore a T-shirt that said it all: "I'm so far down I don't know how to get back up." Suddenly the whole scenario of what happens to some people in our society hit me. I had overheard their stories as they talked to the counselors. While some had fallen out of the world long ago, many had been successful and had led "normal" lives. They felt as surprised as I did to be there, after an unexpected sequence of events had changed everything. They had no home or phone, yet were expected to go to job interviews. That's a tough thing to do when you have no place to get cleaned up, no car to get you there, and no clothes nice enough for an interview, not to mention that you're depressed and full of self-doubt.

Walking out of the government office one day, I realized these people carried the shadow of our society, the hidden polarity of our greed, domination and pride. As never before, I saw the painful duality in it. Some souls have signed on to be at the bottom of the societal barrel, while others are riding high. I looked back on my life and saw that with this recent change I had played out both ends of the spectrum.

Just as we exalt and almost deify those few who have really "made it," we judge and hate, usually subconsciously, those who don't fit our cultural success archetype. I kept thinking about the common judgments that I, too, had allowed to cross my mind when I was at the top, things like *Most of those people are simply lazy. They need to try harder.*

These shared beliefs create a very powerful psychic energetic dynamic in the collective unconscious. Those who "achieve" the idealized success image find that the collective energetic field buoys them up, showering them with adulation, admiration, and the life energy of all who look up to their accomplishments. The myriad of products and services that promise to make us wealthier, more desirable, more intelligent and powerful in the game of the world give testimony to this. Conversely, for those who fall into the downward spiral and get caught in the *I'm an unworthy failure* archetype, the weight of the prevailing cultural judgments can be psychically crushing. To see the devastating effect of believing these projections, one must simply look, with an open heart, into the faces of many homeless people.

As I did, I saw myself. "Successful Barry" was now a distant memory, replaced by relentless inner voices of condemnation, self-hatred and shame. Oh, how different the issue looked from this side! Gone was the aversion to this segment of our society, the buffer of a safe distance between them and me. My heart had been blasted open now that I was rapidly becoming one of them.

It even seemed as if many of my friends had abandoned me. When I told them what was going on in my life, their uneasiness was palpable. Some attempted to change the subject, while others gave seemingly kind, falsely empathetic or vaguely patronizing responses. A few stopped returning my calls. It seemed as though everyone I knew was abandoning me in my hour of need. I imagined that I represented an aspect of themselves they weren't ready to experience, and that I was having to play it out not only for myself, but also for the collective.

There seemed to be no escape from the precipitous descent; the waves of guilt, shame, fear, insecurity and worthlessness had become daily fixtures in my inner landscape. I felt raw and vulnerable as more and more of who I thought I was got stripped away in a never-ending process that felt as painful as surgery without an anesthetic. What remained had always been lurking under the surface, buried there during the recent past of early childhood or the distant past of previous lives. I had tried to rise above it for many lifetimes, including this one, but now there was no escaping it. Even knowing this, I still found it difficult to continuously embrace the process.

As I spiraled downward, I began to feel that death would be easier than continuing here. This wasn't life. I couldn't prostitute myself to make money when my soul had absolutely no remaining draw to the world I encountered nearly everywhere I turned. I had to face that I was too fragile, too far down into a dark night of the soul, to do anything. I felt done with the struggle to find and keep a place in the world. I had no energy left to buoy myself up to even make an attempt to survive. Day after day, not a ray of hope gleamed anywhere.

Barry: Beyond Crucifixion

Each day I prayed for help, and one morning the familiar presence of the Christ came to me more closely and personally than ever before. At times He seemed to be walking with me, just as tangibly as when I walked with a friend or Karen; the only difference was that they had a physical body, while He did not. He became a companion beyond any friend I had ever known, and I felt His warmth and love continually enfolding me. Once He came, He didn't leave, nor did He interfere or try to help in any way. He was simply with me always, walking beside me like an elder brother.

His continuous loving presence conveyed that I was loved completely, without conditions. Christ Jesus saw and knew everything about me. He asked no questions and gave His love and compassion unceasingly, without ever asking anything in return.

This renewed a deep desire that had become somewhat latent in my heart during all the outer travails. I only wanted to be like Him -- to have the love, compassion, peace and wisdom that I longed for but saw nowhere on this Earth. Nothing else seemed even remotely important.

More than ever I was coming to know that "My Kingdom is not of this world." There was so little here that deeply resonated with my soul. The prolonged dark night had escalated into what felt like a crucifixion, which I embraced with the assistance of His presence. The grip on my human life weakened daily. All I wanted was to have the peace that comes from being free of the cares of the world, and to live in the state I experienced in Christ Jesus.

At the time I didn't know that the Divine was in the process of giving me more of what it knew was the only thing any of us really wants. The psychic weight of everything I was enduring felt devastating. It was becoming too much to bear, and I felt almost ready to die.

Then, one day, Yeshua (Christ Jesus) began to speak:

> *Barry, you are coming to discover that the crucifixion is over. It is done — finished. It needed to happen only once, 2,000 years ago. And even then, it was not about my sacrifice and suffering. The message was eternal life — not death.*
>
> *You see, Barry, the ego sees everything backwards. It sees life as death and death as life, when in truth they are One, the never-ending experience of love in my kingdom. Even as you watched the autumn leaves float gently down onto the stream the other day, you saw at first death.*

You felt the sadness and grief of life dying. Then, in the next moment, you saw beyond the veil of form and there revealed was the never-ending process of God moving, dancing, changing her form of experience and expression.

That which you are is eternal. You rest in that which is beyond the comings and goings, beyond the cycle of life and death. In truth there is only Life. But in your realm, you see the changing pattern of life as death. All forms of divine expression change. Nothing is static, for God is always new, always seeking new experience and expression. It is all play, divine play. Every form must always give way to a new, emerging form. Patterns change eternally. But nothing is lost, nothing dies except patterns of experience and expression. Always, what you are lies beyond it all, untouched by everything.

Your only pain is that you believe you are the form, and as the form dies, so do you. In the world of matter, this is particularly pronounced. Forms decay and break down into a seeming nothing. This, too, is appearance, for there is only coming and going. The leaves fall from the tree only to magically reappear anew in the spring. Does the tree weep in autumn? No, it revels in the magnificent splendor of its golden hues. For the tree, there is no death, only a changing expression of Being.

You cannot find this unchanging core of being anywhere but within yourself. It alone is eternal. As you discover it, you find that it holds and embraces all changes. It is a continuity unbroken, always sure, always safe. Rest in this, my brother.

The swirling vortex of change in your life seems to spin outward, quickly taking many things away that you know and are familiar with. There is another movement, a spiral in. This spiral leads you to your core, the undying divinity which you truly are. The faster the forms spiral away, the faster the spiral carries you inward.

You have asked to be free. You have asked to live in the truth of your being. You have created the spiral of becoming. To become what one is, there must be an unbecoming or undoing of what one is not. Thus, the forms that spiral away from you are those that you are not — those that your soul no longer chooses to experience. Let them go. Surrender into the inward spiral to Self. As I have said before:

> *What is real cannot be threatened.*
> *What is unreal does not exist.*
> *Herein lies the peace of God.*

You are getting closer. The truth is only a step away. It awaits you always in the boundless, unchanging ground of your being. When all else is relinquished, you find what always has been, is, and shall ever be.
I AM. I AM that I AM.

The conversations continued for the next few weeks. Finally and fully, I felt seen, loved, and understood by another being. Yeshua was the brother I had always hoped it was possible to have. There was no one in the world who could walk with me as He was doing. I walked with Him in another dimension, even while I felt that "Barry" was dying. Amidst the devastation I sensed the Crucifixion ending, because I was beginning to see beyond it, into the world Yeshua resided in. I knew everything I was going through could only bring me closer.

Barry: The Last Moments on the Cross

One night Karen and I had yet another strained discussion about money. She felt burdened, knowing her small salary wouldn't support two people, and afraid of what would happen if I didn't find some way to make money. Deep in my heart I didn't want to be a burden, nor would I take anything from anyone who didn't want to give it to me. From all appearances, my life was on a steep descent into oblivion. It seemed as if I had been on this path for years, and now the obvious conclusion lay before me. The last thing I wanted to do was to take Karen down with me.

The thought of her going into debt and having to face bankruptcy as I had was too much to bear. Contributing to this would have been out of integrity with the truth of my soul. Nor could I go out to work in the world for a company. The light within dimmed at the thought, and there was nothing more sacred than following the light of the soul.

Despite all my fears of letting go of the seeming security of a roof over my head and a warm human being to share life with, I could not compromise the truth of my soul. The knowing arose that I had to let it all go and be willing to walk out of this life and into the Mystery with no visible support for my human needs.

I called the homeless shelters to inquire how to secure food and lodging. Only one in Eureka would take me, and then for only a few days a week. The rest of the time I would have to be out on my own. *Maybe this is it,* I thought.

During winter in Humboldt County, it could rain for weeks at a time with temperatures in the 30s and 40s. Visions of myself lying huddled in a dark alley, cold, wet and despondent, ran through my mind. My will to live was not strong. I sensed that survival in this body would not have been very likely for long under such conditions. Going to sleep cold and wet, hypothermia settling in...never to awaken in the world again. All that I had come here for -- lost. My soul purpose and destiny to assist in the collective awakening. My union with Karen, my twin soul. All gone.

But even this I could face and embrace, if this was the path God was putting in front of me. It seemed a lot more true to my soul to go out on the street and completely put myself in God's hands, even if it meant I would shortly be leaving this world and all that I loved and cherished most. I felt a deep sense of peace and comfort in letting go and totally surrendering to God. In my heart, I realized what Yeshua was attempting to convey. Yes, my body might drop away like leaves in the fall, but nothing could happen to who and what I really was. I was free!

That evening I went looking for my sleeping bag. Putting some belongings together, I informed Karen of my plans. I was on my way out the door when a shift occurred. Karen softened, and warmth returned. The eternal bond between us emerged, and she knew we were to be together. She asked me not to go out in the street that night, but instead to stay, pray together, and give it all up to God. There was nothing else to do. This is where we always wound up when we stood on the precipice staring into seeming oblivion.

As Karen softened, so did something within me. I let go of my strong intention and dropped into the Mystery. *What is asked for here -- what does God want? I thought it was to let it all go.* The upwelling energy in the core of my being moved toward Karen, surrendering once again into the ever-changing Mystery. I had to trust that the path lay in continuing on together. There must be something yet for me to do here.

The words from a Janis Joplin song came to mind: "Freedom's just another word for nothin' left to lose, and honey, you ain't got nothin' if you ain't free." The Divine, in its all-encompassing love, had given me what I had always asked for -- freedom, and the peace that results from surrendering everything. I had given it all up, yes, and I had nothing left to lose.

Reflection

~ ~ ~

Barry:

The moment I made the decision to give my life totally to God and walk out into the streets to face the very real likelihood of death, if that was what the Divine wanted me to do, I passed through a pivotal initiatory doorway. My soul could no longer be purchased by the fear of death, or even by what it most loved and cherished. There would be no more struggle even to deepen my union with beloved Karen, or to assist in planetary awakening, the core passion of my existence. I was free now on a level I had never experienced. The depth of union with my true, eternal nature had reached a new milestone on the path.

Down, down I had been plummeting for a very long time. For months, a gnawing sense that I might not survive the descent coexisted with the question of what I would be asked to give up if I did. Looking back it is clear that, in a way, I did not survive. And what was asked was everything.

During the Dark Night, we are propelled to the bottom of the figure 8 conveyor belt of consciousness, where we encounter the most fundamental programming that defines the soul's human identity. On the way to the bottom we are brought, one way or another, to the deepest recesses of our attachment and identification. We even face all that forms our sense of self as a soul. All of this must be surrendered if we are to fully incarnate the absolute, pure, unqualified, empty fullness of the true, eternal Self.

It may sound counterintuitive at first, but not only the distorted or "negative" aspects of our being are purged. We are also faced with giving up even what our soul most cherishes. I was asked to relinquish my identity as a catalyst for awakening. I thought this was my role in life, my highest service to God, my purpose for coming to Earth at this time, my destiny. And letting go of being with my twin flame seemed implausible, as coming together in this lifetime seemed to be a critical element in the conclusion of many embodiments. The attachment to these most cherished images and identities had to go; they were the deepest remaining impediments to further realizing the unqualified, free nature of Self.

The Dark Night of the Soul has a starkly overpowering, fateful quality. We are required to completely submit to the process and allow it to take us to the very bottom. Once it starts, there is no turning back, and no question of choice. All resistance is dissolved by the overwhelming power of the process. It can seem as if we are drowning, or being destroyed. Through encountering existential fear and overwhelming powerlessness, hopelessness, and despair, any remaining coping mechanisms are rendered null and void. We see nowhere to look for any sort of outward solace or support. It all must be found within, and even there often nothing is found but a dark void. As we hit the bottom-most layers, we may lose all contact with God and doubt whether the Divine is really there. We even have to let go of the idea that this experience of utter spiritual desolation will ever come to an end. Any will to resist or hope that it may soon be over is overwhelmed by the inexorable force of the descent.

During the deepest part of the Dark Night, the feeling of being "crucified" may become overwhelming. Now, the most fundamental levels of egoic identification are being dissolved. Giving up our ideas, possessions, and relationships is one thing, but surrendering our physical life is the most terrifying of all. We must face the fundamental fear underlying all others: the fear of death.

Even as I entered this seemingly impenetrable darkness, grace was present, both as the darkness and as the light that the Christ brought to illumine it. While all I could see was dissolution and death, He helped me understand that all that was not the true, eternal Self was being spun away, as though I were in a centrifuge that was simultaneously drawing me ever deeper into the ultimate truth of who and what I am. In the darkness, all that I had held as "me" was being dissolved, so that I could experience the total freedom of my eternal, unbound, formless nature. As I realized this experientially, I stepped down off the cross forever.

The foundation of the false self sense lies in our mistaken identification with the physical body. When we believe our very existence is predicated on the body's continuance, we unknowingly buy into the most profound and binding illusion. As we face and go beyond the core fear of death by surrendering our body and physical life fully to God, we sever the deepest attachments that bind us.

This surrender delivers the ultimate gift of the Dark Night. As we come out the other side, the foundational fear upon which all others rest no longer controls our awareness. We know we are truly free, now and forever. When we see that all that we feared was based on an inherent illusion, nothing can ever threaten our existence again.

Because of its overwhelming intensity and death-knell finality to our human self sense, most humans understandably fear the Dark Night. There's even a growing New Age belief that such a deep, demanding passage is no longer necessary, or may not need to be as intense. That may be true for some, as the planetary vibration continues to rise at an ever-accelerating rate. Yet in our experience, the figure 8 of soul evolution cannot be denied. All aspects of our being will inevitably be included in the journey from human self to soul-awakened Self. Spiritual evolution takes place through the process of incorporating all parts and pieces, however distorted and ultimately illusory they may be, into the wholeness of our being. Accordingly, it's likely the Dark Night initiation will continue to occur in one form or another for many on the soul's journey to freedom.

29

An Ascension
into a "Heaven" in the Mountains

Barry: From Crucifixion to Resurrection

As the long crucifixion ended, the intense darkness began to lift, and a feeling of freedom and peace unlike anything I had ever known steadily grew stronger. There was no sense of coming back to "me," as had occurred after previous descents. The sense of "me" had largely vanished, along with any thought of reestablishing one. This new, peaceful emptiness did not want to be disturbed or blemished by any attempt to "do" anything.

Thinking the solace of nature would soothe my wounded psyche, a friend had recommended I look into working as a fire lookout. After making a few phone calls, I was soon hired to staff Eddy Gulch Lookout, high in the Salmon River drainage of northern California. In this remote district, nestled within half a million acres of virtually uninhabited mountainous terrain, salmon and steelhead ran in the fall and winter. Deer, bear, eagles and a variety of other wildlife inhabited the rugged landscape of deep canyons and high mountains. The clouds created an ever-changing skyscape, and to the west a small sliver of the ocean was sometimes visible. Driving to the lookout was like ascending into a heaven on earth.

And I seemed to have been made for this job. So many personal gifts and skills, from excellent distance eyesight to well-developed map-reading ability, coalesced to make this vocation absolutely perfect. There was more time than ever to commune with the inner realms, to walk in pristine nature, to laugh, sing, dance and simply enjoy being alive. To top it all off, the job provided ample financial resources to cover my human needs, even

259

while being on the mountain for only five months a year. Everything about it felt totally, blissfully right.

My hermit nature became even more pronounced after the profound death I had been through. With no more calling to the world, being paid for being on retreat in this beautiful place felt ecstatic beyond imagination. On the mountain, I felt I had ascended into a whole new life. Living in an area so energetically and physically pristine was just what I needed to finally ground all the spiritual openings into my body. On this remote mountaintop, in a building with 360 degree views, my aura could spread out for miles and miles without feeling any impingement from civilization.

My true Self blossomed, coming forth as never before. For the first time, my human soul felt whole, complete, and full as I osmosed something from this pure, undistorted nature that I desperately needed. I was being filled with an invisible essence or presence that was deeply nurturing and nourishing. Walking in the mountains each morning and evening and sleeping on the ground in a tent, I became deeply immersed in the web of life. A feeling of wholeness, stability and peace grew with each passing day. I began to see that much of the chaos and suffering I had experienced all my life was the result of missing what I had deeply needed from Mother Nature.

A new dimension of my soul unfolded on the mountain. Each day brought a greater realization of the oneness of all of life, a woven tapestry of being in which each living being forms an inextricable thread. Subtle sensory perception opened, revealing the essence of the various plants and animals. Interspecies communication flowed, and I began to really "know" these beings. The rabbits greeted me whenever I descended from the tower, and one occasionally came over to chew on my shoe. An owl waited for me to come back from my walks at night and circled me as I walked up the road, often swooping down to within ten feet of my head. At times she flew around the lookout at night, so close that I could see her eyes in the light of the propane lamp as she looked in to say hello. The deer let me approach, and some even slept near my tent at night. Many peaceful encounters with bears and rattle snakes and other creatures of the forest deepened my comfort with the graciousness of Mother Earth.

It was becoming clear that much of the suffering and dis ease I had been experiencing had resulted from not being fully connected to the web of life. My seeking had been in the transcendent worlds of spirit, where I thought the solution for my suffering lay. While there was truth in that, my humanness was harboring another "hole" in the core of my being that could only be filled by the nurturing, feminine grace of the Great Mother Goddess. In th

Salmon Mountains she embraced me deeply, healed me, and made me whole.

Reflection
~-~-~-

Barry:

Something subtle yet profound had shifted after the Dark Night. For the first time in my life, I was no longer suffering. All the previous concerns and obsession with "me" had fallen away, revealing a space that was empty yet paradoxically full of spontaneously arising rapture. Joy and happiness pervaded my experience of each day. If experiencing heaven on Earth was possible while still living in a physical body, this seemed as close to it as I could imagine.

I felt very complete, and knew that life was now to be lived simply for the joy of it. No compulsions remained to do this, accomplish that, or become anything. The world of human culture now seemed a strange, distant realm with which I no longer had any connection. When I had to go to town for groceries and supplies, I found myself leaving as soon as I was done. A sense of hollow emptiness had replaced my previous fascination with the delights of "civilization." Now, I simply existed in and as who I really am, and for the first time in my life I felt whole, complete, in balance, and one with life.

30

A Journey into Enlifenment

Karen: What Next?

With two weeks until the end of fire season, we had no idea where we would go next. Our sublet in town had ended, and a new dwelling-place had not appeared. For the past month I'd been staying at the fire lookout with Barry, luxuriating in long days of reading, playing with art supplies, and simply gazing out over the vast, silent expanse.

One Sunday I found myself cooking up a much bigger lunch than the two of us could ever consume. Just as it was ready to eat, a district fire truck pulled up. When the crew climbed the stairs to the tower, I invited them all to share our meal.

Jacqueline, who worked at the helibase, had never been to Eddy Gulch Lookout, but today she was patrolling the district with the fire crew. As we talked over lunch, she asked what we planned to do after fire season ended. "We don't know," I responded, to which she replied that we should come have a look at her home on the family farm where she and her husband, David, lived. They had just built a new house, she went on, and their former home would soon be available to rent.

During Barry's next days off, we traveled through the remote region to the farm, which sat in a quiet, peaceful valley, surrounded by hayfields and cattle ranches. The house would more than meet our needs, and it was fully furnished, a real boon since we had sold our furniture when we left Ashland. Visiting David's parents, we admired their handicrafts and were gifted with a freshly baked loaf of bread and their equally warm hospitality.

"When have we ever received such a warm welcome?" we asked one another as we drove back to the lookout. "Is Life trying to tell us something?"

Sitting in the tower that evening, we pondered our situation. The house at the farm seemed to be the only option that had presented itself. Were we to go there to live? And if we did, how would that work out? The farm was miles from the nearest sizable town; no employment opportunities existed nearby. We weren't sure we'd find many clients for our soul-awakening work among the farmers and ranchers who would be our new neighbors.

One morning, I asked about it all in meditation. As I sat quietly, turning our situation over to the Divine, I was astonished by the response: *If you go there, the whole world will open unto you.*

Wow! That sounded auspicious. I had no idea how that might happen, but it felt good -- really good. When I told Barry what I had heard, he agreed that moving to the farm seemed to be our next step. It would take years, but the prophetic words did eventually come to pass.

Karen: Getting Grounded -- Fast!

We retrieved our belongings from storage and hauled them to our new home. It was now November of 1998, and the weather had turned very cold. The stovepipe needed immediate repair so we could safely heat the house. With no wood on hand to burn, we borrowed a chain saw and went out into the forest. After bringing home truckloads of wood, we split and stacked it all in the shed, which leaked. We added fixing its roof to the ever-growing list of projects. But first, the house needed cleaning, painting, and significant minor repairs and upgrades, including a front door, to make it livable. All of this had to be dealt with -- right away!

After this initial burst of activity, we began to settle into our new life. We cut more wood, fixed more things, and added decorative touches to the furnished house. Each afternoon, we took long walks out on the road, which received welcome sunlight, or up into the hills behind the farm. The winter was severe that first year, with temperatures well below zero at times. We quickly learned how to coax the most heat out of our precious firewood.

Recalling how much I'd enjoyed being at Barry's lookout, I yearned for the peace and solitude only a mountaintop offers, and decided to seek my own fire lookout position. The next summer I found myself at Parker Mountain Lookout, just across the border in Oregon.

Over time, we got to know Joyce, the matriarch of the farm, who could often be found sitting in a rocking chair hand-stitching quilts when she wasn't canning or baking or making other craft projects. Jerry, her husband, wore bib overalls and a jaunty kerchief around his neck. Each summer the family sold produce from their huge market garden at area farmers' markets, where Jerry was known for his sweet corn. Our new neighbors included some of the grown offspring of this industrious pair, along with an assortment of their children and grandchildren. The farm also provided a home to cows, chickens, horses, mules, small gray birds called chukars, rabbits, and a turkey named Lucky. Barry and I often felt as though we had taken up residence in a three-dimensional Norman Rockwell painting.

We had often heard about the importance of "getting grounded," usually in reference to spiritual seekers whose feet hovered a few inches above the earth. During this time, we lived into a deeper awareness of what that phrase really means. With little experience or training in how to perform many earth-plane tasks, our newfound grounding was hard-won. We frequently felt as though we had entered another dimension of existence altogether. Sometimes, when we were mired in clueless frustration over yet another fix-it challenge, David would calmly show up. With amazing ease and deftness, and not a hint of condescension, he'd solve our latest dilemma within moments.

One day, I assisted Barry while he installed a new bathroom exhaust fan and sunlamp. For him, this involved a complicated process of figuring out which circuits needed to be shut off, climbing into the attic, and connecting and disconnecting many wires before all was operational. I stayed below, handing up tools and parts and steadying the step-stool as Barry made his ascents and descents. Later that day, we met David outside the barn. I expressed appreciation for the way Barry had jumped into this project and completed it with ease.

David looked at me and said, "You could do that, too, if you had to. You'd just crawl up in the attic and work with it until you figured it out. It might take some time, but you'd get it sooner or later."

David embodies that perfect faith and trust in Life, gained through countless experiences with plants, animals, machines, wood, metal, and other materials. When Jacqueline expressed a desire for a bigger home, they looked at architects' plans and said, 'We can do this. We'll figure it out -- we don't need to spend $400 on a plan." Over the next couple of years, they built their house from the ground up, without a blueprint. They bought a timber sale from the Forest Service, went out into the woods and cut down the trees, hauled them back to the sawmill on the farm, milled the wood, and built the house, with very little help from anyone else. Along the way, they learned about wiring, plumbing, tile-laying, carpeting, and every other facet of home construction. Whatever they decided the house needed, they knew they could figure out how to bring it into being. Today the house stands as a monument to what people can do when they believe they can.

I'm not sure I could ever build a house from scratch, as our endlessly inventive neighbors did, or that my destiny lies in that direction. But in moving to the farm I have found reservoirs of strength and resilience I didn't know were there. Loading trucks with firewood, splitting and stacking it, figuring out how to repair things or replace them when they were beyond repair -- all of this has brought me into this earthly existence in ways I never imagined I'd experience in this life.

Barry: Learning to Live on the Earth

One January morning, we awoke to an intense chill. I was unable to see the temperature on the outside thermometer, as the window was nearly iced over. A second glance told me I hadn't been looking low enough on the scale. *Minus 30 degrees?!* Nothing came out of the tap when I tried to take a shower. Calling the neighbors revealed that no one else had water, either. Jerry informed me that the main pump, which draws water from two hundred feet below the ground, had frozen.

There's an unspoken code on the farm that when something like this happens, all the men immediately show up to deal with it. So, into my warmest clothes I crawled. My mind complained, *What am I doing in this picture? I should be in Hawai'i!*

Within the hour, a broken pipe or two had been repaired and the pump was thawed out and running again. Amazingly, it all happened with only a handful of words spoken. Everyone knew what to do, as they always do. They have worked together for years, and are so deeply interconnected that they move as one in an unspoken communion. They seem unaware that this capacity is anything special. They were born and grew up on the land, and their oneness with the earth is a natural part of who they are.

Over the years, we have gradually begun to enter the field of consciousness that everyone on the farm lives within. It is amazingly devoid of frustration, tension, worry, and the belief in "problems." Situations arise, they are dealt with, and life goes on. No one bit of emotional or mental energy is ever wasted. Whatever the issue, it is quietly observed, a solution is sometimes stated, although more often simply known, and, mostly in silence, people move. Soon, order and functionality are restored. Everyone knows that the matter will be resolved, one way or another, if they stay present with the situation. There is no need to push or struggle, for nothing is seen as difficult, much less insurmountable. Afterward, no handshakes, celebrations, or other post-task formalities occur. Their souls are so intertwined that being there for each other is understood to be an essential part of life. It's just business as usual, the Tao of living in communion with life on the farm.

When we first moved in, we inherited Monk, a cat that stayed behind when his family moved to their new home. A day or two later, another cat showed up at the door, and when we let it in, the big, orange feline went right over to Monk. The two cats rubbed against one another the entire length of their bodies again and again, purring loudly, clearly overjoyed to be reunited. When we told our neighbors about this, with her typical generosity Jacqueline responded, "Oh, that's Tiger, Monk's brother. You can have him if you want!" We happily welcomed Monk and Tiger into our lives.

One night, Monk went out the cat door and never came back. With owls, coyotes, bobcats and mountain lions living nearby, pets often don't last long on the farm. We missed Monk very much, but before we even mentioned what had happened to anyone, Jacqueline showed up at our door with a beautiful kitten she had chosen for us. Somehow, she just knew that it was time to bring this new little being into our lives. Cleo grew up to be an irrepressible delight who gave us three kittens that have filled our lives with joy.

In its infinite wisdom, Life knew that living and working in close communion with the Earth would ground all the vaster experiences and realizations we'd been given and open us up to a new dimension of consciousness altogether. When we came to the Farm, we were not very physically sturdy, nor were we deeply connected to the rhythms, flows and innate intelligence of Life. Now, living closer to the land, we began to use our bodies to do things we normally would have acquired with a credit card. Cutting and splitting the wood, for example, involved many days of hard, physical labor. Yet this was more than repaid by the newfound sense of satisfaction we felt seeing the next two winters' worth of warmth stacked up in the woodshed. Even more gratifying was feeling ourselves weaving into the web of intelligence that furthers and nurtures all of life. Rather than hiring others to do things for us, we were becoming active participants in more aspects of our existence than we had ever dreamed possible. Our kind, generous neighbors became our guides and teachers in this new realm of earthy, embodied life.

Karen: Shedding the Spiritual Ego

For decades, we had lived in towns filled with spiritual seekers -- "New Age ghettos," as we jokingly called them. These rarefied environments elevated our spiritual vibration, but also resulted in a somewhat ethereal mode of existence. After many years in such homogenous communities, it wasn't always easy to bridge to people from diverse backgrounds, let alone farmers and ranchers, who were often judged in such places as being at the far end of the vibrational spectrum. While we had developed a measure of spiritual sensitivity, we were also identified with our spirituality; on some level, we thought it was who we were. And being identified, even with "positive" qualities and ways of being, always gets in the way of awakening.

To a degree, the two of us were products of the New Age spirituality that often revolves around creating a more glorified sense of self. Rather than bolstering the self through material acquisitions and worldly success, we, like many others, had focused on developing a more "spiritual" self -- a kinder, gentler, wiser and more loving version of who we had been. But self is self, and this was not getting us free!

It was tough to spot these spiritual dimensions of egoism for they were tinged with soul-qualities, and fueled by aspirations that seemed "good" and "positive." As these bubbles of spiritual identity began to pop, we sometimes felt as though we were losing important parts of who we were, parts other "spiritual" people had appreciated and admired. Were we leaving behind what was best about ourselves in this new place?

Life on the farm, among people who didn't possess the spiritual overlays we'd been surrounded by in the New Age ghettos, was teaching us the difference between the "spiritual" self and the Self. The true Self, we were discovering, exists prior to and beyond all identities. It has no objective nature, and cannot be defined by its outer experience or expression. Resting in the Self, we have no desire to become or acquire anything. To the contrary, as ego-layers peeled off, our existence increasingly focused on the joy of simply being, as all that we thought life was about dropped away.

Living in towns full of "spiritual" people, we had become fairly insulated and spirit-polarized, with well-developed spiritual egos. Life knew just how to balance that out. Being on the farm and working at our fire lookouts has helped us as probably nothing else could have done more effectively to go beyond our idealization of the spiritual at the expense of the material. Living and working among people with different types of awareness and ways life not only grounded us, it also increased our mental-emotional flexibility and openness. Over and over, we have faced and let go of our judgments about "dense," "unspiritual" people and ways of living.

As we got to know David, our landlord and neighbor, we realized that he naturally and effortlessly radiated many of the soul qualities we were only beginning to come into, attributes like perseverance, equanimity, and inner strength. Living on the farm repeatedly shredded any remaining ideas about who was "spiritual" and who wasn't. We realized there are millions of Davids all over the planet, quietly, steadily beaming out the frequencies of love, generosity, and helpfulness. Day after day, without fanfare or recognition, these are the beings who keep our world going.

Karen: Releasing Preferences

It could be said that we moved to the farm in spite of ourselves. In a marked departure from previous moves to places we chose for their beauty or other redeeming qualities, we found nothing that initially presented itself easy and natural to accept, much less embrace. At first, we couldn't even connect with the land itself. It seemed dry and desolate, barren and harsh. We preferred lush, deciduous trees, and all that grew here were scrubby junipers. We missed flowers in the spring, and the blazing foliage of fall. Over and over, our ideas of what is beautiful and what isn't obscured our perception of this new place.

When we first moved to the farm, I was appalled by the piles of discarded machine parts and broken appliances scattered everywhere. I couldn't believe our neighbors would toss a soda can onto the ground when it was empty. All trash, including lots of plastic, was burned, and no one recycled anything.

We spent the first few years complaining about all that was missing from this remote corner of the world. We pined for the places we loved and insisted to God that we didn't belong here. When it became apparent we were not going to be divinely reassigned, we grudgingly resigned ourselves to putting up with this place, although it clearly was not up to our egos' standards. We often asked ourselves, *What are we doing here?*

At these times, we'd recall the first line of the *Hsin Hsin Ming*, a treatise by the Third Zen Patriarch: *The Great Way is not difficult for those who have no preferences.* During the many times we'd read this pithy document aloud to one another, we had often wished it was as simple as those few words made it sound: *Just eliminate those preferences, and life will be easy.* Actually *doing* that proved far more difficult. In countless ways, we liked *this* and not *that*; we felt happy when what we wanted was present, and not so content when it was absent.

It's easy to feel serenely liberated when things around us match our internal preferences. We congratulate ourselves at putting up with minor inconveniences and feel proud of our spiritual progress. But when Life puts us in the midst of a situation that bears little or no resemblance to our idealized images of who we think we are and what our life should look like, we find out how much ego still remains. And that is a humbling experience!

What was left of the ego-mind was sure it knew what was best for us. It had a long list of conditions it felt were essential for us to enjoy life and fulfill our destinies. However, God had another plan for us. It was designed to shave off ever more of the rough bristle of our egoic view of reality. In moving to this place far from any centers of spirituality, at a remove from all that we believed our evolution required, we were presented with the biggest challenge to our egos yet.

But as hard as it was at times to accept that this austere, remote place was our new home, no inner prompting to go anywhere else ever arose. As we sank deeper into our new life, we began to appreciate its gifts, and stopped complaining as much about what the mind insisted were its shortcomings. For instance, we realized all that "junk" lying around the farm in seeming chaos was really an inventory of potential parts for future construction projects and repairs. Amidst the apparent disarray, there was an order and a way to things that slowly emerged as our eyes opened to see it.

The move to the farm slowly, thoroughly emptied us of ever more of what we thought was important, so we could find out what really mattered. As we sank into the ever-present quiet, the "still small voice" of our souls became easier to hear. Complaining about what was missing was supplanted by gratitude for what was present, and ego-ranting gave way to ever-increasing inner peace. We found it easier to remember that we must have been brought to this place because it would support the next steps in our soul-evolution better than anywhere else available.

Karen: The Fullness of the Emptiness

Driving through Los Angeles, we often saw ads on the sides of buses for a well-known gym. They displayed a buff person working out, alongside an astonishing slogan: "You can rest when you're dead." This seemed to be the motto that just about everyone

in L.A. had adopted. But it is by no means confined to that metropolis. When we lived there, we once decided to drive north until
we found some quiet; there, we would spend a couple of days
camping. It took many hours until we finally found a place that was
relatively peaceful. Even there, we did not feel a true stillness.

Buddhist teachings describe the "hungry ghost" syndrome
that plagues those of us caught within the empty, egoic state. Like
many others in the western world, we, too, were addicted to seeking and consuming, looking for the latest "more, better, and different" material goodies. During our first years of living and working at
such a remove from town-life, our cravings reminded us we were
not yet totally free.

I can't wait to get to town, the mind would rant after days of
isolation on a mountaintop. *I want to buy something, go a restaurant, see people. I want variety and stimulation -- a movie, a conversation, a new book to read. I want, I want, I want.*

But when we'd finally get to town, all the shops seemed to
be overflowing with nothingness. There was so much, materially,
yet so little of it had any soul-resonance. We'd pass store after
store full of things -- millions, if not billions of things -- and the vast
majority of it no longer had any relevance to our lives, if it ever had.

When my father, brother, and I visited Sweden in 1996, our
relatives prepared a delicious meal for us. As the plates emptied
and we sat back from the table, our hostess asked, "Is everyone
fed up?" She laughed along with us when we explained that the
colloquial meaning of that phrase has a weary, put-upon edge, not
the pleasant sense of satiety she thought it held. But I liked her
meaning, and Barry and I began to incorporate it into our own conversations. Now, on our trips to town, we know it is time to leave
when we turn to one another and say, "I'm fed up!"

It's not that we don't enjoy the small towns we visit regularly, or the larger cities we travel through from time to time. It's fun
to immerse in that world for a while, but then we are always ready
to leave. There is never a time when we feel, *Wouldn't it be nice to
stay and have more of this?* Once we've gathered in enough urban
stimulation, we are happy to go back to the ground of our being --
the peace, spaciousness, and all-pervading quiet of our country
home. We could never have guessed that these qualities would
become more important to us than how it looks or what the
weather is like.

Even now, many years later, whenever we drive back to
the farm, we feel grateful for the simplicity of our lives. How good it
feels to no longer want so many of the things we used to seek in
town! We feel totally satisfied as we unpack our bags of groceries,
which provide plenty of newness and variety. Walking into our

home after an immersion into the complexity of the world, we feel awash in relaxation, supremely comfortable within our humble little haven on the planet.

Karen: Deepening into the Mystery

Left to our own devices, we would never have found our way to the farm. Not one strategy or plan our minds could ever have come up with would have gotten us here. What brought us to the farm was a willingness to submit to divine grace, a commitment to live in alignment with one simple phrase: *Thy will be done.* We wanted that more than we wanted to use our own wills to conjure up our next step. That had become impossible, for we were all out of ideas about what was next for us. Being stationed at a remote fire lookout precluded getting busy with plans and strategies to get something going. More than that, by this time we had come to know that our own plans were always inferior to the perfection of the divine plan for our lives. Our decade together had taught us that there is indeed an infinitely intelligent, unfathomably loving and powerful Presence that is stewarding our lives far better than we could ever hope to do. So we simply gave the whole thing back to God and waited for further instructions.

Into that vacuum stepped Jacqueline, with an offer of a home to rent. Yet this did not make immediate, perfect sense to us; we still had to live into the understanding of how this next step was the right one for us. Many years passed while we slowly lived into that understanding. At first, our awareness was fixated on the fact that nothing that fed our former way of living was present. No shops or cafes were anywhere nearby, and the few restaurants that did exist served food we didn't eat. Foreign films? Music performances? Theater? All of this would have required hours of driving. There was nothing trendy, "spiritual," or "alternative" going on for miles in all directions.

Yet in this place that no one we knew, least of all ourselves, would have chosen, we discovered gifts that lay hidden in the utter absence of worldly glamours and distractions. In the high desert, where psychic and energetic distortion is largely absent, a subtle field of energy~consciousness unfolded as we became capable of merging with it. Over many years, the emptiness that pervades this remote, undisturbed place on the planet has gently, subtly transformed into a fullness we have never known. It revealed itself only as we emptied, finally landing at that "zero point" where all our seeking for something more, different, or better slowed down to a stop.

Our awareness of that empty fullness continues to expand to this very day. It was always there, hidden beneath the layers of craving and future-thinking that obscured it from our vision. As Christ Jesus said, "Heaven is laid out before you but you cannot see it." Releasing all ideas about the environments we thought would make us happy, we've found that true contentment has nothing to do with our outer circumstances. As we have stopped imaging there might be someplace better suited to our preferences and simply accepted that in this moment, this is where we live, the joy of living in the present has revealed itself ever more fully.

It took many years of living in this sparse landscape for us to drop into our surroundings and develop the deep appreciation for them we now feel. Now, when we return to this spacious emptiness, we feel utterly grateful. The stark, haunting beauty of this place feeds and uplifts the spirit. There is a freedom in the vast, open spaces -- endless room in which the mind can spread out and decompress, releasing all the thought forms that may have swarmed in during our visits to busier areas. Returning home, we feel our awareness stretching out into infinity, free of all questions about why we are here or what it means about us that this is now our home.

Barry: Living into Oneness

Other than being in the presence of an enlightened being, nature is probably the clearest mirror we can find on this planet. Nature is pure life, without overlays; it is as it is. A tree or a bird or a rock forms part of the unchanging Tao of Life. It cannot be other than its essence allows. Nature invites us to drop into the same authenticity, by the very purity of its inherent being. A tree doesn't notice what kind of car we drive, what we're wearing, or whether we have a "great body." We can talk to a deer or a bush, but they don't judge us on how illumined our discourse is.

As we dropped into our new home in the country, our awareness simultaneously landed more deeply within our core essence. The trees, bushes, animals, birds and even the rocks responded, sharing the truth of simply being. Over time, we entered into a newfound communion with all of life and the soul of Creation that animates each form. Our consciousness opened into the omniscient, omnipresent intelligence of Life that prompts geese to lead south in the fall and impels flowers to push up through the moist earth each spring. Within its vastness, all exists as one completely interconnected living beingness. And now, in this place far from anything that had previously given our lives meaning, we began to directly experience that we were a part of this limitless, interwoven oneness.

We discovered we could share this fundamental unity with our fellow humans, too, no matter how different their cultural matrix was from ours. As our masks and ego overlays fell away, the essence that united us with every other being emerged. The more we settled into our new life, the easier it became to connect with any one and everyone, because it wasn't happening from the personality level. We simply showed up in the present moment and shared what there was to share, free of the overlays of trying to be clever or make spiritual points. Like so much else, the need to try to impress anybody with what we knew or who we were was dissolving away.

The lack of personas and posturing among the farmers and ranchers we met was refreshing. Being around these salt-of-the-earth beings helped us to drop any remaining personality acts and get real. Country people, as they often refer to themselves, are astute observers of human nature, and very sensitive to "fake" personas. They have no use for anyone who comes across as having an inflated opinion of himself.

Amidst the simple surroundings of the farm, our own relationship stabilized and strengthened. The many physical-plane tasks this new life presented required us to work together. At first egos clashed and wills collided, but over time, we lived into more harmonious ways of getting things done. As ego-overlays were worn away through karma yoga and simple living, we found it easier to connect soul to soul. Mutual respect replaced faultfinding and perfectionism, and we discovered we could have a lot more fun together when our egos weren't vying for dominance. Through even the most challenging passages, our souls had always counseled staying together, and now we were reaping the fruits of that perseverance.

Barry: Dropping into a Heaven on Earth

Here on the farm, where the clamor of the world's illusion does not overpower the quiet voice of the Divine, we've come to more clearly hear its call in our heart of hearts. With each passing day, we more fully know that It alone is real, and that nothing else has any lasting basis. As the ego-mind continues to dissolve, we are more able to see and love what is real, and find rest and peace in the way things simply are.

True contentment arises from living in as much of heaven on Earth as we have ever known. To our amazement, we did not find this in the idyllic landscape of Hawai'i, or any of the other places our personalities preferred. Through third-dimensional eyes, the outside of the house we live in resembles a chicken coop, and the farm's forty acres are far from aesthetically pleasing. Yet those who are able to look beyond appearances sense something deeply peaceful, nurturing, and even numinous about our humble environs.

Gradually, we've learned that true happiness has little or nothing to do with outer props; it's the field of energy and consciousness that emanates from our souls that creates the experience of serenity and fulfillment. Even when something seemingly disruptive enters in, the underlying communion with Self is like a vast ocean in which the waves of whatever is arising tend to ripple across the surface and then dissipate. Awareness of the always serene, imperturbable core essence grows with each passing day. When remaining imprints of limiting thought and emotion arise, they are more quickly seen as illusion and released through the grace of the luminous presence that emanates with increasing power from the core of our being.

The divine presence within has blossomed to the degree that its inner radiance now outshines anything the world can offer. We watch outer seeking fall away as we discover what is ultimately fulfilling and attractive within. Progressively dying to the false self, our true inner divinity rises up and shines forth, revealing what has always been there beneath the dense opacity of our occluded minds.

The simplest things bring such deep satisfaction in this new life. Whenever we return from a trip, one of the first things we do is drink a glass of water, right out of the tap. We marvel at its clean, pure, taste. It has come from two hundred feet beneath the ground, free of fluoride, chlorine, and everything else city water contains, and imbued with robust, palpable life energy. We look up at the sky -- the clear, blue sky, empty of industrial pollutants. It, too, is full of life energy. We go to bed immersed in stillness and awaken into the deep silence that tells us we are home.

Here on the farm, evenings often find us sitting quietly in our living room, browsing the internet or reading a book, enjoying the warm glow emanating from the wood stove. As we share our thoughts on the many distressing stories that cross our laptop screens, we realize what a stark juxtapose our lives present to what most humans are experiencing. With conflicts raging around the globe, the world cries out for peace. Although a Department of Peace is a beautiful idea, the violence, fear and insecurity that fill the world will only be resolved as one soul at a time awakens and remembers the eternal compartment of peace within.

Jesus Christ's famous words, "My kingdom is not of this world," have taken on new meaning. Living at some remove from the humanly created world makes it easier to recognize it as largely a formation of the ego-mind, spawned in its dream of separation and fear. Although its facades can seem utterly convincing, we are coming to know that this world has no ultimate reality. The scary, powerful-looking apparitions of the separated state are revealed as arising from the ultimately impotent little egos behind the curtain, posing as the Wizard of Oz.

Our daily prayer has become *May we all awaken*. In our hearts and souls, we know this is as certain as tomorrow's rising of the sun. The hand of grace is now lifting up the entire species. As the outer world lists and crumbles before our eyes, the collective awakening simultaneously gathers momentum. People everywhere are rising up to say "Enough!" to power without love as its foundation. The many are letting the few know that they see their tricks, as well as their basis in greed and separation, and they will not be allowed to continue. As we reclaim our "NO!" we simultaneously rediscover our ability to say "Yes!" to what really matters. Life, love, liberty -- the world over, we all want the very same things.

We feel so blessed that somehow, the hand of the Divine touched us and showed us the way back Home. Words are inadequate to express our gratitude for the life that has found us through grace alone. When the illusions of the world are swept aside, the eternal truth of Life stands clearly revealed, as it has always been. How simple, how glorious, how peaceful and brimming over with love.

The neighbors' dog comes by to play and have a treat...love, only love. The turkey runs through the yard on its way to wherever...love, only love. The forest gifts us with wood for the winter to come...love, only love. The floor needs to be swept and the table wiped clean of the remnants of dinner...love, only love. Drifting into the silence each night to awaken into its wonderful peace....all love...only love...the love that is, always has been, and shall forever be...

The Return is this alone, remembering what has long awaited our awakening from the amnesia of Self-forgetting into the awareness of what we always, already are -- the holy sons and daughters of the only One That Is.

Resources

To receive emails when we release subsequent books, CDs, and videos, please join our mailing list on our website. There you can also register for teleconferences and read much more about our offerings.

Birthing the Luminous Self
www.luminousself.com

To order additional copies of *Soul Awakening: The Journey from Ego to Essence* as well as the *Conscious Soul Communion* CD, please visit our website store:

http://www.luminousself.com/store.html

Books mentioned in the text

PART ONE:

Strangers Among Us by Ruth Montgomery

The Dawn Horse Testament Of Heart-Master Da Free John by Adi Da Samraj

A Course in Miracles, Foundation for Inner Peace

Seth Speaks and *The Nature of Personal Reality* by Jane Roberts

Autobiography of a Yogi by Paramahansa Yogananda

Descent to the Goddess: A Way of Initiation for Women by Sylvia Brinton Perera

The Book of Knowledge: The Keys of Enoch by J. J. Hurtak

PART TWO:

Conscious Soul Communion CD, Barry Snyder and Karen Anderson

Step By Step We Climb To Freedom, Volumes 1-3 by Pearl

Original Unveiled Mysteries and *The Magic Presence* by Godfre Ray King
The I Am Discourses by Ascended Master Saint Germain through Godfre Ray King
Available through:
Saint Germain Foundation
www.saintgermainfoundation.org

PART THREE:

The Miracle of Iniki: Stories of Aloha from the Heart of Kaua'i by Anne E. O'Malley and Ellie Radke

Hsin Hsin Ming by the Third Zen Patriarch, Sengstau. The translation we like best is available to read online:
http://allspirit.co.uk/hsinhsinming.html

Acknowledgments

This book could not have been written without the help of the divine beings who have been overlighting our earthly journey for lifetimes. Our inexpressible gratitude goes to Christ Jesus, Mother Mary, Babaji, St. Germain, Amen Bey and the many other ascended beings who have guided our footsteps. Most of all, we offer our limitless love and gratitude to our true, eternal Selves, which are being born into manifestation in this human experience more fully with each passing moment.

A thousand thanks to the Earth angels who have been instrumental in bringing this book into manifestation. Alana Wolfe has participated in this project since 1995, when the earliest version of this book came into being. She has served as a true Keeper of the Flame of this process, and her discerning questions and comments have helped us make this book a far more articulate expression of what we were trying to say. Mahalo nui loa, dear Alana!

We have deeply enjoyed Mary Val McCoy's soulful presence and inspiration during countless teleconferences, and appreciate her encouraging, clarifying responses to early versions of this book. Merci beaucoup, MV!

DeeDee Schneider always let us know when we were on target and when we weren't, both in our writing and in creating the *Conscious Soul Communion* CD. Muchas gracias, DeeDee!

Loving gratefulness goes out to Roger Shaw for his encouragement, guidance, and support over the years. Roger once told us, "Writing is like shooting an arrow straight from the heart." We hope our writing embodies these words.

Finally, we send our heartfelt gratitude to Anna and all the other evolutionary forerunners we have met during soul-awakening sessions and groups. You have blazed a trail for many to come!

Made in the USA
Las Vegas, NV
10 July 2023

74456329R00174